ISRAEL & the NATIONS

The History of Israel
from the Exodus
to the Fall of
the Second Temple

F. F. BRUCE
REVISED BY DAVID F. PAYNE

InterVarsity Press
Downers Grove, Illinois

InterVarsity Press
P.O. Box 1400, Downers Grove, IL 60515
World Wide Web: www.ivpress.com
E-mail: mail@ivpress.com

InterVarsity Press®is the book-publishing division of InterVarsity Christian Fellowship/USA®, a student movement active on campus at hundreds of universities, colleges and schools of nursing in the United States of America, and a member movement of the International Fellowship of Evangelical Students. For information about local and regional activities, write Public Relations Dept., InterVarsity Christian Fellowship/USA, 6400 Schroeder Rd., P.O. Box 7895, Madison, WI 53707-7895.

Cover photograph: Daniel Blatt (mosaic: Pavement at Hammat, Tiberius)

ISBN 0-8308-1510-4

Printed in the United States of America ∞

Library of Congress Cataloging-in-Publication Data

Bruce, F. F. (Frederick Fyvie). 1910-
    Israel and the nations: the history of Israel from the Exodus to
    the fall of the Second Temple/F. F. Bruce: revised by David F.
    Payne.
        p.   cm.
    Originally published: Grand Rapids, Mich.: Eerdmans, 1963.
    Includes bibliographical references and index.
    ISBN 0-8308-1510-4 (permanent paper)
    1. Jews—History—To 70 A.D.   I. Payne, David F. (David Frank),
1931- .   II. Title.
DS118.B75   1998
909'.04924—dc21
                                                        98-22122
                                                        CIP

| 22 | 21 | 20 | 19 | 18 | 17 | 16 | 15 | 14 | 13 | 12 | 11 | 10 | 9 | 8 | 7 | 6 | 5 | 4 | 3 | 2 | 1 |
| 16 | 15 | 14 | 13 | 12 | 11 | 10 | 09 | 08 | 07 | 06 | 05 | 04 | 03 | 02 | 01 | 00 | 99 | 98 | | | |

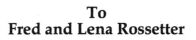

To
Fred and Lena Rossetter

Contents

Reviser's Preface

In July 1963 my good friend and former teacher F. F. Bruce gave me a complimentary copy of the first edition of *Israel and the Nations*; I read it with pleasure and profit. I did not dream then that over thirty years later the publishers would ask me to revise and update it. I have subsequently read and reread it—with pleasure and fresh profit.

The most important aspects of the revision concern factual data and the bibliography. The late F. F. Bruce (he died in September 1990) was always open to argument as well as to evidence, but he had an independent turn of mind, and was not prepared to follow every vogue of scholarly opinion. I have therefore been reluctant to revise his opinions; for example, I have left unaltered his dating of Ezra as he assessed it in 1963, even though he might well have changed his mind in the light of subsequent discussions. Certainly I am confident that he would not share the very sceptical approach to Old Testament history of several recent writers. He did not believe that biblical authors, simply because they had theological purposes, were unreliable as historians.

The English has been simplified, to a limited extent, since it is hoped that this revised edition will have a wide circulation overseas.

Scripture quotations are from the New International Version (except that 'Yahweh' has been preferred to 'the LORD'). Quotations from the Apocrypha are from the New Revised Standard Version (Anglicized Edition).

This revision is offered as a grateful tribute to the memory of an outstanding scholar, teacher and friend.

April, 1996   D. F. P.

Preface to the First Edition

This book has its inception, not in any inward urge on the part of the author (who makes no claim to be a specialist in the greater part of the field which it attempts to cover), but in a request by a group of Scripture teachers for a handbook which might prove useful to them in their work. It is based on two courses of lectures—a shorter one sketching the story of Israel from the Exodus to the Babylonian Exile, and a longer and more detailed one from the Exile onwards. It can accordingly be charged with lopsidedness; but I have reflected that the period treated in greater detail is the period that is less well known to the majority of potential readers of the book, some of whom may therefore be not displeased to have the treatment proportioned thus.

The limited scale of treatment has dictated the complete or virtual exclusion of some important aspects of the history of Israel. While we cannot speak of the nation of Israel before the Exodus, Israel's history cannot be separated from its 'prehistory'—the history of the patriarchal period. The Israelites never supposed that the God who delivered them from Egypt and brought them into covenant relationship with himself was a God of whom no one had ever heard before: to them he was the God of their fathers, Abraham, Isaac and Jacob. The patriarchal period, however, constitutes a subject in itself, especially with the wealth of light that archaeological discovery has shed on it, and deserves separate treatment, by someone better versed in the history of the second millennium BC than the present writer.

Again, throughout this book Israel's religion is dealt with only incidentally, for all its centrality in the life and continuity of the nation. Israel's literary history receives even more cursory treatment. Each of these subjects also deserves a volume to itself. But what is given in the following pages may, I hope, serve in some sort as prolegomena to the volumes in the Paternoster Church History series.

Special thanks are due to Miss June S. Hogg, BA, who typed out the whole work from a none too legible manuscript. I am further indebted for valuable comments to Mr. H. L. Ellison, BD, BA, who read the typescript, and the Revd. A. A. Anderson, BD, BA, who read the proofs; and—last but not least—to my wife, for help with proof-reading and the compilation of the index.

March, 1963   F.F.B.

Introduction

A great many books have been written about the early history of Israel—but very few about other small nations that were her neighbours, such as the Edomites or Moabites. Why should this be so? What was so special about this one small nation of antiquity? Why should the story of Israel still be of interest and relevance to us in the late twentieth century and beyond?

The answer to these questions can be found nowhere but in the distinctive features of Israel's religion. There was something about it that was unparalleled in the surrounding world. An Assyrian king once tried to discourage any resistance on the part of the Israelites by pointing to the uselessness of the gods of greater and more powerful states which he had overthrown. 'Where are the gods of Hamath and Arpad?' (2 Kgs 18:34), he asked. A question which might well be repeated today. Where, indeed, are they? And how does it come about that the God of Israel continues to be worshipped by millions of people in every one of the earth's continents? The Israelites had their own explanation. As they considered their experience of the God of their fathers, they affirmed: 'He has done this for no other nation' (Ps. 147:20). Their affirmation is vindicated by the course of their history.

Yet Israel's national history was not lived out in isolation from other peoples. The Israelites were surrounded by nations greater and mightier than themselves, who impinged upon the life of Israel at innumerable points. It is in the varied response to the challenge presented by these other nations, Asian, African and European, that Israel's own nationhood acquires its special character. Hence the subject of this book is not Israel in isolation but Israel and the Nations.

For much of the period covered in this work, our most important primary sources are the books of the Hebrew Bible, which Christians call the Old Testament. In these books the story of Israel is told as 'sacred history'. That is to say, the narrators' interest was not so much in political developments as in the dealings of the God of Israel with his people. They retain their religious value to this day both for the Jewish people and for the Christian church.

Yet, while these books have come down to us as Holy Scripture, they are also historical source-documents of first-rate worth. The chapters which follow are not concerned with them as canonical writings, but as material for constructing a political narrative. Other source-material has also been used, for which no canonical claims have been made—the writings of secular historians and the inscriptions of ancient cultures contemporary with the life of Israel in the period under review. These last-named documents have come to light as a result of the archaeological research carried out in the Near East for well over a century and a half. Their discovery has enabled us to appreciate, in a way previously impossible, how remarkably faithful is the historical outline preserved in the Hebrew Bible, from the age of the patriarchs to the Macedonian supremacy.

But to our tale.

Chapter One

Israel's Beginnings
(c. 1300–1100 BC)

THE EXODUS

The very first mention of the Israelites in any record outside the Old Testament occurs in an inscription on a pillar set up shortly before 1200 BC by Merenptah, king of Egypt, to celebrate several victories won in the course of his reign. Merenptah boasts of his victory in Palestine over Israel in these words:

Israel is desolate; it has no seed left.[1]

From the way in which the word 'Israel' is written in this inscription, it appears that Israel was not yet a settled nation; so it is reasonable to suppose that the Israelites' exodus from Egypt had taken place not long before, during the same thirteenth century BC.[2] If Merenptah's claim had been accurate, there would be no story of Israel to tell. But ancient commanders, like their more recent successors, often exaggerated the scale of their victories; Israel was not so completely desolate, so totally deprived of all hope of posterity, as Merenptah claimed.

No Israelite battle with Merenptah's army is mentioned in the Old Testament, though it is just possible that his record is connected in some way with the Israelites' exodus from Egypt. It is just conceivable that it is the only official Egyptian account of the events when the Israelites crossed the 'Red Sea',[3] although the context suggests rather that Israel had already entered Canaan.

At any rate, the departure of the people of Israel from Egypt marks their birth as a nation. Some generations previously their ancestors, members of a pastoral clan, had gone down from Canaan to Egypt in time of famine and settled in the Wadi Tumilat. The early kings of Dynasty XIX, Sethos I and Rameses II (c. 1300–1225 BC), drafted them in large numbers into forced labour gangs for the building of fortified cities on the north-eastern frontier of Egypt. They rapidly lost their former manner of life and were in danger of forgetting the faith of their fathers. A few generations more, and they would have been no different from their oppressed fellow-workmen of Egyptian origin. Their ancestral faith, however, was rekindled by Moses, a man of their own race. This Moses had been brought up, through a strange combination of events, at the Egyptian court; but eventually had to flee for his life to north-west Arabia when he was caught supporting the cause of his enslaved kinsmen. In north-west Arabia he became allied by marriage with a priestly family of the Kenite tribe, and in a vision he received a command from the God whom Israel's ancestors had worshipped to return to Egypt and lead his kinsmen out to the place where the vision appeared to him. The land of Canaan, he was told, had been divinely promised to these ancestors, and their God had not forgotten his promise; indeed, God had observed the affliction of their descendants. God was now about to fulfil his promise, and in connection with his purpose he made himself known to Moses by the name Yahweh. This was a name by which the patriarchs had not worshipped him, but which expressed his character as a covenant-keeping God. Moses therefore returned to Egypt, and led his people out of that land into the wilderness of north-west Arabia. Their escape was accompanied by the 'plagues', a series of natural phenomena in which the Israelites saw the controlling power of the patriarchs' God, as he intervened for the deliverance of their descendants. And indeed, Moses in the ordinary way could neither have foreseen nor controlled these phenomena. The fact that they occurred just at that time confirmed God's instructions given to him in his vision and made possible Israel's escape from Egypt in the way in which Moses assured them it would happen.

Moses, in fact, was the first and greatest of the long succession of prophets whose influence upon the religious life of Israel was in the long run so decisive—men who spoke in the name of Israel's God and interpreted the events of the past, present and future in terms of his revealed character and will. But no prophet's influence had such an effect on the national life as that of Moses—so much so that it has been well said that if he had not existed, he would have to have been invented to account for the rise and progress of the nation of Israel. The plagues which afflicted the Egyptians immediately before Israel's departure from their land; the ebbing of the waters of the Red Sea— probably a northerly extension of the Gulf of Suez—which took place in a moment of desperate need and enabled them to cross when they were pursued by the Egyptian chariots and hemmed in by hills to the north and south; the pillar of cloud by day and fire by night which led them to their rendezvous with God; the awe-inspiring phenomena which they saw and heard as they approached the sacred mountain: all these were interpreted to them by Moses as revelations of the power of their God, acting for them in deliverance and providence.

MOUNT SINAI

The Egyptian chariots which pursued the departing Israelites and tried to prevent their escape from Egypt were caught and overwhelmed when the waters returned to their normal limits. The Israelites rejoiced in this fresh display of Yahweh's care for them and marched eastwards by 'the way of the wilderness of the Red Sea' across the head of the Gulf of Aqaba until they reached the sacred mountain known as Horeb or Sinai. Here, near the place where Moses had received his first commission from Yahweh, the people solemnly undertook to keep the covenant into which Yahweh had brought them with himself: he would be their God (as he had already shown himself to be) and they would be his people. The basis of the covenant was an early form of the Ten Commandments or 'Ten Words' in which Yahweh made known his will for his people. The introduction to the 'Ten Words' clearly identified the God who declared his will for them in these words : 'I am Yahweh your God, who brought you out of Egypt, out of the land of slavery.'[4] The God who had done that for them, to whose power and mercy they owed their existence as a people, ought indeed to be accepted as their God: there was none like him among the gods— 'majestic in holiness, awesome in glory, working wonders.'[5] They were right to submit to his exclusive terms, 'You shall have no other gods before me',[6] for what other god was worthy to be mentioned alongside Yahweh?

In paying him worship they were forbidden to attempt to represent his likeness by means of an image; they were to treat his name with the reverence to which he was entitled; they were to reserve for him every seventh day; and in thought and word and deed they were to treat each other in the manner required by the covenant which bound them all together. They were to regard themselves as a holy people—i.e. a people set apart for Yahweh. But Yahweh was a God who was not only incomparably powerful, but also incomparably righteous, merciful and true to his promises; and therefore men and women who were holy to him, reserved for him, must reproduce these qualities in their own life and conduct.

This attitude we may call practical monotheism. Whether other gods— the defeated gods of Egypt or the gods of the Canaanites or of other nations—might have some sort of existence was not a question about which either Moses or his followers were likely to trouble themselves. Their business was to worship Yahweh their God and serve him alone.

Moses has always been considered the first and greatest lawgiver of the Israelites. In his own person he combined the functions of prophet and priest and king; he judged their lawsuits and taught them the principles of their religious duty, not only in the details of sacrificial worship but in many aspects of ordinary life as well. Of course his laws were edited and expanded, issued and re-issued down the centuries that followed, for different situations and changing circumstances; but Israel's law would never cease to be known as the law of Moses. Rightly so: for the principles laid down in his time, before the settlement in Canaan, remained the principles of Israel's law for all centuries to come.

Many of the laws of Moses can be separated into two readily distinguishable groups of laws on grounds of style and content. There are the case-laws or 'judgments', cast in such a form as 'If a man do so-and-so, he shall pay so much'; and there are the statutes, expressed in direct commands and prohibitions: 'You shall (or shall not) do such-and-such'. When these Old Testament laws are compared with other ancient Near Eastern lawcodes, it is to the former group, the case-laws, that parallels are found. This is the form, for example, in which the laws of the Babylonian king Hammurabi (who lived several centuries before Moses) are expressed, like the laws of still earlier codes in that part of the world. But the second type (the statute-laws) with their distinct religious note, though they too have various parallels in ancient documents, are certainly distinctively Israelite.[7]

IN THE WILDERNESS

The undisciplined body of slaves which left Egypt under the guidance of Moses had to spend a generation in the wilderness before they became an organized nation which could invade the land of Canaan as conquerors and settlers. Some Israelites who attempted to raid the Negev about two years after they left Egypt were easily driven back, and had no wish to repeat the experiment. Much of the time that separated the solemn events at Sinai-Horeb from the large-scale entry into Canaan was spent in the oasis of Kadesh, to the south of the Negev. Another name given to this place is En Mishpat, 'the spring of judgment'; the name suggests a tradition that here judgment was pronounced as the Israelites submitted their cases for the decisions of Moses and the judges he appointed. As for the name Kadesh, it simply means 'sanctuary'; the fuller form Kadesh-barnea distinguishes it from other sanctuaries. This suggests that even before the settlement in Canaan the Israelites consisted of a number of tribes who were united in part by a common ancestry but much more so by common participation in the covenant with Yahweh. The outward and visible sign of their covenant-unity was the sacred chest, the ark of testimony, constructed by Moses, housed in a tent-shrine. Some scholars have seen similarities with ancient Greek history; in Greece sometimes a group of states or tribes bound themselves in an 'amphictyonic league', sharing a common sanctuary which served as the centre and focus of their federation.

A tent-shrine was easily moved, and very suitable for a community that was so frequently on the march. Other groups were permitted to enter into the covenant-bond: in particular we know of nomadic communities of the Negev such as the Kenites (to whom Moses' wife belonged), the Kenizzites and the Jerahmeelites who now or later allied themselves with the members of the tribe of Judah. It seems that ultimately these groups merged into that tribe. Closely related to these nomadic groups was another called the Amalekites, but they were hated as bitter enemies of Israel. The hatred lasted for centuries; it can best be explained if they were guilty of some breach of covenant. Alliance with such nomadic groups was a very different thing from alliance with the settled agricultural population of Canaan. The Canaanites practised fertility rituals which attracted many Israelites and which endangered the essential features of the pure Yahweh-worship which Israel learned in the wilderness. Even before they entered Canaan, the Israelites were strictly forbidden to make common cause with its inhabitants.

There was some Israelite infiltration from the south into the central Negev, an area with which the tribe of Judah had earlier links; but the route followed by the main group when they left Kadesh led them south and east of the Dead Sea, where they passed by the territories of their kinsfolk of Edom, Moab and Ammon, who had recently organized themselves as settled kingdoms. They made no attack on these related groups, but they acted quite differently towards two other kingdoms which lay farther north in Transjordan—the Amorite kingdoms of Sihon in Heshbon and his northern neighbour Og in Bashan. They entered the realms of Sihon and Og as hostile invaders, overwhelmed their armies, and occupied their territory (the territory which became the tribal heritage of Reuben, Gad and eastern Manasseh). Part at least of the Israelite community had thus adopted a settled agricultural way of life before the crossing of the Jordan. We are told that Moses gave them a lawcode there in Transjordan which they were to observe in their new territory; so the laws which imply an agricultural way of life need not be regarded as later additions to his lawcode.

INTO CANAAN

There in Transjordan Moses died, after he had commissioned his assistant, the Ephraimite Joshua, to be his successor and to lead the people into Canaan. Joshua led them over Jordan in circumstances which impressed themselves on the national memory alongside the circumstances of their departure from Egypt. When Israel had departed from Egypt, 'the sea looked and fled', as a later poet wrote; now as they came into Canaan 'the Jordan turned back.'[8] The Old Testament records that the drying up of the river was due to a landslide at Adam (modern Ed-Damiyeh), some fifteen miles north of the place where the Jordan runs into the Dead Sea. The fact that it occurred just at this time was evidence to them that the God of their fathers, who had brought them safely out of Egypt, was now bringing them safely into Canaan. The collapse of the walls around the citadel of Jericho, which lay two miles west of the place where they crossed the river, was no doubt caused by the same series of earthquakes which had brought about the landslide at Ed-Damiyeh. To the Israelites it brought further confirmation of the controlling power of Yahweh. Jericho, by the collapse of its walls, lay defenceless before them. As the firstfruits of their conquests in Canaan it was solemnly 'devoted' to Yahweh with all that was in it. The indestructible wealth in the citadel was set aside for the service of Yahweh's sanctuary; the rest was destroyed in a gigantic bonfire.[9] The 'devotion' of Jericho, together with the solemn ritual that preceded the assault, as described in the book of Joshua, indicates that the Israelites were engaged in a holy war; the battles in which they took part both east and west of Jordan were known as the 'wars of Yahweh' and celebrated as such in sacred song.

From Jericho they pressed into the heart of the country, taking one citadel after another, for the news of the fall of Jericho had struck terror into the hearts of many Canaanite garrisons. At one time the Canaanites could have called upon Egypt for help, but Egypt was entering a period of decline and was unable to exercise the control she had formerly claimed over central Canaan. It was only along the western coastal strip as far north as the Pass of Megiddo that Egypt still exercised some measure of control, and even there the Philistine settlement on the Mediterranean seaboard was soon to form a barrier against the extension of Egyptian power.

An alliance of five military governors of Canaanite citadels attempted to bar the Israelites from turning south from Gibeon and the other cities of the Hivites in the central hill-country, which had submitted to them as subject-allies; but it was completely defeated, and the road to the south lay open to the invaders. They were unable to operate in the plains and valleys, where the chariot-forces of the Canaanite citadels were too formidable for them to face; but before long they dominated and occupied the hill-country of the centre and south, and also the Galilaean uplands, north of the Plain of Jezreel. The decisive stroke in the conquest of the north was the storming of the great city of Hazor, formerly 'the head of all these kingdoms.'[10] Hazor is one of several ancient citadels, excavated by archaeologists in recent years, which were destroyed before 1200 BC, and were rebuilt some decades later with thinner walls and a lower standard of material culture.

THE PERIOD OF THE JUDGES

The tribes who settled in the north were divided from the tribes in central Canaan by a Canaanite chain of fortified positions strung along the Plain of Jezreel, from the Mediterranean coast to the Jordan. The central tribes, in their turn, were cut off even more effectually from contact with Judah farther south by the stronghold of Jerusalem, which remained a Canaanite fortress for a further two centuries.

On one notable occasion, the northern and central blocks joined forces in an uprising against the military governors of the Plain of Jezreel,[11] who were steadily enslaving them; and their united rising was crowned with success at the Battle of Kishon (c. 1125 BC), when sudden heavy rain flooded the valley where the river ran and put the horses and chariots of the Canaanites out of action. The lightly armed Israelites swept down upon them and routed them. The inspiration for united action on this occasion came not from the Israelite commander Barak but from the prophetess Deborah. The tribesmen went up to her headquarters in the hill country of Ephraim to have judgment pronounced in their disputes. It was on her instructions that a message was sent at speed throughout the tribes, calling them together for this holy war—'to help Yahweh against the mighty'—as we are told in the ancient triumph song in celebration of the victory which is preserved in Judges 5. The tribes that failed to respond are reproached, but Judah is not mentioned; Judah was too completely cut off from the tribesmen of the centre and north.

When the tribes of Israel remembered their covenant-bond, on an occasion like this, their united strength enabled them to repel their foes. But such united action, even on a smaller scale, was rare. When the danger which caused them to call upon the God of the covenant receded, the tendency was strong to slip back into conformity with the way of life of their Canaanite neighbours, to intermarry with them, to imitate their fertility rites in order to secure regular rainfall and good crops, and to think of Yahweh rather as a *ba'al* or fertility-god than as the God who had delivered them from Egypt and made his nature and will known to them in the wilderness. The bond which united them to their fellow-Israelites was thus weakened, and they became an easy prey to their enemies.

It was not only Canaanite cities in the land itself that tried to make them virtual slaves. From time to time they suffered raids from beyond the Jordan, by their own kinsmen of Moab and Ammon and Edom, and more disastrously by the Bedouin from more distant parts of Arabia, who, riding on camels, raided their territory year by year at harvest time and destroyed their crops. These 'Midianites' or 'Ishmaelites', as they are called in the biblical record, would have made life impossible for the Israelites; but an

Israelite man named Gideon, from the tribe of Manasseh, took leadership and led a small and mobile band against the invaders, took them by surprise, pursued them across the Jordan and killed many of them. The grateful tribesmen invited Gideon to become their king and to found a hereditary monarchy, but he refused. He argued that a monarchy, if it was like the monarchies which governed Israel's neighbours, was alien to the ideals which they had learned in the wilderness. Let Yahweh alone be acknowledged as King in Israel; let him use as his agents not one particular family but the men whom from time to time he might choose, giving them special powers, to rule his people and defend their cause.

From the number of such 'charismatic' persons who arose in Israel in this period and led them back to loyalty to Yahweh and forward to victory against their enemies, the whole period is known as the period of the 'judges.'

One of Gideon's sons, Abimelech by name, did not share his father's views about kingship. (He, however, was the son of a Canaanite woman and had been brought up with his mother's relatives at Shechem.) After his father's death he attempted to succeed to his power, and killed off most of the other members of Gideon's family in the process. For three years he reigned as king from Shechem, but his kingdom did not extend beyond Western Manasseh. His subjects soon grew tired of him, and he met his death in trying to put down their revolt.

NOTES

[1] Cf. DOTT, pp. 137 ff.

[2] It is not impossible that the Exodus had occurred much earlier. The evidence for dating the Exodus and conquest of Canaan is complex yet incomplete, and there are several theories. See J. J. Bimson, *Redating the Exodus and Conquest* (1978), chapter 8; J. Bright, *History of Israel* (3rd ed., 1981), pp. 123 f.; K. A. Kitchen in ABD vol. 2, pp. 702 f.

[3] Literally 'the Sea of Reeds' (Heb. *yam suph*), a name applied to the Gulfs of Suez and Aqaba. Another suggested correlation of Merenptah's claim with the biblical record is that which connects it with the disaster suffered by Israel at Hormah in the Negev (Num. 14:45).

[4] Exod. 20:2.

[5] Exod. 15:11.

[6] Exod. 20:3.

[7] Cf. D. Patrick, *Old Testament Law* (1985), pp. 21 ff.

[8] Ps. 114:3.

[9] The destruction of Late Bronze Age Jericho is very difficult to date archaeologically, owing to the considerable erosion of the site during the centuries that elapsed before the building of Iron Age Jericho (1 Kings 16:34). See K. A. Kitchen in J. J. Bimson (ed.), *Illustrated Encyclopedia of Bible Places* (1995), pp. 165 ff.

[10] Josh. 11:10. The precise date of the destruction of Hazor is a matter of considerable dispute.

[11] Led by Sisera (see p. 9).

Chapter Two

The Philistines and the Hebrew Monarchy (c. 1100–1010 BC)

THE PHILISTINES

The situation which did at last lead to the establishment of a hereditary monarchy in Israel was brought about by invaders from another region—not from the east but the west. The downfall of the Mycenaean and Hittite empires towards the end of the thirteenth century BC uprooted many of the populations of the Aegean lands and sent them sailing over the eastern Mediterranean in search of new homes. One such group was called the Philistines, from the south-west of Asia Minor. Some of the Philistines settled in Crete; others attempted to land on the Egyptian coast, and when they were driven away, sailed east and landed on the Mediterranean coastland of Canaan. Here they were able to settle. They organized themselves in the five city-states of Ashdod, Ashkelon, Ekron, Gath and Gaza—former Canaanite cities. Each of these five city-states was under the control of a ruler whom they called in their own language a *seren* (a word related to the Greek *tyrannos*, cf. English 'tyrant'). The Philistines intermarried with the Canaanite women of the area and quickly adopted the Canaanite language and religion. They were capable military organizers, and when once they had established themselves in their five city states, they began to extend their control over the rest of Canaan. They soon came into contact with the Israelites, and militarily the Israelites were no match for them. Although the Israelites had entered Canaan some time after the beginning of the Iron Age, they were slow in making use of iron. Sisera[1] had had nine hundred chariots with iron fittings, but the Israelite tribesmen who defeated him had never developed similar equipment. There would have been technical and organizational problems; and besides, a chariot force required the use of horses. Horses, as we shall see,[2] were scarcely used in Israel until the reign of Solomon.

The Philistines, however, had mastered the art of iron-working, and when they began to assert their power over the Israelites they made sure that they kept control of all iron-working in their own hands. When the Israelites began to use iron agricultural tools, the Philistines insisted that they must come to Philistine smiths to have them sharpened. They realized that if they permitted Israelite blacksmiths, these workmen might not only make and sharpen agricultural tools, but also weapons of war, to be used in rebellion against their overlords. The Philistines were able to extend their power steadily along all the roads and lines of communication in the land, as far as the eastern end of the Plain of Jezreel. Although they made the Israelites pay them tribute, their domination was not really oppressive; they certainly did not threaten the very existence of the people as the Midianite raiders had done in Gideon's day. Indeed, some of the Israelites were quite content to live peacefully under Philistine domination, as the story of Samson makes plain, and they objected to Samson's attacks on the Philistines, which resulted in Philistine anger not only against him but against his fellow-countrymen as well.

But if the very existence of the Israelites was not endangered by their Philistine overlords, their national survival was in danger. An important sanctuary at this time was at Shiloh, in Ephraimite territory, where the ark of the covenant was housed (in a more permanent structure than the old tent-shrine of the wilderness days) and where the God of Israel was worshipped as 'Yahweh of hosts'. The priestly family in charge of the sanctuary of Shiloh traced its descent from Moses' brother Aaron (who had been chief priest of the tent-shrine in the wilderness). The last of the chief priests of Shiloh, Eli by name, was more than just a priest; at this important sanctuary he also acted as intertribal judge. Near the end of his life, the tribes of Israel decided to resist any further Philistine encroachment, and revolted against their overlords. First they came to Shiloh, no doubt in order to receive the priestly blessing on their enterprise. But after a defeat by the Philistines, they decided that they must have the sacred ark itself, to go before them into battle and (they believed) ensure success against the enemies of Yahweh. But even the presence of the ark was insufficient; they were beaten, and more decisively than before, at Aphek, some twelve miles east of Joppa. The two sons of Eli, who accompanied the ark as it led Israel into battle, were killed in action. Worse still, the ark itself was captured by the enemy. The disastrous news was taken back to Shiloh and caused the death of Eli himself. Shiloh itself with its sanctuary may have been destroyed by the Philistines— the evidence of archaeological research on the site is not clear.

The bond which united the tribes of Israel was broken: the central shrine was destroyed; its priesthood was wiped out (apart from two infants, the grandsons of Eli); and the ark, the very symbol of Yahweh's presence with his people, was in foreign hands. The Philistines had triumphed indeed. It looked as if Israel's glory and national identity had departed for ever.

SAMUEL'S LEADERSHIP

Israel was rescued by the courage and leadership of one man, Samuel. Samuel has often received much less than his due from historians, but his name deserves to stand alongside those of Moses, Joshua and David in the annals of Israel. Samuel was a native of the region of Ramah, in the tribal territory of Ephraim. He had grown up at Shiloh, where he was in attendance at the sanctuary under the direction of Eli. Even before the destruction of Shiloh he had shown a prophetic gift, and when the disaster took place, he proved equal to the task of rallying the shattered morale of his people. He showed them that their God was still with them, even if the sacred ark was in the hands of the Philistines. Indeed, when the Philistines after a short time restored the ark to Israelite territory, Samuel was content to leave it in the obscurity of a private house in Kiriath Jearim, on the border between Judah and Benjamin. It remained there throughout Samuel's lifetime and for several years more. The functions as judge which Eli had carried out could no longer be performed at Shiloh, but Samuel continued to carry them out. He went annually in circuit to the ancient sacred centres of Mizpah in the central highlands (which to some extent served as a new Israelite centre), Gilgal and Bethel, as well as to his own hometown of Ramah. In these places he pronounced judgment on the cases submitted to him.

Although he did not belong to the priestly family, Samuel undertook the priestly duties, without Israelite objections. At Mizpah, Gilgal and Bethel there were ancient altars where sacrifice might be offered, and at Ramah too he erected an altar and sacrificed there. Israel had no capital city, but this one man, under God, served as the focus of national life. He has well been described as 'God's emergency man'.

Under his direction Israel returned to its old covenant loyalty to Yahweh, and with the return of their former faith came a resurgence of national courage. They again confronted the Philistines, and on the battlefield where they had suffered such a crushing defeat a few years before, they defeated the Philistines so thoroughly that for many years the Philistines left the central highlands in peace.

But Samuel grew old, and then the question arose who should take his place. He had two sons who acted as deputy judges for him, but they did not show their father's strict honesty and were suspected of accepting bribes. The people had no desire to be judged by them when Samuel could no longer carry out his duties as judge.

In these circumstances, Israelites once again began to desire to have a hereditary monarchy, just as they had done in Gideon's time, but with greater urgency than before. However, a hereditary monarchy introduced

a principle which was bound to change the character of government in
Israel. Till now they had been ruled by judges raised up by 'the spirit of
God', sometimes from one tribe, sometimes another. But the hereditary
principle meant that their rulers in future would not all have the special
spiritual gifts which Samuel and the judges before him had possessed. In
fact, the Israelite kings would probably resemble the kings of Israel's
neighbours.

But if the Israelite people now wanted a king, there was only one man
who could arrange it, and that man was Samuel. Samuel argued with them,
telling them that their request marked a lack of faith in Yahweh, their true
King—Yahweh had never yet failed to raise up a leader of his choice in time
of need. When they persisted, Samuel agreed to their demand, and nominated as their king a man named Saul, from Gibeah in the tribal territory
of Benjamin. Saul may have been chosen by Samuel some time earlier to act
as military commander under his direction. But Saul came from an obscure
family, and many despised him in spite of his impressive stature. Their
attitude was changed, however, when a sudden cry for help came from
across Jordan, from the men of Jabesh-gilead, who were closely related to
Saul's own tribe of Benjamin. The Ammonite king had threatened to
enslave them. When the appeal came to Saul at his home farm at Gibeah,
he sent a summons to united action throughout the tribes, and arrived with
astonishing speed to give effective help to Jabesh-gilead.

The energy which he showed on this occasion impressed the popular
imagination. The people united to acclaim him as their king, the chosen of
Yahweh, at Mizpah. Not only so, but the approval of Yahweh himself
seemed assured when Saul suddenly showed the prophetic gift and in this
way indicated that he too was an Israelite leader empowered by God's
spirit. Samuel had by no means given up his authority, which was essentially moral and religious in character. If Saul had been content to act as
king—i.e. as judge and military leader—under the old man's guidance, the
combination might have worked out most happily for Israel. Then the
decision to begin a monarchy might have seemed justified. But events
turned out differently.

SAUL'S REIGN

The Ammonite threat had provided Saul with a timely occasion for dem-
onstrating his kingly qualities. But it was the Philistine domination that
chiefly lay behind the people's demand for a king, and it was against the
Philistines that the first two kings of Israel would have to prove themselves.
The Philistines were not, like the Ammonites, related to the Israelites, with

much the same way of life; they were heirs of the ancient civilization of the Aegean. Their chief buildings and temples (like the one at Gaza which Samson brought down upon himself) were constructed on Aegean models. Their leading warriors (like Goliath of Gath) were equipped like Homeric heroes. It was no easy thing to challenge the strength of overlords like these. But the Israelites did so, by the very fact of electing a king. The Philistines knew what that meant, and also knew what action to take.

Then Jonathan, the daring and fearless young crown-prince, took matters into his own hands by killing the Philistine commander at Geba, not far from his father's headquarters at Gibeah. As a result, a Philistine company of soldiers marched in and established itself at Michmash, where they could cut the line of communications between Ephraim and Benjamin. They then set about destroying the Israelite rebels. Saul's men, who were a volunteer peasant army, saw with dismay the revenge that their revolt was likely to bring upon them, and they began to desert. The remainder would soon be left defenceless before the Philistines. But Jonathan, who had done so much to create this crisis, remedied the situation by a daring commando action. Accompanied only by his armour-bearer, he climbed up the rock of Michmash by the steepest ascent. When the Philistine garrison, thinking that a large band of Israelites had come to attack them, came out to deal with them, Jonathan and his armour-bearer killed them one by one at a narrow point where only one man could pass at a time. The garrison panicked, for they imagined that a large army was attacking them. Saul's scouts, looking north from Gibeah towards Michmash, saw the panic. Saul then consulted the sacred oracle, and received a response from the priest that the time was right for attack, so he led his army against the fleeing Philistines and inflicted great slaughter on them. The central territory was once more cleared of the invaders, and for a time Saul's control was firmly established over central Israel. Other enemies, who had taken the opportunity during the Philistine invasion to encroach on Israelite territory from other directions, were pushed back. Saul reached the peak of his success and power.

But the tragedy which increasingly affected the later part of Saul's reign had already begun. At an early point in his campaign against the Philistines, when Saul gathered his army at the sanctuary at Gilgal to receive the divine blessing through Samuel for the commencement of the holy war, Samuel was late in arriving. In order to prevent the army from dispersing, Saul performed the sacrifices himself. By this action he was taking priestly duties away from Samuel, and it led to a growing alienation between the two. The alienation was intensified when Samuel gave a divine communication to Saul commanding him to march into the Negev and to destroy Israel's old enemies, the Amalekites, and Saul failed to 'devote' the whole community to Yahweh. In particular, Saul did not kill Agag the Amalekite king. Clearly it would be wrong to suppose that Saul had humanitarian motives for this—he did not hesitate to slaughter the rest of the Amalekite people, though they were less guilty than Agag. One possible explanation is that Saul had his own ideas about the treatment that kings deserved. Samuel executed Agag with his own hands, and declared to Saul that he had proved unworthy of the kingship and had been rejected by Yahweh.

The tragedy of Saul is that he was a sincerely religious man, deeply concerned to do the will of Yahweh. Samuel's announcement that Yahweh had rejected him as king disturbed his mind, as it would not have done if he had been an irreligious man. He became a victim to melancholia and persecution mania, and needed music to soothe his dejected spirits. It was in this way that he first met the young man who, unknown to him, had been anointed by Samuel as his successor, for David, a member of a family in Bethlehem, a town in the tribal territory of Judah, was a skilful harpist.

David was not only a skilful harpist but a gifted warrior as well. When the Philistines once again began to encroach on Israelite territory, David showed such skill and courage that Saul made him commander of the royal army and gave him one of his daughters in marriage. But his success made him a target for Saul's suspicions—and it is possible that Saul suspected that Samuel saw David as a future king. It was all the more bitter for Saul that his eldest son Jonathan and David were very close friends. But David's personal charm was such that even Saul himself could not resist it, and in his more rational moments he addressed David in terms of warm affection.

Again and again, however, Saul's suspicion returned and showed itself in murderous threats and attacks upon David, until David was forced to take refuge in the wilderness of Judah. There he became the leader of a group of discontented people and fugitives from justice. He organized and trained them until they became a first-class force of fighting men, who were so deeply loyal to David that if necessary they were prepared to die for him. In fact, the name David[3] may have been given to him as a term of affection by his comrades; it has been thought that his personal name was Elhanan.[4] David's cause was greatly strengthened by the arrival of Abiathar, a young priest who fled from the sanctuary of Nob, near Jerusalem, at the time when the whole priestly family there was killed at Saul's command, after they had given aid and comfort to David as he fled from the royal court. Abiathar was a great-grandson of Eli, the last priest of the sanctuary at Shiloh, and he brought with him the intertribal 'ephod', the portable garment or object by which the will of Yahweh could be found.

Several of the men who joined David in the wilderness retreat, in the cave of Adullam, later came to hold high position in his kingdom. Joab later became commander of the army and Benaiah became captain of the royal bodyguard.

Saul saw in David's band of followers a rival force to his own army, and decided that there was no room in one kingdom for both military groups. He therefore took advantage of a spell of inactivity on the Philistine frontier to pursue David into the wilderness of Judah, until David realized that he and his followers could not remain there. He therefore crossed the Philistine frontier and offered the services of his small army as a mercenary force to Achish, ruler of the Philistine city of Gath. Achish, who remembered David's reputation when he led Saul's army against the Philistines, was delighted to have him on his side, and made David's band his personal bodyguard.

By driving David out of Judah Saul brought most of the southern part of his kingdom under his control. He then planned to bring the northern tribes into the unity of Israel as well. They lay north of the Plain of Jezreel, which was controlled by the Philistines. In order to establish his rule effectively over these tribes, therefore, it was necessary to fight a decisive battle against the Philistines. As the Philistine forces prepared for the battle, some of them disliked the presence of David and his men in their ranks. The other Philistine rulers pointed out to Achish that, if David wished to be reconciled with Saul, he now had a marvellous opportunity for doing so—by changing sides in the course of the forthcoming battle. Since David and his men occupied an important position in the Philistine army, it would be very dangerous for the Philistines if they changed sides. These suspicions were probably very sensible, despite Achish's personal confidence in David. We may be sure that David had no wish to fight against fellow-Israelites. Achish was compelled by the other Philistine leaders to dismiss David, who then led his followers back to Ziklag, the town in the south of Judah which Achish had given to them, and awaited news from the north. When news came, a few days later, it was tragic news indeed. The Israelites had lost the fight at Mount Gilboa. Saul with Jonathan and two other sons had fallen in battle, and the Philistine grip on the whole land of Israel was firmer than before (c. 1010 BC).

NOTES

[1] At the battle of Kishon (p. 7).
[2] See page 20.
[3] The most probable meaning of David is 'beloved'. The suggestion, based on the evidence of Old Babylonian inscriptions from Mari on the Middle Euphrates, that it meant 'leader', is now regarded as doubtful.
[4] In 2 Sam. 21:19 the man who killed Goliath, the Philistine giant of Gath (cf. 1 Sam. 17:4 ff.), is called Elhanan.

Chapter Three

The Reign of David
(c. 1010–970 BC)

THE DEFEAT OF THE PHILISTINES

Some of Saul's followers were able to escape to Transjordan, and there they proclaimed Saul's remaining son Eshbaal[1] king in his father's place. Eshbaal remained east of the Jordan, making his court at Mahanaim; there was no place for an independent king of Israel west of the river. In Judah, however, a new king was proclaimed. David, after consulting the oracle of Yahweh, left Ziklag and went to Hebron, an ancient city in the territory of Judah, and his fellow-tribesmen sent a deputation to him there and acclaimed him king of Judah. To the men of Judah, Eshbaal was a distant and ineffective Transjordanian ruler, and a Benjaminite by birth; he could not be compared with their own courageous fellow-Judaean, David.

The Philistines tolerated David's title of king over Judah. He was still their vassal, and the fact that the Judaeans made him their king meant that the tribes of Israel were now divided in their loyalties. A policy of 'divide and rule' seemed sensible to the Philistines. Events seemed to play into their hands still further when war broke out between David's followers and the supporters of Eshbaal. The commander of Eshbaal's army was his uncle Abner. In one of the skirmishes between the two small armies, Abner killed a brother of Joab. A short time afterwards Abner took offence when Eshbaal rebuked him, and led a party of his men over to David's side. David gave him a warm welcome, for many other Israelites were likely to follow Abner's example and desert Eshbaal. Joab, however, seized an early opportunity to assassinate Abner in revenge for his brother's death. David, in dismay, made it as clear as he could that he dissociated himself entirely from Joab's treacherous act, and he himself followed Abner's bier as chief mourner.

With the desertion of Abner, Eshbaal's cause was hopeless. Two of his officers, realizing this, decided to take advantage of the situation by murdering him and carrying his head to David at Hebron, expecting a reward.

The reward they received was a shameful death, which their treachery thoroughly deserved. Eshbaal's death hastened the inevitable conclusion towards which events were already moving. The other tribes of Israel, now left leaderless, sent delegates to David, whom they remembered as their beloved commander during the reign of Saul, and anointed him king over all Israel. The anointing ceremony was accompanied by a covenant in which king and people undertook mutual obligations. The king of Israel was no absolute monarch, in spite of the sacredness of his anointed person; he was as much bound by his covenant to the people as they were by theirs to him.

The Philistines had now to deal with a situation in Israel which had turned sharply to their disadvantage. The tribes were now reunited under a king who was no minor ruler. David could no longer be counted upon as their loyal vassal. They decided that he must be eliminated without delay, and sent an army against him. David withdrew to his old headquarters at Adullam, and from there he made a surprise attack upon them on their way to Hebron, and defeated them at Baal-perazim in the Valley of Rephaim, south of Jerusalem. When he defeated them a second time in the same area, his victory drove them out of Judaean territory. Their dominion over Israel was broken, and would never be renewed.

THE CAPTURE OF JERUSALEM

The ancient citadel of Jerusalem was still in Canaanite hands on the southern border of the tribal territory of Benjamin, between the two separate sections of David's kingdom, Israel and Judah. It was originally a joint Hittite and Amorite city, and its inhabitants called themselves Jebusites. A king who aimed at uniting Israel and Judah into one realm could not afford to leave this foreign region between the two sections. David therefore, having driven the Philistines out of Judah and central Canaan, determined to capture Jerusalem. But this was no easy task; otherwise it would have been taken long before. It was strongly fortified, with steep slopes and strong walls. The citadel stood on the hill Ophel, south of what was later to become the temple area. The defenders of the city were so confident that it was impregnable that they taunted David and his men when they came to besiege it, saying that even the blind and lame among the population would be able to keep the besiegers out. But David was equally confident in the abilities of his soldiers. He announced that the man who succeeded in capturing the fortress would be made commander-in-chief of his forces. Joab, David's nephew, succeeded in leading a band of followers into the city by an unsuspected route, the water shaft[2] by which water was drawn up from the cave forty feet below into which the Gihon spring empties.The idea that this vertical shaft would ever be used as a means of entry by a hostile force was never taken seriously by the Jebusites, until they found the enemy inside their city walls. Their strong fortifications were useless to them now; Jerusalem was at last in Israelite hands. The fortress became known as the City of David, for David made it his headquarters, and the capital of his kingdom.

The importance of David's capture of Jerusalem can hardly be exaggerated. The strategic advantages of the place were now to David's advantage, and we may be sure that care was taken that no future invader should find the same way into the city as Joab did. It served as a centre from which David could dominate the land and complete the conquest of the Philistines. Politically it was admirably suited to be his royal city, for it was neither Israelite nor Judaean. Neither Israel nor Judah could complain that the other part of the nation was favoured in the choice of city. It remained a city-state in its own right, governed by the king of Israel and Judah, who now claimed to be the successor to the city's ancient dynasty of priest-kings. Such a famous sacred city was a worthy capital for the founder of a new dynasty, under which all elements in the population of Canaan were to be united. It had honourable associations in Israelite as well as in Canaanite eyes, for they remembered that Melchizedek, priest of El Elyon, had come out of Jerusalem to greet Abraham after that patriarch had returned from his victory over the invading kings from the east. Melchizedek had given Abraham his priestly blessing and received tithes of the spoil from him. And now David had taken the throne of Melchizedek as king of Jerusalem, as well as the joint throne of Israel and Judah.

But David knew a way in which the sacred reputation of his new capital, already great, might be further increased, especially in Israelite eyes. Since the days of Samuel when the ark of the covenant was restored by its Philistine captors, it had remained in obscurity in Kiriath Jearim. If this important sacred chest, which had given protection to the tribes of Israel in earlier times, were publicly brought to Jerusalem and installed there with due ceremony, Israel and Judah would once more have a single intertribal sanctuary. Jerusalem would become the spiritual centre of the united nation as well as its political and military capital. So David proceeded to carry out this plan. His first attempt to bring the ark to Jerusalem failed, due to the unexpected death of an attendant who laid his hand on the ark to steady it; but three months later the operation was completed without any such disaster, and the ark was brought into the city of David. It was placed in a tent-shrine that David had prepared for it, amid scenes of enthusiastic rejoicing. Here in Jerusalem was a dwelling place for Yahweh of hosts, the God of Israel. Abiathar, a descendant of Eli and the ancient priesthood of

Shiloh, became David's chief priest, and so now priesthood and ark were reunited as they had been in the sanctuary at Shiloh.

The recognition of Jerusalem as a holy city by three world faiths—Judaism, Christianity and Islam—is to be traced back to its capture by David in the seventh year of his reign. Nor must we overlook the extraordinary way in which the names of Zion and Jerusalem have entered into the religious language of Christianity, as symbols of the church both militant and triumphant, and of the heavenly home of the people of God.

From Jerusalem David made himself master of all the land of Israel. Not only were the Philistines expelled from Israelite territory, but they in turn became David's vassals. From their ranks he drew his personal bodyguard of Cherethites and Pelethites. Nor had he a more loyal band of soldiers than the six hundred men of Gath, under their commander Ittai, who were attached to him since the days when he himself had served as a mercenary leader in the pay of the Gittite king Achish.

DAVID'S EMPIRE

But David was not satisfied merely to bring the whole land of Israel under united control for the first time in history. The situation outside the frontiers of Israel gave him the opportunity of creating an empire for himself. His military and diplomatic skills matched the opportunity. The conquest of Edom made David master of the territory as far south as the head of the Gulf of Aqaba. Moab, east of the Dead Sea, was added to his empire. So was Ammon, whose king Hanun foolishly made an enemy of David by insulting the ambassadors whom David sent to congratulate him on his accession to the throne. The whole of Transjordan was now in David's hands, in addition to all the land between Jordan and the Mediterranean. This situation is reflected in the oracle quoted in Psalm 60:6–9:

> God has spoken from his sanctuary:
> 'In triumph I will parcel out Shechem
> and measure off the Valley of Succoth.
> Gilead is mine, and Manasseh is mine;
> Ephraim is my helmet,
> Judah my sceptre.
> Moab is my washbasin,
> upon Edom I toss my sandal;
> over Philistia I shout in triumph.'
> Who will bring me to the fortified city?
> Who will lead me to Edom?

Similar opportunities existed to the north of his kingdom. There were no powerful rulers at this time in the valleys of the Nile or of the Euphrates and Tigris to control the highway that ran from the Egyptian border to Carchemish. Hadadezer, king of Zobah, a state to the north of Damascus, had given assistance to the Ammonites against David. Therefore, when Rabbah, the Ammonite capital, had fallen to David's men, and David had set the crown of Ammon on his own head, David turned against Hadadezer, and defeated him. He also defeated the army of Damascus, which came to Hadadezer's help. Zobah and Damascus had to pay tribute to David, and garrisons of David's troops were placed in Damascus and other Aramaean cities. Farther north lay the Hittite kingdom of Hamath on the Orontes, whose king Toi was quick to enter into friendly relations with David, and became in effect his vassal. David's sphere of influence now extended from the Egyptian frontier on the Wadi el-Arish ('the Wadi of Egypt') to the Euphrates; and these limits remained the ideal boundaries of Israel's dominion long after David's empire had disappeared.

David also entered into alliance with his neighbour to the north-west, Hiram, who was king of Tyre and overlord of Phoenicia. This alliance was economic rather than military, and was beneficial to them both. The Phoenicians could import grain from the fertile parts of David's kingdom and other merchandise through the Gulf of Aqaba, while David had some share in the profits of the wider Phoenician sea trade. He also hired Phoenician architects to build in Jerusalem royal buildings worthy of the ruler of such an empire.

David's conquest of the Aramaean kingdoms beyond his northern border gave him the opportunity to acquire a small chariot-force of a hundred chariots and horses. This was small by comparison with the forces developed by Solomon and later kings of Israel. But it was the first sign of a new development which was later criticized by the far-sighted prophets of Israel. The introduction of the horse into the western Asian states, from the eighteenth century BC onwards, created a division in the free population (as also happened later in Greece and Rome and mediaeval Europe). The men who owned horses—the chivalry or the 'knights'—were inevitably accorded a higher rank than citizens who did not possess horses, and this social change endangered the free equality of Israel's covenant-constitution. This effect did not show itself in the time of David, for he seems to have reserved his hundred horses for military purposes only. He did not have a horse for his own use. Earlier rulers in Israel had ridden on white donkeys, and David compromised to the extent of riding on a mule, in other words a cross between a horse and a donkey.

POLITICAL PROBLEMS

David's court now began to present a visible contrast to the simplicity of the fortress at Gibeah which had been Saul's headquarters throughout his reign. We are able to read a wonderfully vivid and honest picture of David's court life, thanks to the court chronicler whose account is preserved in 2 Sam. 9–20 and 1 Kings 1–2. David began to copy the style of other eastern kings, and the unhappiest aspect of his court-life was the domestic rivalry between the children of his numerous wives—a rivalry which was to continue to the closing moments of his life.

In the later part of David's reign two serious revolts broke out against his authority. Of these the first and more serious was organized by one of his own family, in fact his favourite son Absalom (who was by this time probably the oldest surviving son). Absalom prepared the way for his revolt carefully. He set out to win the affection of the people, especially in Judah, to undermine their loyalty to his father. When he thought the right time had come, he had himself proclaimed king in Hebron, which had been David's earlier capital and Absalom's own birthplace. The situation was so serious that David and those who remained loyal to him (including his Philistine bodyguard) had to escape to Transjordan, leaving Jerusalem to Absalom. Absalom knew that his position was not secure so long as his father was alive and active, so he led an army across the Jordan against him. This rebel force was completely defeated, and Absalom himself was killed by Joab, despite David's orders to his men to do no harm to Absalom. Joab believed that he knew David's best interests better than David himself did—and in this instance he was certainly right. With the death of the usurper, the rebellion came to nothing, and first Israel and then Judah renewed their allegiance to David and escorted him back in triumph to Jerusalem.

It may have been partly as a gesture of conciliation that David transferred the chief command of his army from Joab to Amasa, another of his nephews, who had commanded the rebel army; but probably David could not forgive Joab for killing Absalom. Very soon Amasa had to take military action in David's service. Northern Israelites were enraged because David allowed the Judaeans to take the lead in escorting him back to his kingdom, despite the fact that these same Judaeans had been Absalom's chief supporters. A man named Sheba inflamed the northerners' resentment and led a fresh revolt. He was a member of the tribe of Benjamin to which Saul had belonged. Before David was well established again at Jerusalem, his army had to crush this second revolt. At an early stage in operations, Joab found an opportunity to assassinate Amasa, and took over the command from him. Joab then pursued Sheba through all the tribes of Israel until at last he besieged him in a city near the northern frontier of the kingdom. The men of that city saw that it would be wise to get rid of their embarrassing guest, so they killed Sheba and threw his head over the wall to Joab. Thus the second revolt collapsed.

The last conspiracy in David's reign was not directed against his authority but concerned the succession to the throne. David, now about seventy years of age, lay on his deathbed. His oldest surviving son, Adonijah, believed that he was the proper successor to his father, and several of his father's most loyal servants thought so too, including both Joab and the priest Abiathar. But Adonijah and his supporters knew that when David died, other brothers would challenge Adonijah's succession to the throne. They decided to have Adonijah proclaimed king while his father was still alive and thus present the nation with a situation they could not alter. The proclamation was accordingly made, with sacrifice and feasting, at a place about a quarter of a mile south-east of Jerusalem called 'Serpent's Stone'—possibly the place where kings of Jerusalem had been installed in the Jebusite era.

But while the ceremony was going on, and shouts of 'Long live King Adonijah!' could be heard, news of what was happening came to Nathan the prophet. He informed Bathsheba, David's favourite wife. David had already promised her that her son Solomon would succeed him as king. This succession would certainly be more pleasing to the people of Jerusalem, who would prefer to be ruled over by a native of their city (as Solomon was) rather than by a son born to David before he became king of Jerusalem. Adonijah and his supporters were probably well aware of this, for when the proclamation ceremony was arranged, no invitation was sent to Solomon, nor yet to those court officials—Zadok the priest, Nathan the prophet and Benaiah, captain of the royal bodyguard—who were known to support Solomon's claims.

Bathsheba entered the king's presence and reported Adonijah's action. David acted quickly. He ordered that Solomon, mounted on David's special mule, should be escorted by the royal bodyguard down to the spring Gihon (the Virgin's Fountain) in the Kidron valley and proclaimed king there. So it was done, and when Zadok the priest poured the anointing oil on Solomon's head, the roar of acclamation was so loud that Adonijah and his guests heard it where they were feasting nearly half a mile away. Immediately afterwards a messenger arrived and told them what had happened, and the guests in dismay broke off their banqueting and went home in haste. Adonijah himself fled for sanctuary to the altar at the central shrine, and stayed there, clinging to its horns until he received a personal assurance from Solomon that his life would be spared.

Solomon's succession was thus assured, and before he died the old king knew that his wishes had been carried out.

NOTES

[1] He is called Ish-Bosheth in 2 Samuel, but Eshbaal in 1 Chr. 8:33; Eshbaal is probably the original form of his name.

[2] The meaning of the very rare Hebrew word *sinnor* in 2 Sam. 5:8 is uncertain, but 'water shaft' remains the most likely interpretation (as in NIV, NRSV, REB).

Chapter Four

Solomon and His Successors
(c. 970–881 BC)

SOLOMON'S ACHIEVEMENTS

Solomon's reign had not long begun before he got rid, by one means or another, of those who had supported Adonijah's claim as well as the luckless Adonijah himself.

Solomon was no warrior, as David was, but he determined to exploit the commercial possibilities of the empire which his father had conquered and bequeathed to him as a glorious inheritance. He used much of the wealth of the empire to develop a much more elaborate and ostentatious style of court life than his father's. He gathered a very large harem; many of the women were daughters of neighbouring princes and chieftains with whom he had political and commercial agreements. He engaged in a magnificent building programme in Jerusalem. The complex of buildings which constituted his new court included his royal palace; a palace for his queen, who was a daughter of one of the last kings of the weak twenty-first Egyptian dynasty; the 'hall of pillars' or assembly room, the throne-room of justice, and a treasury or armoury, called 'the house of the forest of Lebanon,' probably because it was panelled in cedar-wood. But more important and imposing than any of these was 'the house which King Solomon built for Yahweh' north of the citadel of Jerusalem, on a site which David his father had bought from its Jebusite owner. David had used it as a place of sacrifice at a time when Jerusalem was devastated by a pestilence. Here was a natural rock-altar where, according to later Jewish tradition, Abraham had prepared to offer up Isaac his son.[1] And here was erected the great temple of Solomon, on a spot where sacrifices were to be offered to the God of Israel with only two interruptions[2] for a thousand years.

In order to carry out this elaborate architectural programme, which took twenty years to complete, Solomon hired workmen from Hiram of Tyre, his father's friend, with whom he maintained a close alliance. But the consequence was that Solomon fell heavily into debt and had to mortgage part of his territory to Hiram.

With the aid of Hiram and his Phoenician fleet, Solomon also developed the commercial opportunities which arose from the fact that the trade route from the Mediterranean to the Red Sea and Indian Ocean passed through his kingdom. Solomon himself had a fleet of merchant ships based in Aqaba, which sailed with the Phoenician fleet to the Red Sea and Indian Ocean ports, bringing home from 'Ophir'[3] almug wood and precious stones, and from other parts 'gold, silver and ivory, and apes and baboons'.[4]

Copper was used lavishly for the vessels used in the temple. Copper was readily available for mining in the south of Solomon's kingdom, and it is tempting to suppose that Solomon was able to make use of it. Indeed, the first archaeologist to excavate at Aqaba, on the Red Sea, thought that he had found the remains of a very large refinery dating from the time of Solomon; but in fact the building was a storehouse, and no direct evidence of mining operations in Solomon's time has yet been found.[5] However, we do know that further north in the Jordan Valley molten metal was cast to make such vessels: 'The king had them cast in clay moulds[6] in the plain of the Jordan between Succoth and Zarethan' (1 Kgs 7:46).

Solomon also gained wealth from other sources. He acquired large revenues because his kingdom lay across the main route from Egypt to Asia Minor and Mesopotamia, and the trade routes across the Syrian and Arabian deserts. One valuable source of income was the horse and chariot trade with Asia Minor, in which he acted as middleman. 'Solomon's horses were imported from Egypt [or perhaps Cappadocia] and from Kue [probably Cilicia]—the royal merchants purchased them from Kue. They imported a chariot from Egypt [? Cappadocia] for six hundred shekels of silver, and a horse for a hundred and fifty. They also exported them to all the kings of the Hittites and of the Aramaeans.'[7]

Trade with Egypt was fostered by Solomon's alliance with the Egyptian king, his father-in-law. When Solomon received the Egyptian princess in marriage, he received a handsome dowry with her, for her father captured the city of Gezer from the Canaanites who occupied it, and handed it over to Solomon who rebuilt and fortified it. Other cities which Solomon fortified (apart from Jerusalem itself) were the strategic stronghold of Megiddo, Hazor in the far north, Beth-horon in the central area, and Baalath and Tamar in the territory of Judah.

Solomon not only acquired a large revenue from the horses and chariots which passed through his hands; he also built up a large force of chariots and horses for himself. The narrative of 1 Kings 10 refers to the cities which Solomon built for his chariots and horsemen. We may be sure that Solomon's horses were better housed than many of Solomon's ordinary citizens.

But the ordinary income of his empire and the revenue which came to him from commerce were not sufficient to maintain the expensive establishment which Solomon set up and the building programme which occupied so much of his long reign. He found it necessary to impose increasingly heavy taxes on his subjects, and to compel some of them to be labourers. At first this forced labour was supplied by his non-Israelite subjects but later it was extended to Israelites as well. 'He sent them off to Lebanon,' we are told, 'in shifts of ten thousand a month, so that they spent one month in Lebanon and two months at home' (1 Kgs 5:14). This system (known as a corvée system) was a serious departure from the ideals of early Israel, when every citizen had been free. Many Israelites regarded it as a breach of Yahweh's covenant which bound king and people alike. Nothing did so much to alienate the tribes of Israel from the dynasty of David. Moreover, the kingdom of Israel was divided into twelve administrative districts, largely, but not entirely, following the old tribal boundaries. Each of these districts was administered by a royal commissioner, and was responsible for food supplies to the court for one month each year.[8]

Israel and Judah enjoyed peace throughout the reign of Solomon, but the prosperity and joy which accompanied that peace at the beginning turned to disillusionment towards the end of his reign. He placed on his realm burdens too heavy to bear, and the kingdom split up after his death. Nevertheless, the memory of his earlier years, before the burden of forced labour and taxation became so heavy, was cherished by the people for many years. In later years, when Israel and Judah fell into harder times, the hope of a future glorious golden age was based to a large extent on the memory of the time when peace and prosperity were established by David and Solomon, who ruled the territory between the wadi at Egypt's frontier and the great river Euphrates. The coming King was pictured as combining in his person the military genius of David and the arts of peace associated with Solomon.

We may well believe that one of the arts of peace which flourished under Solomon was literature of various kinds. The architectural achievements of his reign were Phoenician rather than Israelite, but the national epic and the court-chronicle flourished, together with the 'wisdom' for which Solomon became renowned in all succeeding ages. We read that he 'spoke three thousand proverbs and his songs numbered a thousand and five.' His knowledge of the natural world made him famous among all his neighbours and more distant peoples as well.[9] Yet the features of his reign that mattered most for Israel at the time were those that showed a departure from the ancient ideals of the nation.

SOLOMON'S ENEMIES

Towards the end of Solomon's reign a change of dynasty took place in Egypt. The weak twenty-first dynasty (to which Solomon's father-in-law belonged) came to an end, and a new and ambitious king, Shoshenq by name—or Shishak, as the biblical narrative calls him (c. 945–924 BC)—took the double crown as first ruler of the twenty-second dynasty.[10]

In earlier centuries ambitious kings of Egypt had often looked towards Asia to enlarge their territory. The Mediterranean coastal road ran north to Megiddo, where it turned east through the pass into the Plain of Jezreel and crossed the Jordan, to turn north again and run through Syria as far as Carchemish, where the Euphrates could be forded. But when Shishak came to the throne this road, from his own frontier as far as the Euphrates, was controlled by Solomon. It was therefore to his advantage to weaken Solomon's power. His chief method was to encourage any movement for independence that showed itself among Solomon's subject-peoples. And there was no lack of such movements. Early in Solomon's reign a former officer of Hadadezer king of Zobah, Rezon by name, led an independence movement which made its headquarters at Damascus, and he became the founder of a royal dynasty which ruled in Damascus for two hundred years. Again, Hadad, crown prince of Edom, who had been carried to Egypt as a child when David conquered Edom, grew up at the Egyptian court and in due course returned to Edom with Egyptian support to lead a revolt in his native land.

These enemies of Solomon were not Israelites. A more serious threat to him was the encouragement which Shishak gave to Jeroboam the son of Nebat. Jeroboam was one of Solomon's officials. He had shown skill in organizing repairs to the fortifications of Jerusalem, and so Solomon put him in charge of the corvée provided by the tribes of Ephraim and Manasseh. But there were prophets, opposed to the new features of Solomon's policy, who saw that Jeroboam was an able man who could win the loyalty of the nation. One of them, Ahijah of Shiloh, acted out a prophecy which put this suggestion in Jeroboam's mind. When Solomon got news of this, Jeroboam escaped to Egypt, and remained there under Shishak's protection until Solomon died.

THE DIVISION OF THE KINGDOM

Solomon's death (c. 930 BC) coincided with the collapse of David's empire, and was followed by the division of the united kingdom of Israel and Judah itself. The long separation of Judah from the northern tribes made them think of Judah as almost alien territory. When a Judaean dynasty acquired supreme power, the situation called for special qualities of diplomacy and consideration if the loyalty of the northern tribes was to be retained. Unfortunately, the northern tribes now had good reason to suspect that Judah was being increasingly favoured at their expense. When, therefore, the tribes came together after Solomon's death to elect his successor, great care and tact were called for if the unity of the realm was to be maintained.

The tribal delegates met at Shechem, one of the most sacred of the holy places in central Canaan. The dynasty of David still retained some limited support in the north; its prestige was still very great. The people were prepared to accept Solomon's son Rehoboam as king if he was willing to return to the terms of the ancient covenant which his father's oppressive measures had recently broken. But Rehoboam, with almost incredible folly, refused to give them the satisfaction which they requested. He refused to promise to lighten the burden which Solomon had placed upon them. The reaction was immediate and violent. The northern tribes threw off their allegiance to a dynasty which would not recognize that it had obligations to its subjects. They did not have far to look for an alternative choice to Rehoboam. Jeroboam had recently come back from Egypt; in fact he was the man who took the lead among the tribal delegates who stated their conditions to Rehoboam. There at Shechem they proclaimed Jeroboam king; and there he made his capital.

Rehoboam, seeing the hostility of the delegates, hurried home in his chariot to Jerusalem. He had good cause to seek the safety of Jerusalem, for when he tried to assert his authority over the rebel tribes by sending the officer in charge of the corvée to the delegates, they showed what they thought of him and his royal master by stoning him to death.

As a result of his folly, Rehoboam was left with a tiny kingdom, consisting of the tribe of Judah and the small tribe of Benjamin on its northern boundary; Jerusalem was situated in Benjaminite territory. However, he still had important resources; he still had great wealth and a powerful army at his command, and he prepared to invade the northern territory and suppress the revolt by force. But a spokesman of the prophetic party forbade him to do so, and such was the respect due to the prophets that Rehoboam abandoned this plan. The division between the two parts of the nation was permanent.

The immediate cause of the division was economic: the people were tired of the burdensome taxation and forced labour which they had to endure under Solomon, and they saw no prospect that his son Rehoboam would lighten their burdens. The jealousy of the northern tribes against Judah was another cause, and another was the actions of Egypt. But the intervention of the prophets must not be forgotten. Samuel the prophet had played his part in preparing the way for David's rise to power, and in succeeding generations members of the prophetic guilds which Samuel probably founded continued to remind the kings of both north and south that the principles of 'democratic Yahwism' must not be disregarded.

The kingdom, then, was divided politically, but religiously it was united by means of the intertribal covenant. The ark, the symbol of this unity, was enshrined in the temple at Jerusalem, which thus remained the central sanctuary of the nation as a whole. If Jerusalem, with its temple, had been the religious capital and nothing else, this unity might have been preserved. But Jerusalem was also Rehoboam's political capital, and the temple was his royal chapel as well as being the central shrine for all Israel. Jeroboam was afraid that if the northern Israelites continued to visit Jerusalem for religious purposes, some of their old feelings of loyalty to the house of David might revive. He therefore raised two ancient sanctuaries in his realm to the status of national shrines. One was the sanctuary of Dan, in the extreme north, where the priests traced their ancestry back to Moses. The other was the sanctuary of Bethel, near the southern frontier of his kingdom, whose sacred associations were even more ancient, going back to Abraham and Jacob, both of whom had offered sacrifice there. Such rival sanctuaries to that at Jerusalem were against the principles of Israel's worship and a breach of Israel's covenant; Jeroboam's action was certainly divisive. But to make matters worse, in both these sanctuaries golden images of bull-calves were installed, probably intended to serve as the visible pedestal for the invisible throne of Yahweh. These images broke the principle laid down for Israel's worship in Exodus 20:4, and represented a dangerous assimilation of Canaanite religious practice (although among the Canaanites a visible image of the god rested on the animal).

It may be asked whether there was any difference in principle between the use of bull-calf images to support Yahweh's invisible presence and the use of cherubs for the same purpose in the holy of holies at Jerusalem. The answer probably is that the cherubs were symbolic beings (originally representing the storm-winds) and their images were therefore not 'in the form of anything in heaven above or on the earth beneath or in the waters below',[11] whereas the bull-calf images were all too closely associated with Canaanite fertility ritual. It appears from the ritual texts of Ugarit that El, the supreme god of the Canaanite pantheon, was sometimes represented as a bull (*shor*), and known as Shor-El.[12]

At any rate, Jeroboam's elevation of the shrines of Dan and Bethel to be rivals to Jerusalem, and his installation of the golden bull-calf images in these shrines, are both attacked throughout the narrative of the book of Kings, and repeatedly described as 'the sins of Jeroboam the son of Nebat, which he had caused Israel to commit'.

WEAKNESS AND DEFEAT

In the fifth year after the division of the kingdom (c. 925 BC), the Egyptian king Shishak invaded Palestine. We have two accounts of the invasion: the Judaean account preserved in 1 Kings 14:25 ff. and in 2 Chronicles 12:1 ff., and an Egyptian account preserved on a pylon of the temple of Amun at Karnak.[13] The Judaean account concentrates on the fact that Shishak took away the ceremonial shields of gold in Jerusalem, carried by the royal bodyguard when the king entered the temple. They could only be replaced by shields of bronze. The Egyptian account gives us further information: in addition to a relief picturing Shishak's victory there is a list of conquered cities of Asia, of which about 120 names are legible. A number of these are identifiable as Israelite cities. It is plain that his invasion was not confined to Judah, for the list includes cities which he took in the northern kingdom as far north as Megiddo and the Plain of Jezreel and eastward across the Jordan. Probably Jeroboam, whom Shishak regarded as his vassal, did not pay him sufficient respect but acted as an independent king; and so he as well as Rehoboam suffered at Shishak's hands.

The southern kingdom in particular was gravely weakened, both in money and in manpower, as a result of Shishak's invasion. The kings of Judah could no longer think seriously of reconquering the rebellious Israelite tribes to the north. This did not lead them to make peace, however; it led them to seek allies. They found them in the kings of Damascus, the successors of the Rezon who founded a dynasty there in the reign of Solomon. Abijah, Rehoboam's son, gained the help of Tabrimmon, king of Damascus, against Israel, and the alliance was renewed between their sons, Asa and Benhadad I respectively. The kings of Israel were forced to keep watch on their southern and north-eastern frontiers simultaneously. If they tried to take offensive action against Judah, they had to expect an invasion from the north. So in about 890 BC, Baasha fortified the frontier town of Ramah as an outpost against Judah. Probably he also wanted to prevent any of his own subjects going over to Judah; the reputation of Jerusalem and of the dynasty of David was still strong! The king of Judah at the time, Asa, responded by sending a message to Damascus. Benhadad then invaded Israel and overran a good part of the territory north of the Plain of Jezreel. Baasha had to hasten north to deal with this greater threat, and during his absence the king of Judah organized compulsory work parties from Judah who demolished the fortifications of Ramah and carried away all the material to build two fortresses in his own Benjaminite territory against the northern realm.

The name of Asa is also associated with a religious reformation in Judah. He got rid of Canaanite cultic objects and institutions which had become part of Yahweh-worship at various local shrines ('high places') throughout the land. Stern measures were adopted even in his own household. Maacah was deposed from the important position of queen-mother because she maintained a shrine of her own with an image or sacred pole representing the Canaanite goddess Asherah.

Despite its weakness, the southern kingdom remained loyal to the house of David, which remained in power as long as the kingdom itself lasted, a period of 340 years after the death of Solomon. There was much less political stability in the northern kingdom. Only two dynasties—those founded by Omri about 881 BC and by Jehu forty years later—lasted for more than two generations. Jeroboam's son was assassinated by Baasha, one of his army officers, in the year after he succeeded to the kingdom. When Baasha had reigned twenty-four years, his son and successor died in the same way. A few years of civil war followed between various rivals for the succession; the survivor, Omri, was one of the greatest kings of the northern kingdom.

NOTES

1 It was only later that 'the land of Moriah' of Gen. 22:2 (perhaps originally the land of Moreh or Shechem) was identified with Mount Moriah, the name given to the temple hill in 2 Chr. 3:1.
2 That is, after the destruction by Nebuchadrezzar in 587 BC, and during the profanation under Antiochus Epiphanes, from 167 to 164 BC.
3 Probably modern Somalia. An area in southern Arabia or even India are also possibilities.
4 The Hebrew word in 1 Kgs 10:22 is *tukkiyyim*, which may be connected with Sinhalese *tokei*, 'peacock', or (more probably) with Egyptian *kyw*, a kind of monkey.
5 On the whole, little has yet been found in Palestine dating from Solomon's reign; but as P. R. S. Mooney states, 'Material remains of his ascendancy may everywhere remain meagre, but at no point does what survives invalidate the record of the Old Testament' (K. M. Kenyon, *The Bible and Recent Archaeology* (rev. ed. 1987), p. 107.
6 Or 'clay ground' (NRSV) or 'foundry' (REB).
7 1 Kgs 10:28 f. 'Egypt' should perhaps be replaced by 'Musri,' a district in S.E. Asia Minor. Cf. NIV margin, where the name is spelled 'Muzur'.
8 1 Kgs 4:7–19.
9 1 Kgs 4:32 ff.
10 The identification of Shishak with Shoshenq I remains probable in spite of some recent doubts; see D. M. Rohl, *A Test of Time* (1995), chapter 7, for a very different identification.
11 Exod. 20:4; Deut. 5:8.
12 It is relevant to recall here the Greek myth of Europa and the bull, since it has links with Phoenicia. In this myth Europa, the daughter of a Phoenician king, was abducted by the god Zeus in the form of a white bull.
13 Cf. ANET, pp. 263 f.

Chapter Five

The Dynasty of Omri
(881–841 BC)

OMRI'S REIGN

The civil war in the Northern Kingdom which followed the assassination of Baasha's son in 884 BC came to an end with the victory of Omri, commander-in-chief of the armed forces. Omri reigned only eight years after his triumph, but during his brief reign he gave his kingdom a direction, by internal consolidation and foreign conquest and alliance, which it continued to follow during the forty years that his dynasty lasted.

One important internal measure was the choice of a new site for the capital of his kingdom. Jeroboam had fixed his capital at Shechem, probably because of the ancient prestige of the place (the place where Abraham built his first altar after arriving in the land of Canaan). Later the capital was moved to Tirzah, about seven miles north-east of Shechem.

But Omri found a more suitable position and built the city of Samaria, seven miles north-west of Shechem. Samaria had the same central advantages as Shechem and Tirzah, but it also occupied a strong strategic position and its natural strength was increased by fortification. The wisdom of Omri's choice was shown on several occasions during the remaining century and a half of the Northern Kingdom's existence, when Samaria resisted several sieges conducted by well-equipped armies.

Omri extended his control in Transjordan by imposing tribute upon the land of Moab, which had regained its independence since the time when David conquered it. He renewed Solomon's policy of alliance with Phoenicia. This alliance was confirmed by the marriage of his son Ahab to Jezebel, daughter of the Phoenician priest-king Ethbaal (887–856 BC). No doubt this alliance gained some commercial advantages for Israel, but its religious consequences were very serious. Indeed, the prophetic party considered Omri a greater offender against Yahweh than any of his predecessors, surpassed only by his son Ahab himself.

It was a common practice that a foreign princess who married the ruler of a neighbouring state should have facilities for practising her native religion in her new home. So Solomon's many foreign wives had shrines provided for their native cults on the western slope of the Mount of Olives—an action which is attacked by the writer of 1 Kings 11. Even if such a practice was normal diplomatic conduct elsewhere, the prophetic party would have preferred no foreign alliances at all rather than alliances which brought foreign cults into the presence of the God of Israel.

AHAB AND ELIJAH

At least the religious practices of Solomon's wives had made little impact on the life of his subjects. It was a very different matter with the religious practices of Ahab's wife. Phoenicia was a powerful state, and it was expected that great respect would be paid to Phoenicia's gods, and especially to Melqart,[1] the chief god of Tyre. Jezebel was devoted to the worship of Melqart.

It is unlikely that the royal court had any plan to make the worship of Melqart the dominant or sole form of worship in Israel. Ahab, although he patronized the new cult, appears to have been a Yahweh-worshipper, to judge by the names borne by those of his children whose names we know—Jehoram[2] ('Yahweh is high'), Ahaziah ('Yahweh has taken hold'), Athaliah ('Yahweh is exalted'). But Jezebel was plainly not content to have a private shrine where she herself might practise her own religion. She appears to have organized the worship of Melqart on a fairly large scale and maintained a large staff of cultic officials, who enjoyed positions of influence at court. The worship of Melqart was essentially Canaanite in character, and its introduction into Israel led to a great revival of the old Canaanite worship of Baal and Asherah. Melqart himself was, from one point of view, the Tyrian counterpart of Baal, and in fact is called Baal throughout the Biblical narrative. To a large extent the result was a fusion of this Tyro-Canaanite cult with Israel's religion, so that many of the ordinary people departed from the purer forms of Yahweh-worship. The prophets of Yahweh protested against this apostasy, but their protests were treated as treason because the apostasy was supported by the royal court. At Jezebel's instigation many of these prophets were put to death.

The leader of these protesting prophets was Elijah, a man of exceptionally powerful personality, who announced a three years' famine throughout the land as a divine judgment for the apostasy. This made him the special target for Jezebel's enmity. He had to take refuge from her anger, first in Transjordan and later in Phoenicia. After three years he returned to Israel to lead the people back to Yahweh-worship.

The impressive occasion when the 'fire of God' came down on Elijah's sacrifice on Mount Carmel and convinced the people that Yahweh and not Baal was the true God is described in 1 Kings 18. The summit of Carmel, a range of hills which juts out into the Mediterranean, was an ancient holy place. Elijah did not build a new altar there, but repaired an old Yahweh-altar which had fallen into ruin. But even as he did so, he made his sacrifice at the same time as the daily afternoon offering in the temple at Jerusalem. It is true that 1 Kings 18 records no protest by Elijah against the cults of Dan and Bethel; but we should not assume therefore that he approved of them. These were corrupt forms of Yahweh-worship; but at the time the dangers of Baal-worship were a far more serious matter, and Elijah's active opposition concentrated on them.

The people who gathered on Carmel accepted Elijah's challenge not to waver any longer between two opinions. They acclaimed Yahweh as the real God, and at Elijah's orders slaughtered the cult-officials of Baal in the Kishon ravine at the foot of the hill. These events were followed quickly by the ending of the long drought and a downpour of rain, which again showed the people that they were right to return to covenant-loyalty. But Elijah, despite all that Yahweh had done on Carmel, panicked when Jezebel threatened to kill him, just as he had killed the prophets of Baal. He fled south to Arabia, where he held communion with God and received fresh encouragement at the sacred hill of Horeb, the place where Yahweh had appeared to Moses four hundred years earlier. With renewed strength, he returned to his homeland, to put into effect a plan of action which would lead to the destruction of the dynasty of Omri. He saw this as the only way to purify the land completely of the Baal cult.

The prophetic opposition to the policy of the house of Omri was not concerned simply with the external forms of the national religion, but with its social content as well. The covenant with Yahweh safeguarded the rights and privileges of ordinary Israelite citizens. But the influence of foreign alliances led to a weakening of the covenant in this respect too. Solomon's alliances had weakened Israel's covenant, and this weakening in turn had led to the break-up of the kingdom. The story of Naboth the Jezreelite clearly illustrates the same process at work in Ahab's reign.

Ahab had a country house at Jezreel in the Plain of Jezreel. Near his estate lay the small vineyard of Naboth, a freeborn Israelite of that town. Ahab thought that Naboth's vineyard would make a useful addition to his own estate, and he offered to buy it from Naboth at a good price or to give him a better vineyard in exchange. Ahab was perfectly free to make such an offer, and Naboth was equally free to accept it or reject it. Naboth rejected it. The vineyard was one which had come down from his ancestors; he did not choose to let it go, even for the sake of getting a better vineyard somewhere else. When Naboth said 'No', Ahab accepted his refusal: he could do nothing else. He was displeased, and went home and sulked; but he knew that Naboth was completely within his rights by the ancient law of Israel. The idea of violating that law did not occur to Ahab. But Jezebel his wife was used to a very different idea of kingship. 'Is this how you act as king over Israel?' she scornfully asked. Then she bribed false witnesses, who accused Naboth of blasphemy and treason in front of the elders of Jezreel; and in this way she brought about Naboth's judicial murder by stoning. His vineyard was confiscated and became crown property. When Naboth was dead, Jezebel announced to her husband that he could now take possession of the vineyard he desired without any obstacle. The king went to inspect his new property, where he was met by Elijah the Tishbite, recently returned from Horeb. From Elijah's lips the conscience-stricken monarch then heard a frightening sentence pronounced on himself and his family—a sentence which involved their total and shameful extermination.

And the prophets continued their opposition to the house of Ahab until this extermination was completed.

YEARS OF WARFARE

There had been an armed struggle against Damascus for several decades (with one important interval, described below). Ahab was wise enough to avoid fighting a war on two fronts. Instead of having to defend himself against both Syria to the north and Judah to the south simultaneously, he ended the quarrel with the dynasty of David. He made an alliance with King Jehoshaphat of Judah (c. 870–845 BC), Asa's son, and strengthened it by giving his daughter Athaliah as wife to Jehoshaphat's son Jehoram. (We are not told that Athaliah's mother was Jezebel, but Athaliah's subsequent behaviour suggests that she was.) The restoration of peace on Jehoshaphat's northern frontier enabled him to reconquer Edom, to the south. When the kingdom of Judah was strong, Edom was regularly conquered; but whenever Judah was weak, the Edomites asserted their independence. The Judaean conquest of Edom now, and their alliance with Ahab, and Ahab's alliance with Phoenicia, meant that the trade-routes between the Mediterranean and the Red Sea via the Gulf of Aqaba were open again.

When Benhadad of Damascus invaded Ahab's kingdom with a large army, Ahab succeeded in inflicting two successive defeats on him, one outside the walls of Samaria, and the other the following year at Aphek in the Plain of Jezreel. After the second battle Benhadad had to plead for his life. Ahab granted him peace on condition that he restored the Israelite cities which his father, Tabrimmon, had captured. A second condition was permission for Israel to establish bazaars with special rights in Damascus. So peace was made, and lasted for three years.

During these three years an event took place which would in any case have compelled the small states of Syria to forget their private quarrels and unite to meet a common danger. Assyria had been weak for two centuries because of raids by Aramaean nomads, but it grew strong about 900 BC under a succession of vigorous kings, who sent Assyrian armies westwards from the Tigris to the Mediterranean Sea. In 853 BC one of these kings, Shalmaneser III (858–824 BC), was confronted by a coalition of Syrian and Cilician states at Qarqar on the Orontes. Shalmaneser's record of the battle has survived, and it gives us information about the identity of these confederate kings and the size of the forces supplied by each of them. Among the twelve kings who fought him he mentions Benhadad of Damascus—or, as he calls him, Adad-idri (the equivalent of the Biblical name Hadadezer)—and Ahab of Israel. While Benhadad supplied the largest force of soldiers (20,000 men), Ahab supplied the largest chariot-force (2,000 chariots). Ahab is credited with supplying 10,000 soldiers—a large figure compared with the armies supplied by some of his stronger allies. The heritage of Solomon in horses and chariots had not been lost or wasted: the stables at Megiddo were still maintained at a high level of efficiency.[3]

Shalmaneser claims a sweeping victory. The corpses of his foes, he says, covered the plain of the Orontes and dammed the stream itself. But the fact that he did not pursue his alleged advantage but returned home suggests that his confederate opponents were far from ineffective.

When the Assyrians retreated, the alliance against them quickly broke up. It was not long before Ahab and Benhadad resumed their own battles. The Israelite frontier city of Ramoth-gilead in Transjordan had remained in Benhadad's control in spite of the terms of the truce three years earlier. Ahab decided to make an effort to recapture it, and King Jehoshaphat led a military force from Judah to co-operate with him. The narrative of 1 Kings 22 draws a memorable picture of the two kings sitting robed upon their thrones at the gate of Samaria, while obliging prophets foretold complete success for the enterprise—until the honest Micaiah ben Imlah described the vision in which he had seen the people of Israel scattered on the mountains like sheep without a shepherd. Ahab sensed that the truth lay with the one independent prophet rather than with the four hundred who had given a more comfortable response. So he disguised himself when battle was joined at Ramoth-gilead, and went on the battlefield looking like an ordinary chariot-soldier. But when 'someone drew his bow at random' and his arrow pierced Ahab between the joints of his armour, the king recognized that no disguise could protect him from his predicted destiny. Yet his last hours were worthy of a royal warrior: he had himself propped up in his chariot till the evening, to prevent his troops from panic if they knew their king was mortally wounded. At sunset he died from loss of blood and the battle was broken off.

His son Ahaziah succeeded him. The only recorded event of his short reign is his attempt to co-operate with Jehoshaphat to send a merchant fleet from Aqaba to import a cargo of gold from Ophir. The ships never set sail, since they were wrecked in a storm while they were still in harbour at Aqaba.

Ahaziah died in consequence of a fall in the year after he became king, and was succeeded by his brother Joram. Joram is credited in the Hebrew record for his attempts to discourage Baal-worship in Samaria. In particular he removed a sacred pillar or *massebah* which his father had erected in honour of Melqart.

THE REVOLT OF MOAB

Ahab's death had been the signal for a revolt of the Moabites, who had been made tributary by his father Omri. The tribute was paid in sheep and wool, the main sources of Moab's wealth. Year by year King Mesha of Moab had to pay to his Israelite overlord 100,000 lambs and the wool of 100,000 rams. We are told in 2 Kings 1:1 and 3:5 that when Ahab died Moab rebelled against Israel. This brief statement is considerably enlarged in Mesha's own account of the revolt, recorded on the victory monument which he set up at Dibon near his frontier with Israel. This monument is often called the Moabite Stone. It was discovered in 1868. In his inscription Mesha explains that the period of Moabite subjection was due to the fact that Chemosh, the god of Moab, was angry with his people; similarly he praises Chemosh for the success of his revolt and for the victories which Mesha won when he tried to extend his territory at the expense of Israel in Transjordan. The rebellion was, in fact, a holy war in Moabite eyes, and the frontier towns taken from Israel were 'devoted' to Chemosh—just as Jericho had once been devoted to Yahweh. Here is part of the inscription:

> I am Mesha the son of Chemosh-[kan], king of Moab, the Dibonite. My father reigned over Moab for thirty years and I became king after my father. I made this high place for Chemosh at Qorhah, [a high place of] salvation, because he saved me from all my assailants and caused me to see my desire upon my enemies. Omri, king of Israel, oppressed Moab many days, for Chemosh was angry with his land. His son succeeded him and he too said, 'I will oppress Moab'. In my days he spoke th[us], but I saw my desire upon him and his house, and Israel utterly perished

for ever. Now Omri had taken possession of the land of Medeba and [Israel] dwelt in it during his days and half the days of his son, forty years; but Chemosh restored it in my days. I built Baal-meon and made the reservoir in it, and I built Qiryathen. Now the men of Gad had dwelt in the land of Ataroth for long, and the king of Israel had built Ataroth for himself. But I fought against the city and took it, and I killed all the people in the city, a spectacle for Chemosh and Moab. And I took captive from there the altar-hearth of David and dragged it before Chemosh in Qeriyoth. And I settled therein the men of Sharon and the men of Mahrath. Then Chemosh said to me, 'Go, take Nebo against Israel'. I went by night and fought against it from daybreak till noon, and I took it and killed them all—seven thousand men, boys, women, [girls] and female slaves, for I had devoted it to Ashtar-Chemosh.[4] I took the vessels of Yahweh from there and dragged them before Chemosh. Now the king of Israel had built Jahaz and he dwelt there while he fought against me; but Chemosh drove him out before me. I took two hundred men of Moab, all of them chiefs, and led them up against Jahaz, and I took it to annex it to Dibon. I built Qorhah, the wall of the woodlands and the wall of the mound; I built its gates, I built its towers and I built the royal palace; and I made the two reservoirs for water inside the city. There was no cistern inside the city of Qorhah, so I said to all the people, 'Each of you make a cistern in his house.' I had ditches dug for Qorhah by Israelite prisoners. I built Aroer and made the road by the Arnon; I built Beth-bamoth, for it had been demolished; I built Bezer, for it lay in ruins, [with] fifty me[n] of Dibon; for all Dibon owes allegiance to me. I reigned over hundreds of cities which I annexed to the country. I built Medeba, Beth-diblathen and Beth-baal-meon, and I led up there the sheep-breeders of the country . . .[5]

In 2 Kings 3 we have the story of an attempt made by Joram, with the aid of his ally King Jehoshaphat of Judah and Jehoshaphat's vassal the king of Edom, to bring Moab back under his control. The Moabites were losing until Mesha in desperation offered his firstborn son as a sacrifice to Chemosh on the city wall. The spectacle of this desperate act of prayer to his god gave courage to the hard-pressed Moabites for one final effort, which changed the course of the battle and drove back the Israelites and their allies.

The story of the battle is also interesting for the part that the prophet Elisha plays in it, directing the strategy of the confederate forces. Elisha had been the attendant of Elijah, and he had succeeded his master as chief prophet in the land of Israel. The prophetic guilds recognized his leadership. He was to prove a reliable adviser to the kings of Israel for several decades, especially after the fall of the house of Omri. In fact, he played a large part in starting the revolt which led to its downfall.

Soon after the campaign against Moab, Jehoshaphat died and was succeeded as king of Judah by his son Jehoram, son-in-law to Ahab. This Jehoram was a weak king, and during his reign Edom rebelled against Judah and established its independence once more.

JEHU'S RISE TO POWER

The hostilities which were renewed between Israel and Damascus in the year of Ahab's death continued for a long time, with fluctuations this way and that. At one point during the reign of Joram the Damascene army penetrated into the heart of the land of Israel, and besieged Samaria. They were about to capture it, due to famine, when they heard a rumour that an army of Cilicians and Hittites from the north was coming to the assistance of the Israelites. At this, they abandoned the siege suddenly—to the immense and bewildered relief of the people of Samaria, who had been reduced to cannibalism by the severity of the famine.

In this continued fighting Ramoth-gilead remained a disputed city. Here Damascene and Israelite troops continued to oppose each other throughout the reigns of Ahab's sons. And it was here in 841 BC that the prophets' determination to destroy the family of Ahab was fulfilled.

The commander of the Israelite army at Ramoth-gilead was Jehu the son of Jehoshaphat the son of Nimshi. Several years before, when the prophet Elijah received a communication from God at Horeb in 'a gentle whisper' which was more powerful for destruction than wind, earthquake or fire, he received several commands. The first was to anoint Elisha as his successor in the prophetic office; and then he was instructed to anoint this Jehu as king of Israel and a man called Hazael as king of Damascus. Elijah did in fact take Elisha as his disciple and successor, but the two other acts of anointing he did not carry out himself. Instead, he left it to Elisha to carry out these commands. Hazael, formerly an officer of Benhadad I, had already succeeded his master. We are told how Benhadad fell ill and sent Hazael to Elisha (whose fame as a prophet was well known in Syria) to ask if he would get better. Elisha replied that the illness was not a mortal one; but he added that Benhadad would die none the less. Hazael pretended not to understand what he meant. Elisha then told him plainly that he would be king of Syria, and wept as he thought of all the damage and death that Hazael would cause to Israel. Hazael left Elisha, and when he arrived back at the palace he assassinated his sick master by pressing a wet cloth on his face, and took the throne for himself.[6]

That left only the anointing of Jehu to complete the threefold command of Yahweh. Elisha sent a member of a prophetic guild to Ramoth-gilead with a small flask of oil, and told him to request a private interview with Jehu. The prophet obeyed, and when Jehu and he were alone, he poured the oil over Jehu's head, hailed him in Yahweh's name as king of Israel and exterminator of the family of Ahab—and fled. Jehu's fellow-officers laughed at him about the visit of this madman, but when Jehu told them what had happened, the idea appealed to them immediately. They blew the trumpet, and proclaimed Jehu king, placing their military cloaks under his feet as he stood on the steps of the barracks.

The only justification for such a conspiracy must be its success.

Treason doth never prosper. What's the reason?
For if it prosper, none dare call it treason.

But treason indeed it was on Jehu's part. Not only did he rebel against the king to whom he had sworn loyalty, but by leaving his post at Ramoth-gilead he weakened the frontier defences of Israel in a manner that he and his successors had good cause to regret for many years.

Jehu's first task, however, was to take over the royal position he had claimed. Joram had recently been wounded in battle against the Damascenes, and was recovering from his wounds at his summer palace at Jezreel. His nephew Ahaziah, king of Judah (who had succeeded his father Jehoram the year before), was paying him a friendly visit. Suddenly the approach of a party of charioteers was reported to the two kings. They both set out to meet the party, expecting to receive important news from the battle-front, since the leader of the party was said to be Jehu himself. But when they reached the charioteers, they learned the truth. Joram received a forbidding answer to his query 'Have you come in peace?' 'Treachery, Ahaziah!' he called out to his nephew, and they both turned to flee. Too late: Joram was pierced to the heart by an arrow, and died on the spot (the spot, the narrator notes, was the former vineyard of Naboth). Ahaziah was also shot at and fatally wounded. Jehu showed his reckless nature; he gave no thought to any possible international reactions to the murder of the king of another country. 'Shoot him too!', he shouted (perhaps because he was a grandson of Ahab). Ahaziah died of his arrow-wound at Megiddo, and his body was carried home to Jerusalem for burial.

Meanwhile Jehu continued his task of wiping out the royal family. Jezebel, the queen-mother, was in residence at Jezreel, and met her death with queenly dignity: nothing in her life deserves as much admiration as her courage when she was killed. The other members of Ahab's household at Jezreel were massacred, but most of his family lived at Samaria, the capital. When they received a letter from Jehu, the elders of Samaria realized that they now had a new master, and that they must win his favour. The best way to do so, they decided, was to present him with the heads of the sons of Ahab. So the male descendants of Ahab, seventy in all, were slaughtered, and their heads were sent to Jehu at Jezreel. Next, about forty relatives of Ahaziah of Judah were also slaughtered; they had not heard about the rebellion and were on their way to greet the royal family of Israel. So the dynasty of Omri was wiped out. It was a popular dynasty; that is why Jehu thought it necessary to leave no member of the family alive in case he might become a focus for the people's loyalty.

But the extermination of the family of Ahab was also the policy of the prophetic guilds; it was retribution for the hostile action which Jezebel had once taken against them.

Another task was important for the prophetic party: Baal-worship too must be wiped out. This foreign cult had declined during Joram's reign, but Melqart still had a shrine in his honour in Samaria. Jehu therefore made his way to Samaria claiming to be a religious reformer. His claim was strengthened by securing the co-operation of Jonadab the Rechabite, leader of a very strict puritanical group. (This group related to other Yahweh worshippers in much the same way as Islamic fundamentalists relate to other Muslims.) These Rechabites had not abandoned the desert way of life to become farmers in Canaan, as other Israelites had done at the time of the settlement. They continued to live in tents, they sowed no seed, planted no vineyards and drank no wine. In fact, they abstained from everything that had the remotest connection with the Canaanite fertility-cults, and above all they detested Baal-worship.

On arriving at Samaria, Jehu acted cruelly and deceitfully. He proclaimed a solemn assembly in honour of Baal, pretending that he would patronize Baal-worship even more than Ahab had done, and celebrate a splendid sacrifice in his honour. When a large number of worshippers had gathered together on the appointed day—many of them no doubt simply wanting to please the new king—they were treacherously massacred. The Baal shrine and all its installations were destroyed; every relic of the Tyrian cult was suppressed.

In this way Jehu carried out the prophetic programme. But the manner in which he did it—the wholesale massacres and the treachery of the suppression of Baal-worship—was unpardonable. A century later another prophet, Hosea, announced in Yahweh's name that retribution would fall upon the house of Jehu because of the bloodshed at Jezreel.

NOTES

[1] Phoenician *melk-qart*, 'king of the city'.
[2] Abbreviated as Joram, by which form he is referred to below (pp. 37 ff.), to distinguish him from his namesake Jehoram, king of Judah (pp. 35, 39, 40).
[3] Excavations at Megiddo were at one time thought to have revealed the stables built in Solomon's reign. However, the buildings date from Ahab's reign, and may have been storehouses rather than stables.
[4] The female consort of Chemosh.
[5] See translation and notes by E. Ullendorff in DOTT, pp. 195 ff.
[6] 2 Kgs 8:7–15.

Chapter Six

The Syrian Wars and the Rise of the Prophets (841–745 BC)

THE SYRIAN WARS

When King Ahaziah of Judah died at Megiddo of the wound inflicted by one of Jehu's archers, his mother Athaliah, the daughter of Ahab, saw the opportunity to seize power for herself in Jerusalem. She was able to secure the support of the royal bodyguard, and had all the royal family massacred. Only Ahaziah's six-month-old son Joash was overlooked. He and his nurse were smuggled out of her way and the infant prince was brought up in the temple buildings.

The worship of Melqart appears to have flourished in Jerusalem during Athaliah's reign of six years: this suggests that she was a daughter of Jezebel. But in the seventh year there was a popular revolt, led by the priest Jehoiada, who succeeded in getting the royal bodyguard to transfer their loyalty from Athaliah to the young prince Joash. They guarded the temple while the boy Joash was brought out and proclaimed king of Judah. Athaliah did not learn what was happening until it was too late. When she came into the temple with a cry of 'Treason!' on her lips, she was immediately rushed out and put to death as soon as she was outside the sacred courts. The installation of Joash as king was marked by a three-fold covenant-ceremony between Yahweh, the king and the people.

In the Northern Kingdom, the dynasty of Jehu lasted for nearly a hundred years. At the beginning of Jehu's reign, Shalmaneser III of Assyria paid a return visit to the west, and Jehu is recorded as one of the western rulers who paid him tribute. He is called 'Jehu son of Omri' in the Assyrian account though he was the man who had exterminated the dynasty of Omri, but the title simply meant that he was king of 'the land of Omri'. Jehu probably welcomed the Assyrian protection against his Damascene neighbours to the north-east, and thought it worth the price of the tribute paid. But Shalmaneser returned to Assyria, and after 839 BC no Assyrian army appeared in these western lands for nearly forty years. No protection came from that direction against the Syrians. Jehu's sudden departure from Ramoth-gilead to seize the throne for himself had weakened the Israelite defences there, and the many deaths that accompanied his revolt weakened the state internally. The Syrians steadily encroached on Israelite territory during the reign of Jehu (841–814 BC) and the situation reached a climax under his son Jehoahaz (814–798 BC). Hazael of Damascus and his son and successor Benhadad II pressed home every advantage, until it looked as if Israel's independence as a nation would be lost altogether. Jehoahaz found that he could muster no more than 10,000 infantry, with fifty horsemen and ten chariots. These figures show clearly the extent of Israel's decline since Ahab's reign—he had been able to send two thousand chariots to the confederate army that faced Shalmaneser at Qarqar.

The Syrians invaded Israel from the north and east. They occupied all Transjordan and infiltrated down the western coastal plain as far south as Gath. Their control of Gath was a threat to Jerusalem, and Joash had to buy protection for his capital city with the treasures of his temple. This action seems to have angered the priests and the people, and he was assassinated about 800 BC. Other enemies of both Judah and the Northern Kingdom profited by their distress. The Ammonites, for example, encroached from the south-east upon Israel's territory east of Jordan, massacring the population to acquire more living space for themselves. But when the fortunes of Israel reached their lowest point, 'Yahweh provided a deliverer for Israel.'[1] This deliverer can be identified as the Assyrian king Adadnirari III, who in 804 BC led an expedition against Syria, in the course of which he raided Damascus and made it tributary. Syrian pressure on Israel relaxed. Jehoash, who succeeded Jehoahaz as king of Israel (c. 798–782 BC), was able to drive back the Syrians and to recover the Israelite cities which they had taken during his father's reign.

All through the long-drawn-out troubles of these years Israel had one man whose morale and confidence in Yahweh never wavered. The prophet Elisha was a tower of strength to his people, and when at last he lay on his death-bed, King Jehoash came down to see him and wept over him. 'My father! My father!' he cried, 'The chariots and horsemen of Israel!'— echoing the words spoken by Elisha himself when his master Elijah was taken from him. Elisha's last words predicted Israelite victory over the Syrians, and Jehoash inflicted three defeats on them.

Jehoash also captured Jerusalem, after receiving a foolish challenge from Amaziah, the successor of Joash as king of Judah. Amaziah had conquered Edom, and thought himself strong enough to fight against Israel. But he was beaten and made tributary, and a large part of Jerusalem's fortifications were dismantled. Amaziah was discredited and had to flee from Jerusalem, where the people made his son Uzziah[2] king in his place (c. 791–740 BC). A few years later Amaziah was assassinated at Lachish, where he had been able to hold out for some time after leaving Jerusalem.

About the same time as Uzziah was proclaimed king in Jerusalem, Jehoash of Israel died and was succeeded by his son Jeroboam II (c. 782–745 BC). Uzziah and Jeroboam II both enjoyed long and prosperous reigns. After the death of Adadnirari III in 782 BC the Assyrians were inactive for forty years, but Damascus was now too weak to undertake renewed aggression against Israel and Judah.

ISAIAH AND MICAH

Uzziah regained Elath on the Gulf of Aqaba and fortified it. He reasserted Judaean supremacy over the Philistine cities of the Mediterranean coastland. The agricultural economy of Judah received special attention. The prosperity of the kingdom may be judged from the variety of consumer goods enjoyed by the people in the cities. The character of his reign is reflected in the early oracles of the prophet Isaiah, a native of Jerusalem who was called to his prophetic ministry 'in the year that King Uzziah died'.[3] The list of female finery in Isaiah 3:18 ff. suggests a high level of material prosperity and sophistication among the upper classes. But the underlying condition of the Israelite people was not so healthy as the outward adornment might suggest. The wealth was concentrated in the hands of the few, who had extended their property at the expense of the poorer citizens:

> Yahweh takes his place in court;
> he rises to judge the people.
> Yahweh enters into judgment
> against the elders and leaders of his people:
> 'It is you who have ruined my vineyard;
> the plunder from the poor is in your houses.
> What do you mean by crushing my people
> and grinding the faces of the poor?' declares the Lord,
> Yahweh Almighty.[4]

> Woe to you who add house to house
> and join field to field
> till no space is left
> and you live alone in the land.[5]

The poor were also deprived of justice when they went to the lawcourts; the rich people who had taken their property were able to bribe dishonest judges:

Your rulers are rebels,
companions of thieves;
they all love bribes
and chase after gifts.
They do not defend the cause of the fatherless;
the widow's case does not come before them.[6]

Woe to those who make unjust laws,
to those who issue oppressive decrees,
to deprive the poor of their rights
and rob my oppressed people of justice,
making widows their prey
and robbing the fatherless.[7]

Isaiah was a city dweller. The oppression of the poorer peasants is even more vividly described by his contemporary prophet, the countryman Micah, who lived in the south-western part of the kingdom of Judah:

Listen, you leaders of Jacob,
you rulers of the house of Israel.
Should you not know justice,
you who hate good and love evil;
who tear the skin from my people
and the flesh from their bones;
who eat my people's flesh,
strip off their skin
and break their bones in pieces;
who chop them up for the pan,
like flesh for the pot?[8]

Peasants who owned small properties tended to be more and more at the mercy of their wealthier neighbours. One bad harvest was a disaster; two or three in succession might make life impossible. They were then forced to mortgage their smallholdings to wealthy neighbours, who would seize an opportunity to foreclose, and then add the small holding to their own estates, while the peasants and their families were compelled to work for them in virtual slavery.

AMOS AND HOSEA

This was the developing situation in Judah. It happened too, and on a larger and more alarming scale, in the northern realm, where the peasants had already suffered from the Syrian invasions.

Jeroboam II continued his father's work of winning back Israelite territory from Syria. He completed the reconquest of Transjordan as far south as the Dead Sea, while to the north he extended his power as far as the Hamathite frontier-post of Lebo-hamath (Lebweh). Yet his reign, for all its political importance, is only briefly outlined in 2 Kings. He is condemned for his maintenance of the bull-calf cults in the shrines at Dan and Bethel; and his victories are presented as a merciful relief from the Damascene invasions: Yahweh 'had seen how bitterly everyone in Israel, whether slave or free, was suffering; there was no-one to help them. And since Yahweh had not said he would blot out the name of Israel from under heaven, he saved them by the hand of Jeroboam.'[9]

Some of the details of his reign can be learned from the prophetic oracles of Amos and Hosea. They mention some details of his military career, such as the reconquest of the Transjordanian cities of Lo-debar and Karnaim.[10] But they are most concerned with the religious and social condition of the nation. There was a superficial prosperity, but it had been gained by the richer citizens at the expense of the small independent peasants, who had previously formed the biggest sector in the nation. King Ahab had not taken Naboth's vineyard by force because he respected the covenant laws; but this respect had now disappeared. The rich landowners had discovered ways to get hold of vineyards like Naboth's without breaking the law:

This is what Yahweh says:
'For three sins of Israel,
even for four, I will not turn back my wrath.
They sell the righteous for silver,
and the needy for a pair of sandals.
They trample on the heads of the poor
as upon the dust of the ground
and deny justice to the oppressed . . .

They lie down beside every altar
on garments taken in pledge.
In the house of their god
they drink wine taken as fines.'[11]

Rich men and their wives lived in ease and luxury on the wealth which they had extorted from the poor, with no thought for the misery they caused or for the effect on national life:

Woe to you . . .
You lie on beds inlaid with ivory
and lounge on your couches.
You dine on choice lambs

and fattened calves.
You strum away on your harps like David
and improvise on musical instruments.
You drink wine by the bowlful
and use the finest lotions,
but you do not grieve over the ruin of Joseph.
Therefore you will be among the first to go into exile;
your feasting and lounging will end.[12]

Yet these same people were extremely thorough in their religious obser-
vances. An enormous number of sacrifices to Yahweh were offered on the
altars at Dan and Bethel and other sanctuaries in Israel. The note of praise
rose regularly and loudly from tongue and harp. Was not this the worship
in which Yahweh delighted? So they thought, but the voice of Yahweh
through his prophet told a different story. Their unrighteousness and
disregard of covenant-obligations corrupted their devotions and made
them abominable in his sight:

I hate, I despise your religious feasts;
I cannot stand your assemblies.
Even though you bring me burnt offerings and grain offerings,
I will not accept them.
Though you bring choice fellowship offerings,
I will have no regard for them.
Away with the noise of your songs!
I will not listen to the music of your harps.
But let justice roll on like a river,
righteousness like a never-failing stream![13]

They talked complacently about the Day of Yahweh—the day when Yahweh would deal in judgment with his enemies. But did they not realize that
Yahweh's judgment would be carried out in righteousness, and that wrong-
doing would be punished wherever it was found? And if God found such
sins in Israel, they would be punished more severely than others, for other
nations had not enjoyed the knowledge of Yahweh and his will as Israel had
done. Yahweh had no favourites; as he had brought up Israel from the land
of Egypt, so too he had brought their neighbours, the Syrians and the Philistines, from their former lands and settled them in their present territories.
And just as he had driven out the former inhabitants of Canaan before Israel
because of their sin, he would for the same reasons dispossess Israel too.

The external form of worship was valueless without those inward and
practical virtues which were lacking in Israel. Amos would have agreed
completely with the words of Micah in Judah:

What does Yahweh require of you?
To act justly and to love mercy
and to walk humbly with your God.[14]

But that was not all: the external forms of popular worship themselves were corrupted by imitation of the old fertility cults of Canaan which blinded them to moral values. The worst feature was ritual prostitution, practised at the solemn festivals:

Father and son use the same girl
and so profane my holy name.[15]

Further details of these practices are given by Hosea, whose own wife was seduced by them. But it was Hosea's forgiving love for his erring wife that revealed to him the persistence of Yahweh's love for his unfaithful people. Yahweh planned to bring them back to their old covenant-loyalty, but first their addiction to Canaanite idolatry must be broken. This could only be achieved by being uprooted and carried away from their land, back to the wilderness to renew their loyalty to their God, who had first made himself known to them and won their love there.

THE DECLINE OF THE NORTHERN KINGDOM

In a situation of this kind, as T. H. Robinson has pointed out,[16] one of two things is bound to happen, and either way involves ruin. Either the point will come where the downtrodden peasants will revolt, and overthrow the oppressive ruling classes; or if they are too depressed and hopeless even to do this, then the nation has rotted from inside and will fall, an easy prize, into the hand of the first aggressive invader who comes that way.

Ill fares the land, to hastening ills a prey,
Where wealth accumulates, and men decay.

The 'hastening ills' came swiftly after the death of Jeroboam II about 745 BC. His son Zechariah reigned only six months, and was then assassinated at Ibleam, in the Plain of Jezreel, by Shallum ben Jabesh, apparently one of his military officers. The dynasty of Jehu thus came to an end in the fourth generation. It ended as it had begun, in rebellion and assassination. Not long before, Hosea had been commanded to give his first-born son the symbolic name of Jezreel, 'because I will soon punish the house of Jehu for the massacre at Jezreel, and I will put an end to the kingdom of Israel. In that day I will break Israel's bow in the Valley of Jezreel.'[17] Amos too had foretold that Yahweh would 'rise against the house of Jeroboam' with the sword;[18] it was in fact this prophecy that finally angered the chief priest of Bethel, and made him send Amos back to his own home in Judah.

But Shallum did not enjoy the kingdom long; in a month's time he too was killed by another military leader, Menahem ben Gadi. Menahem made himself king, subdued the cities which tried to obstruct him, and by a display of great cruelty made sure that there would be no rebellion against his rule.

NOTES

[1] 2 Kgs 13:5.
[2] Also called Azariah.
[3] Isa. 6:1.
[4] Isa. 3:13–15.
[5] Isa. 5:8.
[6] Isa. 1:23.
[7] Isa. 10:1 f.
[8] Mic. 3:1–3.
[9] 2 Kgs 14:26 f.
[10] Amos 6:13.
[11] Amos 2:6–8.
[12] Amos 6:4–7.
[13] Amos 5:21–24.
[14] Mic. 6:8.
[15] Amos 2:7. Other interpretations of this verse have been offered; above all, Amos was concerned about the abuse of defenceless women. Cf. D. A. Hubbard, *Joel and Amos* (1989), pp. 142 f.
[16] W. O. E. Oesterley and T. H. Robinson, *A History of Israel* (1932), vol. 1, pp. 366 f.
[17] Hos. 1:4 f.
[18] Amos 7:9.

Chapter Seven

The Fall of the Northern Kingdom
(745–720 BC)

ASSYRIAN VICTORIES

Within the quarter of a century that followed the fall of the house of Jehu, the Northern Kingdom collapsed. Amos and Hosea had foretold what would happen: the plumb-line of God was set against the wall of the state of Israel, and revealed that it was hopelessly crooked and ready to fall.

> The high places of Isaac will be destroyed
> and the sanctuaries of Israel will be ruined.[1]

The people had lost their former cohesion: social corruption was followed by political anarchy, and the swift succession of kings reflected the instability of the nation:

> So in my anger I gave you a king,
> and in my wrath I took him away.[2]

One strong push was sufficient to bring down the building in ruin, and the push was administered by the Assyrians.

About the same time as the dynasty of Jehu fell in Israel, a new ruler had seized supreme power in Assyria. This was a man named Pulu, who, when he became king of Assyria, assumed the throne-name Tiglath-pileser, which had been held by two earlier kings of Assyria. One of these, Tiglath-pileser I (1115–1077 BC), had been a great conqueror in his day, and probably Pulu took the same name because he hoped to achieve similar successes.

For the first few years of his reign Tiglath-pileser III engaged in campaigns against his northern neighbours in Armenia, in the land called Urartu (the biblical Ararat). Then, having secured his northern position, he turned west and invaded the numerous states of Syria, as his predecessor Shalmaneser III had done a century before. The rulers hastened to make their submission and pay tribute to the invader. From Cilicia to Arabia Tiglath-pileser III lists them: they included Hittite, Aramaean, Phoenician and Hebrew rulers, including

Rezin of Damascus, Menahem of Samaria, Hiram of Tyre, and (after stubborn resistance) Azariah of Judah. This expedition is usually dated in 738 BC, but probably took place four or five years earlier.[3]

The Israelite account is found in the Biblical narrative: 'Then Pul[4] king of Assyria invaded the land, and Menahem gave him a thousand talents of silver to gain his support and strengthen his own hold on the kingdom. Menahem exacted this money from Israel. Every wealthy man had to contribute fifty shekels of silver to be given to the king of Assyria. So the king of Assyria withdrew and stayed in the land no longer.'[5] Menahem felt the need of foreign assistance after his seizure of the Israelite throne, so he was glad of Assyrian support, even at the price of tribute. But the manner in which he raised the sum was certain to make him even more unpopular: he imposed a capital levy of fifty shekels (one mina) on each of the richer men in the kingdom, 60,000 in all.

Unlike previous Assyrian kings who had campaigned in the west for a few years at a time, Tiglath-pileser III intended to establish more permanent control. Where local monarchs were able to keep their kingdoms loyal to Assyria and pay the tribute he demanded, he left them in possession. Other areas were organized as Assyrian provinces, ruled by Assyrian governors. Their responsibility was to maintain peace and collect and deliver the tribute regularly. This extension and maintenance of imperial power depended on the Assyrian army, a superbly organized body of fighting men. The states of the west had never seen anything like the efficiency and speed of this army:

> Not one of them grows tired or stumbles,
> not one slumbers or sleeps;
> not a belt is loosened at the waist,
> not a sandal thong is broken.
> Their arrows are sharp,
> all their bows are strung;
> their horses' hoofs seem like flint,
> their chariot wheels like a whirlwind.[6]

The Assyrian army consisted of the regular soldiers, together with the militia who were mobilized in time of war. The regular soldiers wore a uniform or tunic, crossbelt, plumed helmet, kilt, and high boots. The militia were distinguished by the conical shape of their helmets. A company of infantry consisted of twenty-five files; each file comprised two men—an archer, and a spearman with a shield; these two stayed close together in battle. There were also units of chariots, slingers and engineers. The engineers were of considerable importance, for the Assyrians specialized in siege warfare.

Tiglath-pileser inherited this instrument of aggression from his predecessors, and developed it in order to carry out his imperial policy. Assyrian military operations were accompanied by ruthless brutality. Some earlier kings had shown great brutality to all whom they attacked, but Tiglath-pileser and his successors used cruelty as a planned policy. Any state or kingdom which submitted immediately to the Assyrians, and then remained loyal, received relatively mild treatment, though they were heavily taxed. But those states which resisted were crushed with great severity. The worst fate was reserved for those who, having sworn to be loyal, broke their oath and rebelled. These were treated as criminals against god and man; they had committed perjury, not merely against the Great King but against the Assyrian god Ashur. So their punishment— rulers and citizens too— was mercilessly cruel, as a warning to others.

Menahem remained the faithful vassal of Tiglath-pileser for the duration of his reign, as also did his son and successor Pekahiah. But there were other men and parties in the west which were not willing to remain under Assyrian domination, and these found supporters in the land of Israel. One Transjordanian military officer, Pekah by name, determined to bring Israel into an anti-Assyrian alliance headed by Rezin of Damascus. He therefore staged a revolt against Pekahiah, assassinated him, and seized the crown for himself.

THE INVASION OF JUDAH

There seemed to be a good opportunity to throw off the Assyrian yoke, since Tiglath-pileser was once more engaged in fighting against the people of Urartu. But the rebels had not realized that this Assyrian king was not the kind of man who was content to make occasional raids in the western territories, collect as much tribute from them as possible, and then go home and forget about them. Even so, they wanted to strengthen their forces; and so they tried to bring Judah into the alliance against Assyria. They asked the Judaean king, Ahaz, grandson of Uzziah, to join them. When he refused, they decided to use force. They invaded Judah with the intention of deposing Ahaz and placing on the throne in Jerusalem a Syrian named Tabeel, a man who could be trusted to carry out their will. This invasion of Judah from the north gave Edom the opportunity to regain its independence and to occupy the Judaean port of Elath (734 BC).

The invasion of Judah by the united army from Damascus and Samaria threw the court at Jerusalem into a panic. There was one man there—the prophet Isaiah—who saw that the Syro-Ephraimite policy was certain to fail. He urged his king and people to keep calm and trust in Yahweh, but he was not heeded. Ahaz thought he had a better plan: he would send to Tiglath-pileser and invite him to help.

This, as Isaiah insisted, was an unnecessary and foolish move. It was unnecessary, because Tiglath-pileser was certain in any case to march west as soon as he could and deal with this anti-Assyrian revolt. Ahaz's invitation would bring him no sooner. The folly of Ahaz's plan lay in the fact that it would draw the attention of Tiglath-pileser to the kingdom of Judah and bring Judah into the Assyrian sphere of control. Otherwise he might not have paid much attention to the small state in the hill country, which was some distance from the main lines of communication. But Isaiah's motives were not primarily concerned with geography or politics; they were religious. He knew that the Assyrian connection would have disastrous results for the moral and spiritual condition of his fellow-countrymen. The proper course for Judah to pursue was not foreign entanglement, but steadfast trust in God. He was convinced that if Ahaz and his people would only place their faith in God, they would certainly be upheld and preserved. But if they called in the Assyrians, the Assyrians would eventually bring destruction and not aid.

ASSYRIAN CONQUEST

Isaiah's advice, although he gave it in the name of Israel's God, was ignored. Ahaz had made up his mind, and he carried out his own plan. Tiglath-pileser's armies soon came and crushed the rebellion. Damascus was taken, and its monarchy was abolished. Its first king had been named Rezin, and the last king too was a Rezin. This kingdom was transformed into the Assyrian province of Damascus. The Israelites saw their fate approaching, and realized how disastrous Pekah's policy had been. They decided to act before Tiglath-pileser came, and they quickly assassinated Pekah and chose a new king, Hoshea, who immediately offered his submission to Tiglath-pileser (732 BC). This wise action, just in time, allowed him to preserve part of the kingdom of Israel; but all the territory north of the Plain of Jezreel and the Israelite lands in Transjordan were detached from the kingdom and made into Assyrian provinces—called Megiddo, Karnaim, and Gilead. The upper classes of the population of these areas of Syria and Israel were deported to other parts of the Assyrian empire and replaced by colonists from elsewhere. This policy of deportation was begun by Tiglath-pileser, and followed by his successors in the Assyrian and Babylonian empires, as a means of discouraging revolt. Any natural leaders of rebellion would come from the upper classes, so if they were removed far from their homelands they would have less opportunity and less inclination to start a revolt. As a short-term policy, this plan seemed promising: people would not be so ready to fight for a foreign land, and in this way the will to resistance would be broken. But after many years of this policy, the whole empire was full of discontented communities of displaced people. When at last there was a conqueror (Cyrus) who had sufficient political wisdom to allow exiles to return home, he was assured of immediate popularity at no cost to himself.

The deportation of Israelites from the northern and Transjordanian territories was so thorough that these territories lost their Israelite character. The Transjordanian provinces have remained predominantly Gentile ever since. The territory north of the Plain of Jezreel remained predominantly Gentile until it was conquered and judaized by a Hasmonaean king at the end of the second century BC.[7] The change in the population of that area is indicated by the name now given to it—'the circuit (Heb. *galil*) of the nations,' as it is called in a passage of Isaiah which mentions this depopulation but looks forward to a day of glorious hope for the same land, in words which the First Evangelist finds fulfilled in the Galilaean ministry of Jesus:[8]

> Distressed and hungry, they will roam through the land; when they are famished, they will become enraged and, looking upward, will curse their king and their God. Then they will look towards the earth and see only distress and darkness and fearful gloom, and they will be thrust into utter darkness.

> Nevertheless, there will be no more gloom for those who were in distress. In the past he humbled the land of Zebulun and the land of Naphtali, but in the future he will honour Galilee of the Gentiles, by the way of the sea, along the Jordan.[9]

Only the central portion of the land, around Samaria, was left as the diminished kingdom of Israel, ruled by Hoshea as Tiglath-pileser's vassal. 'The country of the house of Omri', says Tiglath-pileser, '. . . all its people [and their possessions], I carried away into Assyria. Pekah their king they had overthrown; Hoshea as king over them I placed. Ten talents of gold and . . . talents of silver I received as tribute from them.'[10]

APOSTASY IN JUDAH

Among the other kings from whom Tiglath-pileser received tribute at the same time he mentions 'Jehoahaz' of Judah. This Jehoahaz is the biblical Ahaz. One may wonder whether the shorter form of his name in the Bible is due to the fact that the biblical scribes considered that a king guilty of such apostasy against Yahweh did not deserve to retain in his name the element Yahweh (of which Jeho- or Yeho- is a reduced form, the whole meaning 'Yahweh has taken hold'). For when the rebellion was crushed, the Great King held a ceremony at Damascus, and his tributaries, Ahaz included, were summoned to meet him there.

And now it became all too clear what Ahaz's request for Assyrian aid involved. It meant that the kingdom of Judah became tributary to Assyria, and so lost its political independence. That was bad enough; but there were religious effects as well. The Assyrians did not compel the peoples they conquered to worship Assyrian gods, and so Ahaz's citizens were free to worship as before. However, some Mesopotamian religious practices had already penetrated Israel, and to some extent Judah too, and undoubtedly Ahaz's foolish action gave them greater prestige and popularity than before. As John McKay has written, 'It would indeed be surprising if it had been otherwise'. It would not have been politically easy for a king of Judah to suppress Assyrian cults. This situation in turn seems to have given encouragement to local idolatrous cults.[11]

A cult to the chief Assyrian god Ashur was established at Damascus; and the same happened in Samaria. It was not important to the Old Testament prophets that the kings of Moab and Ammon should set up the cult of Ashur alongside those of Chemosh and Milcom. But that Ahaz should set up an altar of Ashur in the temple of the God of Israel at Jerusalem involved a denial of the first principle of the covenant: 'You shall have no other gods before me (i.e. in my presence)'. The apostasy which began with Ahaz was to have devastating consequences for the realm of Judah. It brought about a corruption of the national character which two religious reformations could not put right, and which could only be purged at last in the furnace of the Babylonian exile. In the light of this sequel, we can see how right Isaiah was to oppose Ahaz's policy. 'Ahaz had paid a staggering price for survival, not only in monetary terms but most especially in the moral and spiritual compromises which his bargaining had required.'[12]

THE FALL OF SAMARIA

Towards the end of his reign, Tiglath-pileser conquered Babylon. The control of that ancient and sacred city greatly increased his personal prestige. He had himself solemnly installed as king of Babylon by taking the hand of Marduk, the chief deity of Babylon, in the temple of Esagila on the Babylonian New Year festival in the spring of 729 BC.

When Tiglath-pileser died in 727 BC, he was succeeded by his son Shalmaneser V. The change of king was quickly followed by unrest in Syria, under the influence of Egypt. Tefnakht, a ruler in the western Delta (727–720 BC), attempted to establish a unified kingdom in Lower Egypt, for the country had been split up among a number of local princes. He was worried by the fact that the Assyrians were in control of the Asian frontier of Egypt. One of the vassals of Assyria who was inclined to listen to Egyptian persuasion was Hoshea, whom Tiglath-pileser had confirmed as king in Samaria. Hoshea withheld his annual tribute from Assyria and at the same time probably tried to purify the national worship of Assyrian influences, if this is what is meant by the limited commendation given him in 2 Kings 17:2, that the evil which he did in the eyes of Yahweh (by maintaining the Bethel cult) was 'not like the kings of Israel who preceded him'. But he found, as many rulers in western Asia discovered in the following century and a half, that Egypt could not be relied upon to give any effective military aid to those who supported Egypt by rebelling against the Mesopotamian power.

> Ephraim is like a dove,
> easily deceived and senseless —
> now calling to Egypt,
> now turning to Assyria.[13]

Hoshea was summoned to the Great King's presence and thrown into prison (724 BC). An Assyrian army besieged his city of Samaria, and so strong were the defences of the city that even experts in siege warfare like the Assyrians took three years to storm it. About the end of the siege there was a change of dynasty in Assyria, and Sargon II, the new king who displaced Shalmaneser, claims the capture of Samaria as his own work:

> At the beginning of my reign, in my first year, ... I besieged and captured Samaria. I carried captive from the midst of it 27,290 people. Fifty chariots I took there to be an addition to my royal force ... I returned and caused more people than formerly to dwell there; I settled in the midst of it people from lands which my hands had captured. I appointed my officers over them as governors; I imposed tribute and taxes on them after the Assyrian manner.[14]

The last part of the former kingdom of Israel was now reduced to the status of an Assyrian province under the name of Samaria. An Assyrian governor was appointed to administer the area, who increased the tribute which was demanded from the Israelite people there. The upper classes were deported to eastern parts of the Assyrian empire, and replaced by settlers from other parts of the empire—from Hamath, north Arabia and Babylonia after several Assyrian campaigns between 720 and 710 BC. (Further colonists were sent there by later kings of Assyria—Esarhaddon and Ashurbanipal.)

These settlers when they first arrived were worshippers of various foreign deities, but in the land of Israel they soon learned 'the law of the God of the land'.[15] They intermarried with the Israelite population whom they found there and became indistinguishable from them. Since Samaria, originally the name of the capital city, was now the name of the whole province as well, all the inhabitants of the province came to be called Samaritans.

The deportation policy of the Assyrian kings had important linguistic consequences. Aramaic, which was spoken in the majority of the states between the Euphrates and the Mediterranean, became the most common language of communication in western Asia, and retained that status for several centuries.

If Assyrian conquest meant the domination of the Assyrian gods, it also meant the weakening and ultimate disappearance of the gods of the conquered peoples. The Assyrians supposed that the God worshipped in Israel and Judah was another petty divinity like the gods of Hamath and Arpad and the gods of all the other states overrun by the Assyrian armies. The gods of these small states would disappear if the nations who worshipped them lost their national identity. But the God of Israel was the Living God, whose survival did not depend on the well-being of his people. Not only the gods of Hamath and Arpad, but the gods of Assyria as well, have disappeared: the God of Israel lives.

NOTES

[1] Amos 7:7–9.
[2] Hos. 13:11.
[3] Cf. E. R. Thiele, *The Mysterious Numbers of the Hebrew Kings* (3rd ed., 1983), chapter 7.
[4] Note that here the biblical writer calls the Assyrian king by his personal name; elsewhere he calls him by his throne-name.
[5] 2 Kgs 15:19 f.
[6] Isa. 5:27 f.
[7] See page 171.
[8] Matt. 4:15 f.
[9] Isa. 8:21–9:1.
[10] DOTT, p. 55.
[11] Cf. J. McKay, *Religion in Judah under the Assyrians* (1973), pp. 69 f.
[12] Cf. E. H. Merrill, *Kingdom of Priests* (1987), p. 407.
[13] Hos. 7:11.
[14] DOTT, p. 59. The Assyrian records suggest that Samaria fell in 722 and was recaptured two years later.
[15] The literal translation of the phrase in 2 Kgs 17:26 f. (the NIV paraphrases).

Chapter Eight

Hezekiah and the Assyrian Peril
(721–686 BC)

REVOLTS AGAINST ASSYRIA

Sargon's accession to the imperial throne of Assyria occurred at about the time of the capture of Samaria and the deportation of its inhabitants. Elsewhere, it was the signal for revolts in many parts of the empire. In Babylon a Chaldaean prince from the land at the head of the Persian Gulf, Merodach-baladan by name, led a successful revolt against the Assyrian overlordship, and had himself solemnly installed as king of Babylon on the Babylonian New Year's Day, 1st Nisan, 721 BC. He strengthened his position by allying himself with the king of Elam, which lay along the eastern shore of the Gulf. When Sargon attacked the allies, he was defeated, and Mero-dach-baladan ruled in Babylonia for twelve years.

In Syria and Palestine, too, a number of states which had been tributary to Assyria revolted, under the leadership of the city of Hamath. Sargon's campaigns against these were more successful. Hamath was treated with special severity; its population was deported (many of them to Samaria) and replaced by settlers from Assyria, Armenia and Media. Farther south some of the Philistines—Gaza in particular—had revolted at the instigation of Egypt. When the Egyptians marched to their aid, they were defeated and thrown back at the frontier town of Raphia (720 BC). The other Philistine cities continued quietly, and wisely, to pay tribute.

For several years after 720 BC Sargon was kept busy on the northern frontier of his empire—in Armenia and eastern Asia Minor. His northern and western neighbours in those parts (including the peoples called in the Bible Meshech, Tubal and Togarmah) were gravely weakened about this time by raiders called the Cimmerians (the biblical Gomer) from the step-pelands of southern Russia and the Crimea. So Sargon was able to take advantage of the situation, and to secure his northern frontier from the river Halys in Asia Minor to the Elburz mountain range in north-west Iran. For some years he had no trouble with revolts in Syria and Palestine—partly because of the stern lesson he had taught the vassal-states in 720 BC, partly because of a revolutionary situation in Egypt. The Nubian king Piankhy invaded Egypt shortly after the Egyptian defeat at Raphia in 720 BC, and pressed steadily into the territory ruled by the Egyptian king Osorkon IV. Under pressure from the Nubians and threatened by Sargon's armies, Osorkon in 716 BC sent Sargon a present. But it was no use: the Nubians encroached more and more on Egyptian territory, until the time came when Sargon could describe Egypt as belonging to the land of Nubia. For several decades (c. 715–664 BC) Egypt was dominated by a Nubian dynasty (the XXVth). Once they had established control of the whole of Egypt, this new dynasty followed ancient practice and urged the border-states to revolt against their Mesopotamian overlords.

In 711 BC the people of Ashdod accepted a Greek soldier as their ruler and revolted against Assyria. An Assyrian army came to besiege Ashdod and stormed the city. Hezekiah, son of Ahaz, who by this time had succeeded his father as king of Judah, was inclined to listen to Egyptian persuasion and join in the revolt. He and his people were solemnly warned by the prophet Isaiah against paying any attention to Egypt. Isaiah added force to his warning by an acted prophecy, walking without clothing or shoes, like a prisoner of war, to demonstrate not only that Ashdod would fall to the Assyrians but also that the Egyptians themselves would be conquered and led captive in the same way.[1] According to Sargon's own account, Judah was in fact involved in this revolt. The Greek ruler of Ashdod, he says, tried to persuade the rulers of Judah, Edom and Moab to join his revolt, and also asked for the aid of 'Pharaoh king of Egypt, a prince who could not save them.' In their accurate assessment of the value of Egyptian aid, the Assyrians talk like Hebrew prophets! And in fact when the Greek fled for refuge to Egypt, the Egyptian king thought it wise to deliver him up to Sargon. Ashdod was now made the headquarters of an Assyrian governor, who had the greater part of Philistia as his province. The king of Ekron, however, who had remained loyal to Assyria, was confirmed in his position as Sargon's vassal. It has sometimes been suggested that the description in Isaiah 10:28–32 of an Assyrian army advancing on Jerusalem from the north is linked to these events:

They enter Aiath;
they pass through Migron;
they store supplies at Michmash.
They go over the pass, and say,
'We will camp overnight at Geba.'
Ramah trembles;
Gibeah of Saul flees.

Cry out, O Daughter of Gallim!
Listen, O Laishah!
Poor Anathoth!
Madmenah is in flight;
the people of Gebim take cover.
This day they will halt at Nob;
they will shake their fist
at the mount of the daughter of Zion,
at the hill of Jerusalem.

HEZEKIAH'S REVOLT

Whether Hezekiah took part in the revolt of 711 BC or not, there is no doubt that he took a leading part in an anti-Assyrian revolt some years later. Sargon died in 705 BC, and was succeeded by his son Sennacherib. As usual, the accession of a new Assyrian king resulted in widespread revolts, and the new king had to spend the first years of his reign crushing the revolts systematically in province after province of his empire. Merodach-baladan, whom Sargon had expelled from Babylon in 710 BC, returned and made himself king once more. He took an active part in stirring up revolts elsewhere. The biblical record tells how he sent an embassy to Hezekiah, apparently to congratulate him on his recovery from a serious illness, but actually (we may suppose) to find out whether Hezekiah would support the anti-Assyrian cause. Egypt was also busy as usual persuading local rulers to revolt. Isaiah warned the king against listening to either Merodach-baladan or the Egyptian king Shabako. He recommended a policy of patience:

In repentance and rest is your salvation,
in quietness and trust is your strength.[2]

But the pro-Egyptian party at court was too influential, so the prophet's warnings were ignored—until the disaster that followed proved his policy right. Luli king of Tyre, Sidqia king of Ashkelon, whose realm stretched as far north as Joppa, the kings of Moab and Ammon, and Hezekiah all withheld tribute from Assyria. The king of Ekron refused to join them, remaining faithful to his overlord, but the people of Ekron rebelled against him, deposed him, handed him over in chains to Hezekiah for safe keeping at Jerusalem, and joined the revolt against Assyria.

An anti-Assyrian policy made it easier to purify the national worship of Assyrian cultic elements. Hezekiah had probably begun this policy even earlier in his reign, and had also endeavoured to purify Judah from old

Canaanite ritual practices. To do this more effectively, he proceeded to close down the local sanctuaries in the kingdom of Judah, concentrating the national worship at Jerusalem. Even at Jerusalem he purified the temple worship in other ways: he destroyed the bronze serpent Nehushtan, a sacred object which had been revered for many years. He went further: now that the northern monarchy had fallen, he invited the Israelites from the provinces of Samaria and Megiddo to join their southern kinsmen in worship at Jerusalem, but these proposals met with a poor response.

Hezekiah also took steps to reinforce the defences of Jerusalem. In particular, he improved the city's water-supply by having a new channel cut to carry the water from the Virgin's Fountain[3] to the upper pool of Siloam in the south-east quarter of the city. These precautions were wise. It would have been even wiser to have followed Isaiah's advice and not revolted, but having revolted he was right to expect an Assyrian siege. And before long the Assyrian army came.

Methodically, Sennacherib crushed the revolts in the various parts of his empire. In 702 BC he expelled Merodach-baladan from Babylon, and installed an Assyrian prince as vassal-king there. Then he turned west, and marched to Phoenicia. The Phoenician cities which had revolted under the leadership of Tyre made their submission to the Assyrian king. The mainland city of Tyre was taken and the island part of the city was besieged for five years. From there Sennacherib marched south down the coastal road. As he went, Acco, Joppa and Ashkelon submitted to him. He next advanced on Ekron. An Egyptian force, marching north in response to the urgent appeal of the men of Ekron, was defeated at El-tekeh, in the Judaean foothills. Ekron submitted to the conqueror, those who had mutinied against their king were executed, and the king himself was handed over by Hezekiah and restored to his throne.

It was now the turn of Judah to suffer for her part in the revolt. All the fortified places in the kingdom, forty-six in number, were taken and over 200,000 of their inhabitants were driven from them as refugees. Jerusalem itself was closely besieged. The whole realm was reduced to a wilderness, and the capital was left amid the desolation 'like a hut in a field of melons',[4] says Isaiah—like a toolshed in an abandoned allotment. Hezekiah realized too late the folly of listening to his pro-Egyptian counsellors; in humiliation, he sent an embassy to Sennacherib offering his submission and agreeing to accept any conditions which the Assyrians chose to impose. Sennacherib imposed a crushing tribute on him, and reduced the size of his territory by giving parts of it to the king of Ekron and other faithful vassals of the Philistine coastal region (701 BC). Judah was so severely affected that, in the words of Isaiah:

Unless Yahweh Almighty
had left us some survivors,
we would have become like Sodom,
we would have been like Gomorrah.[5]

ISAIAH'S ENCOURAGEMENT

But the economic distress of the land was accompanied by a period of spiritual renewal, under the guidance of Isaiah. The disaster had tragically confirmed his warnings. And Isaiah's presence and encouragement were to prove a true tower of defence to Jerusalem when Sennacherib later decided to get rid of the Judaean monarchy and make the realm an Assyrian province. In the earlier stage of events Hezekiah was in the wrong, having broken his oath under the influence of his pro-Egyptian advisers; but now Sennacherib was guilty of unprovoked aggression against Jerusalem:

Woe to you, O Destroyer,
you who have not been destroyed!
Woe to you, O traitor,
you who have not been betrayed!
When you stop destroying,
you will be destroyed;
when you stop betraying,
you will be betrayed.[6]

Isaiah urged Hezekiah and his people to put their trust in God—he would be their defence against the Assyrians. Thanks to the faith of Isaiah, the morale of people and king did not break. An Assyrian army sent against Jerusalem to carry out Sennacherib's new policy received a report that an Egyptian force was marching against them, and changed direction to the coastal road. There, near the Egyptian frontier, the Assyrian army was ravaged by what appears to have been an attack of bubonic plague. Operations against Judah were stopped; and Hezekiah ended his days in peace.

It was in these days of hardship for Judah and Jerusalem that Isaiah had his vision of an era of perfect righteousness, peace and prosperity, not only for all Israel but for the other nations of earth too, under a prince of the house of David. His vision would be of far-reaching importance in shaping the outlines of Israel's messianic expectation. But, as events quickly proved, the fulfilment of that vision was not for the near future.

NOTES

1   Isa. 20:1 ff.; cf. DOTT, pp. 60 ff.
2   Isa. 30:15.
3   i.e., the spring of Gihon.
4   Isa. 1:8.
5   Isa. 1:9.
6   Isa. 33:1.

Chapter Nine

Apostasy and Reformation
(686–621 BC)

MANASSEH'S REIGN

Hezekiah was succeeded by his young son Manasseh, who for most of his long reign was the obedient vassal of Assyria. He accepted all the religious as well as the political implications of such a policy, and his reign was in complete opposition to the reforming policy of his father; he reverted to the policy of Ahaz. Ahaz's reign had been short, and there was therefore not enough time for his religious policy to create its worst effects, although his whole policy brought disaster enough on his people. But Manasseh's long reign—he reigned for at least forty-five years after his father's death[1]—gave ample time for Canaanite religious thinking and practice to become normal and acceptable to most of the people. The moral effects could not then be reversed, not even by a subsequent reformation, like that which his grandson Josiah carried out. Nothing would put matters right except the refining effects of national collapse and exile. The worship of the sun and other planetary divinities ('the host of heaven') became an integral element in the national cult in the Jerusalem temple itself. The local sanctuaries, which had been closed by Hezekiah, started up again, and the old Canaanite ritual flourished there the worship of Baal and Asherah, along with such practices as necromancy, ritual prostitution and even, on occasion, human sacrifice. Manasseh himself, like Ahaz before him, is said to have offered up his son as a sacrifice, presumably on some occasion of grave national peril.

All this was naturally opposed and denounced by the prophetic party, who saw that the royal policy meant a serious decline from pure Yahwism; but those prophets who opposed it were executed. Such stern penalties were no doubt considered to be in the national interest; it was feared that an anti-Assyrian movement would bring down the anger of Assyria on Judah once again. The foreign alliances, against which Isaiah had warned Ahaz and Hezekiah, created insoluble problems for Judah.

Sennacherib died in 681 BC, assassinated by two of his sons, and was

succeeded by his youngest son Esarhaddon. The most outstanding feature
of Esarhaddon's reign (680–669 BC) was the Assyrian conquest of Egypt.
This conquest reached its climax in 663 BC, under Esarhaddon's son and
successor Ashurbanipal (669–627 BC), when Thebes, the chief city of Upper
Egypt, was destroyed by the Assyrians. The Nubian control of Egypt which
had lasted for half a century was thus brought to an end. The fall of Thebes
is described by the Hebrew prophet Nahum, when he addresses the
Assyrian capital Nineveh and predicts a similar fate for her:

> Are you better than Thebes,[2]
> situated on the Nile,
> with water around her?
> The river was her defence,
> the waters her wall.
> Cush and Egypt were her boundless strength;
> Put and Libya were among her allies.
> Yet she was taken captive
> and went into exile.
> Her infants were dashed to pieces
> at the head of every street.
> Lots were cast for her nobles,
> and all her great men were put in chains.[3]

Yet the Assyrian conquest of Egypt, complete as it was for the time being,
did not last long. Ashurbanipal governed the country through a noble
Egyptian family that had shown its loyalty to him. But by 654 BC this family,
beginning with Psamtek I, was able to assert Egyptian independence of
Assyria and rule the country as the Twenty-Sixth Dynasty. Ashurbanipal
was unable to prevent Psamtek from doing this, because he was faced at
the same time with revolts among his northern vassals and with a war
against Elam on the east. Under Ashurbanipal the Assyrian empire reached
its widest extent: his power stretched from Sardis in the north-west and
Thebes in the south-west to Susa in the east. But the empire began to fall to
pieces even in Ashurbanipal's lifetime.

    Manasseh is mentioned in the records of both Esarhaddon and Ashur-
banipal. Esarhaddon lists him among twenty-two kings of the western
lands who were obliged to supply labour and building material for the
construction of his new palace at Nineveh. Ashurbanipal includes him in
a similar list of twenty-two kings who brought him gifts and escorted him
when he marched against Egypt early in his reign. The Hebrew Chronicler
preserves the account of an occasion when Manasseh was taken as a captive
to Babylon by officers of the Assyrian king.[4] It is not certain to what period
of his reign this event belongs, but we can probably link it with the revolt

against Ashurbanipal by his own brother in the years 652–648 BC, a revolt which caused widespread unrest. Another possibility is that the king of Assyria who brought Manasseh to Babylon was Ashurbanipal's successor Esarhaddon, who was king of Babylon as well as of Assyria, and treated it as a second capital.[5]

THE DECLINE OF ASSYRIA

Esarhaddon and Ashurbanipal are both mentioned in the book of Ezra as sending further settlers to the province of Samaria. Under Ashurbanipal ('the great and noble Osnappar' of Ezra 4:10) settlers were sent from as far east as Babylonia and Elam after he had attacked Babylon in 648 BC, and captured Susa, the Elamite capital, in 645 BC.

The inner weaknesses in the Assyrian empire were increased by the invasion of its northern territories by raiders called the Scythians from the Russian steppelands. They are first mentioned in Assyrian records in Esarhaddon's reign, but it was towards the end of Ashurbanipal's reign that they became a serious danger to the empire. Egypt and Lydia had gained their independence several years before; Media later did the same, and Elam, so recently conquered by Assyria, was seized by the Persians, an Aryan nation farther east. In 626 BC a Chaldaean prince, Nabopolassar, established himself as independent king of Babylon and founded a powerful dynasty there.

A vivid picture of the Scythian invasion is given by the Greek historian Herodotus,[6] although it is uncertain how accurate his account is. According to him, the Scythians dominated western Asia for twenty-eight years, in the course of which they marched down the Mediterranean coastal road as far as the Egyptian frontier (where they were repulsed by Psamtek), and on their return plundered the temple of Astarte at Ashkelon.

The threat of such an invasion by northern barbarians may provide the background for the language of the young prophet Jeremiah when he describes the situation at the time when he was called to the prophetic ministry in 626 BC. In that year the word of Yahweh came to him:

'From the north disaster will be poured out on all who live in the land. I am about to summon all the peoples of the northern kingdoms,' declares Yahweh. 'Their kings will come and set up their thrones in the entrance of the gates of Jerusalem; they will come against all her surrounding walls and against all the towns of Judah. I will pronounce my judgments on my people because of their wickedness in forsaking me, in burning incense to other gods and in worshipping what their hands have made.'[7]

For the present, however, Judah and Jerusalem had a period of relief from

powerful enemies; and the judgment from the north, when it came, was not
the work of Assyria but another nation. Meanwhile the outlook was gloomy
and menacing:

> Sound the trumpet throughout the land!
> Cry aloud and say:
> 'Gather together!
> Let us flee to the fortified cities!'
> Raise the signal to go to Zion!
> Flee for safety without delay!
> For I am bringing disaster from the north,
> even terrible destruction.
> A lion has come out of his lair;
> a destroyer of nations has set out.
> He has left his place
> to lay waste your land.
> Your towns will lie in ruins
> without inhabitant . . .
>
> I looked at the earth,
> and it was formless and empty;
> and at the heavens,
> and their light was gone.
> I looked at the mountains,
> and they were quaking;
> all the hills were swaying.
> I looked, and there were no people;
> every bird in the sky had flown away.
> I looked, and the fruitful land was a desert;
> all its towns lay in ruins
> before Yahweh, before his fierce anger . . .
>
> At the sound of horsemen and archers
> every town takes to flight.
> Some go into the thickets;
> some climb up among the rocks.
> All the towns are deserted;
> no-one lives in them.[8]

JOSIAH'S REFORMS

Manasseh had died in 641 BC and was succeeded by his son Amon, who
continued his father's policy. But new influences were emerging at court.

The assassination of Amon in 639 BC and his replacement by his eight-year-old son Josiah are probably signs of the beginning of a new anti-Assyrian policy. By the time Josiah was old enough to take personal control of his kingdom, the Assyrian grip on Palestine was weak (due mainly to the Scythian invasion). Josiah was thus free to initiate and carry out a policy of religious reformation such as his great-grandfather Hezekiah had been prevented from completing successfully.

The outstanding event of Josiah's reformation, and the one which gave the chief impetus to its most notable features, was the discovery of 'the book of the law' in the temple while it was being repaired in the eighteenth year of the king's reign (c. 621 BC). Even before this date he had begun to purify his kingdom of the idolatrous objects which defiled it. In Jerusalem particularly he cleansed the temple of all the apparatus of sun-worship and the other planetary cults which had been established there during the long period of Assyrian domination when his grandfather Manasseh was king.

The 'book of the law' was handed by the chief priest Hilkiah, who found it, to Shaphan the royal secretary, who read it in the king's hearing. There is little doubt that the book must have been a copy of Deuteronomy (as Jerome long ago realized[9]) or at least the law-code which forms the central part of Deuteronomy (chapters 12–26). The actions which King Josiah immediately took in order to fulfil the commands of the book were all based on laws and instructions which can be found in Deuteronomy.

The reading of this book alarmed and dismayed the king. These commands were the commands of Yahweh, but the nation had been guilty of far-reaching disobedience to them, and would deserve the judgments which the book pronounced against those who failed to keep the divine law. Josiah's recent actions against pagan worship now appeared to be quite inadequate; there was much in the religious life of the nation which needed radical reform if the commands of this book were to be obeyed. But no one was alive who could remember any attempt to obey them; perhaps it was now too late. An urgent message was sent to Huldah, a prophetess, to consult her on the matter and receive a response from Yahweh. The response was unpromising: the idolatrous worship denounced in the book had gone so far that it must inevitably be punished by God. But that judgment would not fall upon Josiah himself, because when the book was read to him he had truly repented of the sins committed by his people and his predecessors in ignoring the commands of God.

Josiah therefore set out to institute a thorough-going reformation. A solemn assembly was held in the temple, at which the newly-discovered book was read publicly, and the king led the chief representatives of the nation in binding themselves by a firm covenant to carry out all the things commanded by God in the book. Their act was in effect a reaffirmation of the earlier covenant inaugurated in the wilderness in the days of Moses, when the people of Israel heard the law for the first time and undertook to obey it. But was this reaffirmation of the covenant sufficient to cancel the evil brought about by generations of idolatry? The conduct of the nation in the years that followed proved that it was not.

The king quickly began to carry out his covenant. The temple had already begun to be purged of the Assyrian cult; but there were many other pagan installations of a Canaanite type: these too must be removed.

Josiah demolished the shrine in the Valley of the Sons of Hinnom, south of the city, where a fertility cult had been carried on for many years, sometimes involving human sacrifice. The valley which had been polluted by its presence was ceremonially defiled in order that the cult might never be re-established there. Where formerly fires had burned on the *topheth* or altar-hearth of Molech, now fires of another kind were to burn, for the place became the common refuse dump and incinerator of Jerusalem. The constant fires which burned there led to the name Valley of Hinnom (Heb. *Ge-Hinnom*) later being used as the name of the place (*Gehenna*, in its Greek form) where the wicked are to be punished in the world to come, just as the Garden of Eden (Paradise) supplied the name for the future home of the blessed.

Similar radical measures of reformation were carried out in the other cities of Judaea; idolatrous cults and priesthoods were suppressed everywhere. Josiah also carried his reforming campaign beyond his own frontiers. Now that Assyrian control in the west was weakening, he was free to enter the province of Samaria without fear of Assyrian anger. He did so, and in particular he destroyed the rival sanctuary at Bethel, just over the border, which Jeroboam I had made the southern of his two national shrines. Other local sanctuaries in the province of Samaria were similarly treated.

But the abolition of the remains of Canaanite worship and the destruction of idolatrous sanctuaries were not enough. Josiah went further: the purity of Judah's worship could be best safeguarded if the sacrificial worship of the kingdom were concentrated exclusively in the Jerusalem temple, where the king and his ministers could superintend it. The local sanctuaries of Yahweh throughout the kingdom were therefore closed down. Hezekiah, some eighty years before, had attempted a similar policy, but he had been unable to complete it effectively because of the Assyrian invasion. The Assyrians could now be safely ignored, and Josiah carried out his radical reformation unhindered by foreign interference. The closure of the local sanctuaries of Yahweh would involve considerable hardship for the priests who served these shrines, but probably the king intended that they should be attached to the priesthood of the Jerusalem temple. Both the centralization of the national cult and the attachment of the priests from outside Jerusalem to the central shrine were prescribed in the Deutero-nomic law.[10] But while the Jerusalem priests no doubt welcomed the centralization of worship at their own shrine, they must have been reluctant to share either their priestly duties or their income with a large number of priests from the sanctuaries which had been closed down. So the priests of the local sanctuaries evidently remained where they were.

When the initial stages of the reformation had been completed, a special celebration was held at the passover season of 621 BC. The passover was held in accordance with the distinctive Deuteronomic regulations[11] as a festival at the central shrine; the passover lambs for the whole kingdom were slaughtered in Jerusalem and not (as previously) at several centres throughout Judah. The novel character of this passover is emphasized by the statement in 2 Kings 23:22 that 'not since the days of the judges who led Israel,[12] nor throughout the days of the kings of Israel and the kings of Judah, had any such Passover been observed.'

THE MESSAGE OF THE PROPHETS

One important element of Josiah's reformation which would never be lost was the production, in its final form, of a historical document covering the period from the beginnings of the settlement in Canaan down to Josiah's reign. It appears in our ordinary versions of the Old Testament as the books of Joshua, Judges, Samuel and Kings. The presentation of the history in these books is so dependent on the ideals and laws of Deuteronomy that they are commonly referred to nowadays as the 'Deuteronomic History'. This history, however, was by no means composed at this time without the use of earlier records; most of the material incorporated in it had probably existed in written form for many years. Many of the earlier records must have been contemporary—or nearly so—with the periods covered by them. In the Hebrew Bible these books are called the Former Prophets, and this title tells us something about their purpose. They are not intended to be a secular chronicle, but a record of Yahweh's dealings with his people Israel, presented from the prophetic viewpoint. Probably members of the pro-phetic guilds compiled most of this history. The reign of Josiah, after the discovery of the Deuteronomic law in the temple, is the most likely back-ground to the publication of this invaluable record.[13]

In carrying out his reforming work Josiah could count on the support of some at least of the prophetic party. Two young prophets in particular appear to have supported him enthusiastically. One of these was (it appears) a distant cousin of his, Zephaniah by name. Zephaniah's prophetic ministry should probably be dated a little earlier than Josiah's reformation. Several of the reforms instituted by Josiah are predicted in the book of Zephaniah, such as the abolition of the planetary cult and the relics of Baal-worship, and the removal of the *kemarim*, or priests of the idolatrous shrines.

More important than Zephaniah is Jeremiah, whose prophetic ministry also began, as we have seen, about the time of the Scythian menace, five years before the reformation. Jeremiah himself belonged to the priestly family of Anathoth (in the tribal territory of Benjamin). The family was probably descended from Abiathar, who was exiled there at the beginning of Solomon's reign. Jeremiah must have approved of the king's reform so far as it went. He was only too well aware of the idolatrous tendencies of those local sanctuaries which Josiah suppressed, even if they were sanctuaries dedicated to Yahweh and not the Canaanite fertility gods. In the oracles which belong to the earliest period of his ministry, he denounces several of the abuses which were put down by Josiah—the many false gods worshipped with incense throughout the cities of Judah, the installation of Asherah-poles and cult-pillars, idolatrous altars, and the ghastly cult of Molech in the Valley of the Sons of Hinnom.

When Jeremiah saw these abuses being abolished by the king, how could he fail to approve of what was done? And yet, despite his approval, he was convinced that all this work of reformation was insufficient to cure the disease from which the nation suffered. It did not go far enough; it did not touch the national conscience. He recognized the sincerity and honesty of Josiah himself. But there were many others who accepted the reform simply because the king had set the example. Inwardly they resented his interference with forms of worship handed down by their ancestors. The covenant in which Josiah so solemnly led his people after the discovery of the law-book was no more than a repetition of the covenant of Moses' day, and suffered from the same defects. It could not change the people's nature, and would be maintained in the future with no more success than the original covenant at Sinai. A covenant of a different kind—a new religious relationship—was what was needed, and in due course Jeremiah foresaw the nature and strength of this better covenant:

> 'The time is coming,' declares Yahweh, 'when I will make a new covenant with the house of Israel and with the house of Judah. It will not be like the covenant I made with their forefathers when I took them by the hand to lead them out of Egypt, because they broke my covenant, though I was a husband to them,' declares Yahweh. 'This is the covenant I will make with the house of Israel after that time,' declares Yahweh. 'I will put my law in their minds and write it on their hearts. I will be their God, and they will be my people. No longer will a man teach his neighbour,

or a man his brother, saying, 'Know Yahweh', because they will all know me, from the least of them to the greatest,' declares Yahweh. 'For I will forgive their wickedness and will remember their sins no more.'[14]

More than six hundred years had passed since the old covenant was begun in Moses' day; another six hundred years would pass before the new covenant which Jeremiah foretold was inaugurated (as the New Testament teaches) by Jesus of Nazareth. But just before the national catastrophe, which nobody foresaw with such terrible clarity as Jeremiah did, this gleam of light was given to illuminate the future with divine hope.

For the immediate future, however, the outlook was very discouraging, in spite of Josiah's zealous example. The demoralization of previous reigns had gone too deep to be reversed by any such reform as the one he put into effect. So long as he lived he maintained the religious purity which he had so vigorously established; but his reformation did not survive after his death. Jeremiah was totally correct in his diagnosis of his people's sickness.

NOTES

[1] The 55 years assigned to Manasseh in 2 Kings 21:1 may include up to 10 years during which he was co-regent with his father; so Thiele, *The Mysterious Numbers of the Hebrew Kings* (3rd ed., 1983), pp. 176 ff. It is generally agreed that his reign as sole king was no more than 45 years.

[2] Heb. No-Amon; 'No (Egyptian *Nut*), the city of the god Amon'.

[3] Nah. 3:8–10.

[4] 2 Chr. 33:11–13.

[5] Cf. H. G. M. Williamson, *1 and 2 Chronicles* (1982), pp. 391 ff.

[6] *History*, i. 103 ff. For possible evidence of Scythian presence in Judah, see E. Yamauchi, *Foes from the Northern Frontier* (1982), p. 99.

[7] Jer. 1:14–16. We must not say, however, that Jeremiah's first stimulus to prophecy was provided by the Scythian invasion itself. The effective occasion of his call may have been Josiah's first steps in reformation, begun in the preceding year (2 Chr. 34:3). See J. Bright, *Jeremiah* (1965), pp. lxxix f., for the circumstances of the prophet's call to ministry.

[8] Jer. 4:5–7, 23–6, 29. This is not the only place in Old Testament prophecy where an invasion by northern barbarians is used as a symbol of divine visitation (cf. Ezek. 38–39; Joel 2:20).

[9] Commentary on Ezekiel 1:1.

[10] Cf. Deut. 12:5–14; 18:6–8.

[11] Deut. 16:1–8.

[12] The Chronicler states that 'the Passover had not been observed like this in Israel since the days of the prophet Samuel' (2 Chr. 35:18); the explicit mention of Samuel may be more significant than appears on the surface.

[13] Originally the Deuteronomic history may have ended with the account of Josiah's passover, at 2 Kings 23:23; the following narrative of the last days of the kingdom of Judah will then be an appendix or series of appendices to the main narrative, completed about 561 BC (the date of the last event to be recorded).

[14] Jer. 31:31–34. On the authenticity of the oracle see J. Bright, *Jeremiah* (1965), pp. 284 f.

Chapter Ten

Last Days of the Kingdom of Judah (621–587 BC)

THE BATTLE OF MEGIDDO

As Assyrian power steadily weakened, King Josiah was able to assert his independence, to carry out his reformation and to extend his control over the former province of Samaria, at least as far north as the Plain of Jezreel. But other nations in the Near East were gaining power, and the freedom of Judah was to be short-lived.[1]

In 616 BC Nabopolassar, founder of the new Chaldaean dynasty at Babylon, invaded Assyrian territory, but the Assyrians received help from an unexpected supporter. Another former subject of their empire, King Psamtek of Egypt, had no wish to see a strong successor to Assyrian power established on his Asian frontier. A weakened Assyria suited him well, and enabled him to extend his influence over the Syrian provinces, which had formed part of the Egyptian empire long ago. For the next eleven years, therefore, the Egyptians took action in western Asia as allies of the Assyrian empire, hoping to preserve it despite the blows directed against it by its enemies.

Nabopolassar had to withdraw in face of Psamtek's approach, but later in the year he routed an Assyrian army east of the Tigris. Next year he made an attack on Ashur, the former capital and most sacred city of Assyria, but failed to capture it. The city fell in 614 BC, however, when attacked by the Median king, Cyaxares. Media, like Assyria, had suffered considerably from the Scythian incursion, but had made a speedy and vigorous recovery. The fall of Ashur was followed by a Medo-Babylonian alliance, which was cemented by the marriage of the Median princess Amytis to the Babylonian crown-prince Nebuchadrezzar. In the summer of 612 BC the allies attacked Nineveh, which fell in August of that year after a siege of two and a half months. The destruction of the imperial city was hailed with delight by all the peoples of western Asia who had had to endure so much cruel oppression by the Assyrians. The victory chant of Nahum must have found a widespread echo:

> Woe to the city of blood,
> full of lies,
> full of plunder,
> never without victims!
> The crack of whips,
> the clatter of wheels,
> galloping horses
> and jolting chariots!
> Charging cavalry,
> flashing swords
> and glittering spears!
> Many casualties,
> piles of dead,
> bodies without number,
> people stumbling over the corpses.

> O king of Assyria, your shepherds slumber,
> your nobles lie down to rest. Your people are scattered on the
>   mountains
> with no-one to gather them.
> Nothing can heal your wound;
> your injury is fatal.
> Everyone who hears the news about you
> claps his hands at your fall,
> for who has not felt
> your endless cruelty?[2]

The Assyrian state survived the collapse of its capital city by a few years, thanks to the continued support of the Egyptians, who were now more anxious than before to have an Assyrian kingdom (or what remained of it) as a buffer between the Egyptian sphere of influence and the rising powers east of the Euphrates.

For two years Ashur-uballit II, the last Assyrian king, maintained himself at Harran, but Harran too fell in 610 BC. In the summer of 609 BC Ashur-uballit endeavoured unsuccessfully to recapture it, with the aid of Psamtek's successor, Necho II. As Necho marched north to help Ashur-uballit, his advance through Palestine was blocked at the Pass of Megiddo by King Josiah. Josiah must have made good use of the few years since 626 BC in developing a new Judaean army. In his opinion the weakening and disappearance of Assyrian power were essential for the maintenance of his own kingdom's independence, and so he determined to oppose Egypt's continued attempts to delay or reverse the process of Assyrian collapse. At Megiddo, then, this patriotic king endeavoured to block the Egyptian army's advance. His motives were good, but his political wisdom must be questioned. He refused to listen to Necho (who had no wish to fight him), fought him in battle, and was fatally wounded by the Egyptian archers. He was carried home to Jerusalem, and all Judah lamented his untimely death. They had very real reasons to lament him, although they probably did not fully realize it immediately, because the death of Josiah marked the end of Judah's independence. The prophet Jeremiah joined in the general mourning over so good a king, but it is noteworthy that Jeremiah's praise of Josiah lists his personal qualities but makes no mention of his reformation. Addressing an unworthy son of Josiah, he asks:

> Did not your father have food and drink?
> He did what was right and just,
> so all went well with him.
> He defended the cause of the poor and needy,
> and so all went well.
> Is that not what it means to know me?
> declares Yahweh.[3]

There is a strange similarity between the death of Josiah and that of Ahab, a very different type of king. Both were fatally wounded by enemy archers and carried home in their chariots to their capital cities; and they both disguised themselves on the battle-field, and perhaps for the same sort of reason. There are some grounds for thinking that Josiah's expedition to block Necho's way at Megiddo was opposed by the faithful prophetic party.

JEREMIAH'S PREACHING

A successor to Josiah was immediately elected, and the people probably had good reason to ignore his eldest son Eliakim and give the crown to his second son Shallum, who took the throne-name of Jehoahaz. But his reign was brief. Necho failed to recapture Harran for Ashur-uballit; but he tried to establish the frontier of his own sphere of influence at Carchemish. When the campaigning season came to an end, he marched south from the Euphrates, and summoned the new king of Judah to his presence at Riblah, a Hamathite city on the main road. There he put Jehoahaz in chains, to be taken captive to Egypt. In his place he made the older brother Eliakim king in Jerusalem under the name Jehoiakim. Josiah's foolish action thus resulted almost immediately in his country's becoming an Egyptian vassal-state.

Jeremiah, who had so recently mourned the death of Josiah, now took the view that Josiah's death had been a happier fate than that of his unfortunate successor Jehoahaz, who would have to spend the remainder of his days in captivity in Egypt.

> Do not weep for the dead king, or mourn his loss;
> rather, weep bitterly for him who is exiled,
> because he will never return
> nor see his native land again.[4]

Jehoiakim soon showed his subjects that Necho had appointed as their king an oppressive and ungodly tyrant. Although the land was crushed by the heavy tribute which Necho imposed upon it, Jehoiakim built a new luxurious palace for himself, using forced labour.

> Woe to him who builds his palace by unrighteousness,
> his upper rooms by injustice,
> making his countrymen work for nothing,
> not paying them for their labour.
> He says, 'I will build myself a great palace
> with spacious upper rooms.'
> So he makes large windows in it,
> panels it with cedar,
> and decorates it in red.
> Does it make you a king
> to have more and more cedar? . . .
>
> But your eyes and your heart
> are set only on dishonest gain,
> on shedding innocent blood
> and on oppression and extortion.[5]

And now it became clear how superficial the religious reformation under Josiah had been. Now that Josiah himself was no longer alive and on the throne, all the old idolatrous practices came flooding back into the nation's life. The prophets who protested were not only disregarded; their lives were endangered.

Early in Jehoiakim's reign the prophet Jeremiah raised his voice in the temple court in Jerusalem and made one of his most daring pronouncements.[6] Because of the sin of the people, he declared, that sacred temple, which was intended to be a blessing to all the nations, would become on the lips of all the nations an example of a sacred building cursed by God.

He pointed to the earlier shrine at Shiloh, which had been destroyed long before because of Israel's rebellion against Yahweh in days gone by—its derelict site remained as a warning to all who cared to pay heed. In the same way, he declared, the temple at Jerusalem would go down in ruin unless there was a speedy repentance. Jeremiah challenged the protest that this was Yahweh's own house and that God could never allow it to suffer such a fate. How, he asked, could they imagine that Yahweh would give them the protection of his house when, as soon as Josiah was dead, they went back to their former ways, burning incense to Baal, making cakes for the 'queen of heaven' and pouring libations to other gods. If they sought security, they must deal justly with one another, cease to oppress helpless people, and turn away from idolatrous worship. But if they persisted in theft, adultery and perjury, what was the use of coming to Yahweh's temple, imagining that it guaranteed their safety? 'Has this house, which bears my Name, become a den of robbers to you? But I have been watching! declares Yahweh.'[7]

These words really shocked the people. It seemed the height of blasphemy, to speak such words against the holy house of Israel's God. Many, in particular the priests and the temple prophets, demanded the blasphemer's death. But when Jeremiah was put on trial for blasphemy, he was acquitted because the secular judges recognized that he had not spoken of his own volition but 'by the word of Yahweh'. They reminded his accusers about the prophet Micah's prediction of the destruction of Jerusalem and its temple in Hezekiah's reign. Micah was not put to death, they pointed out; on the contrary, king and people had listened to his words and repented, and so the threatened disaster was averted.

There were obviously some people in the land who maintained the standards of justice set by Josiah. Jeremiah was acquitted. In this he was fortunate. We are told of another prophet, Uriah by name, who prophesied in the same terms as Jeremiah. King Jehoiakim condemned him to death. When Uriah fled for refuge to Egypt, Jehoiakim had him extradited and beheaded, and his body was thrown into a common grave. Jeremiah did not suffer the same fate because of the protection given him by a high officer at court, Ahikam ben Shaphan (perhaps the son of that Shaphan who was secretary of state under Josiah).[8]

NEBUCHADREZZAR'S VICTORIES

Necho's domination of western Asia did not last long. In the early summer of 605 BC a Babylonian army, led by the crown-prince Nebuchadrezzar, launched a surprise attack on Carchemish and crushed the Egyptian army which was based there. The survivors were pursued all the way to the frontier of Egypt, and might have been pursued farther, but for the fact that just then Nebuchadrezzar received news that his father Nabopolassar had died (August 16). He hurried back to Babylon with a few attendants, by the shortest route across the desert, to secure the throne for himself. The remainder of his forces returned home by the longer route, via Carchemish. They took with them captives from the Egyptian army and hostages from the states of western Asia which had recently been vassals of Egypt, including some of the noblemen of Judah.[9] So after one single battle all those states passed from the Egyptian into the Babylonian sphere of influence.

When Nebuchadrezzar returned to the west in the year after his victory at Carchemish, Jehoiakim formally submitted to him. At the time this made little difference to Jehoiakim; he simply paid tribute now to Nebuchadrezzar instead of Necho. It certainly made no difference to his despotic behaviour, or to his dislike of the prophets of Yahweh.

In the year of the battle of Carchemish Jeremiah had warned the people of Judah and Jerusalem that because of their persistent refusal to repent, they would undergo seventy years of servitude under the Babylonians. In the following year there was a dramatic occasion when his secretary Baruch, having written down at Jeremiah's dictation all the oracles which the prophet had delivered during his twenty-three years' ministry, read them aloud to the people assembled at a solemn fast in the temple. The king heard of this, and the scroll was borrowed from Baruch and read to the king as he sat in his winter house in front of a charcoal brazier. As the reader 'read three or four columns of the scroll, the king cut them off with a scribe's knife and threw them into the brazier, until the entire scroll was burned in the fire.'[10] Some of his courtiers who had more respect for the word of God than their master tried to persuade him not to burn the scroll, but he refused to listen. In his folly he 'thought the penknife was mightier than the pen'.[11] He behaved as if the destruction of the scroll could cancel the divine oracles that had been written on it. He gave orders for the arrest of Jeremiah and Baruch, but they had been taken safely into hiding and could not be found. Jeremiah used his time in hiding to dictate his oracles to Baruch again, and further oracles containing the same message were added to those that had been written down on the first scroll. The warnings of Jeremiah, like those of the other prophets of Yahweh, were intended to lead the people to repentance, in order that the threatened disasters might be avoided; but there was little hope of repentance and deliverance when the prophetic message received such contemptuous treatment.

Jehoiakim perhaps made some attempt to extend his realm at the expense of his weaker neighbours in the years that followed Carchemish. At last they banded together and attacked him and brought him captive before

Nebuchadrezzar (who visited the area year by year to collect the tribute from his new vassals). An event of this sort is implied by the prophet Ezekiel's poetic description of a Judaean ruler's career:[12]

> He prowled among the lions;
> for he was now a strong lion.
> He learned to tear the prey
> and he devoured men.
> He broke down their strongholds
> and devastated their towns,
> The land and all who were in it
> were terrified by his roaring.
> Then the nations came against him,
> those from regions round about.
> They spread their net for him,
> and he was trapped in their pit.
> With hooks they pulled him into a cage
> and brought him to the king of Babylon.
> They put him in prison,
> so his roar was heard no longer
> on the mountains of Israel.

But if this interpretation of Ezekiel is right, Jehoiakim must have been upheld by Nebuchadrezzar, who perhaps regarded his attacks on his neighbours as directed against supporters of Egypt.

In 601 BC Nebuchadrezzar led an army to the Egyptian frontier to fight against Necho, but this time he suffered severe losses, from which he took eighteen months to recover. Many of his new vassals immediately withheld tribute from him, including Jehoiakim. But when Nebuchadrezzar had repaired the losses in his manpower and equipment, he marched west again, and defeated the rebels one by one. He dealt first with Arab tribes east and south of Judah, and meanwhile incited Jehoiakim's neighbours to attack him. Then a Babylonian army laid siege to Jerusalem; Nebuchadrezzar himself arrived while the siege was in progress. Not long before the siege began Jehoiakim died (in December 598 BC). He was succeeded by his son Jehoiachin (otherwise called Jeconiah). The city was taken on March 16, 597 BC, and Jehoiachin, with many members of the royal family and the leading statesmen and courtiers, was taken captive to Babylon. So too were many other members of the higher ranks of Judaean society—three thousand in all. Among the captives was the prophet Ezekiel. The temple treasures were carried off from Jerusalem to be placed in the temple of Marduk in Babylon. Gold objects which were too large to be transported easily were cut up.

Nebuchadrezzar had now reasserted his sovereignty over all the territory between the Euphrates and the Egyptian frontier. It was perhaps at this time that a despairing letter was sent by the king of one of the Philistine city-states to his former overlord Necho,[13] imploring him to send help to a loyal vassal before the king of Babylon came and set up a governor of his own. But no help could be sent: 'the king of Egypt did not march out from his own country again, because the king of Babylon had taken all his territory from the Wadi of Egypt to the Euphrates River.'[14] Assyria had disappeared for ever; the Babylonian empire now covered all the southern area of the former Assyrian empire, while the Median empire took over its northern provinces. It continued to expand westward through Asia Minor until in 585 BC the river Halys was fixed as the common frontier between the Median dominions and the Lydian empire farther west. The kings of Babylon and Cilicia acted as intermediaries on this occasion between the Median and Lydian kings.

ZEDEKIAH'S REVOLT

Nebuchadrezzar appointed Jehoiachin's uncle Mattaniah to rule over the diminished population of Judah, with the throne-name of Zedekiah, and exacted a solemn oath of loyalty from him. Actually Zedekiah was a regent rather than king in the full sense of the word, for Babylonian records show that Jehoiachin, even in captivity, continued to be regarded as the legitimate king of Judah. His fellow-exiles too still regarded him as their king, as is evident from the book of Ezekiel, where dates are reckoned by Jehoiachin's regnal years.

It was an unwise act on Nebuchadrezzar's part to deport so many of the leading statesmen of Judah with Jehoiachin. This meant that those who were left as advisers of the new ruler were men of less wisdom and maturity. Many of them had learned nothing from recent experience, and still expected that Egypt would restore national independence to Judah. Zedekiah, having sworn an oath of loyalty to the Babylonian king, wished to keep it, but he was too weak to resist his foolish advisers. There was in fact one man in Jerusalem whose clarity of vision was undimmed—the prophet Jeremiah. If his advice had been heeded, even at this late date the worst disasters might have been avoided. Jeremiah warned the king and his advisers that their one hope of salvation lay in remaining obedient and loyal to Nebuchadrezzar. But his wise advice was rejected, and Jeremiah was considered a defeatist and a traitor.

At last the temptation to turn to Egypt proved too strong, and Zedekiah was persuaded to rebel against Nebuchadrezzar.[15] He hoped that Egyptian aid would protect him and his people against the inevitable Babylonian attack. But at the end of 589 BC a Babylonian army arrived, the kingdom of Judah was overrun, Lachish[16] and other fortified cities were quickly stormed, and Jerusalem was besieged.

THE SIEGE OF JERUSALEM

Even during the siege Jeremiah maintained that only in submission to the Babylonians was there any hope for the king and people of Jerusalem. For this he was fiercely attacked by the pro-Egyptian party, and accused of treason. At one time, indeed, it seemed that the pro-Egyptian policy was going to be vindicated, for Hophra (the Apries of the Greek historians), who became king of Egypt in 588 BC, sent an army to the relief of Jerusalem. The Babylonian army withdrew for a short time.[17]

But the people of Jerusalem showed no sign of repentance. On the contrary, they seized the opportunity provided by the raising of the siege to do a particularly cruel action. When the siege began, the richer citizens freed their slaves—probably not so much as an act of kindness as to avoid the responsibility of feeding them in the difficult conditions of the siege. But when the Babylonian army departed from Jerusalem, these citizens swiftly changed their minds and re-enslaved those they had just released. Jeremiah was shocked by this act of treacherous oppression, and declared that it had sealed the citizens' doom: the Babylonian army would return and reduce the city with the aid of famine and plague, until they stormed and destroyed it together with its inhabitants.[18]

Jeremiah himself took the opportunity provided by the raising of the siege to go out to his native town of Anathoth. But he was arrested as he was leaving the city by the north gate and accused of deserting to the enemy. He was thrown into prison, where he remained until the fall of the city.

As he had foretold, the Babylonians quickly defeated the Egyptian army that had come to the relief of Jerusalem, and then resumed the siege of Jerusalem. Jeremiah continued to insist that the city's only hope of survival lay in submission to the Babylonians. This insistence enraged the king's advisers, who attempted to take Jeremiah's life. Although the king himself was personally inclined to listen to the prophet, he confessed that he was unable to overrule his ministers. The siege continued, and the city began to endure the horrors of famine. The plight to which the people were reduced is movingly told by one who shared it himself—the author of the book of Lamentations:

> My eyes fail from weeping,
> I am in torment within,

my heart is poured out on the ground
because my people are destroyed,
because children and infants faint
in the streets of the city.
They say to their mothers,
'Where is bread and wine?'
as they faint like wounded men
in the streets of the city,
as their lives ebb away
in their mothers' arms. . . .

Because of thirst the infant's tongue
sticks to the roof of its mouth;
the children beg for bread,
but no-one gives it to them.
Those who once ate delicacies
are destitute in the streets.
Those nurtured in purple
now lie on ash heaps. . . .

Now they are blacker than soot;
they are not recognised in the streets.
Their skin has shrivelled on their bones;
it has become as dry as a stick.
Those killed by the sword are better off
than those who die of famine;
racked with hunger, they waste away
for lack of food from the field.[19]

Even the ultimate horror of cannibalism was not absent from the city's last days.

THE FALL OF JERUSALEM

At last, in early August, 587 BC, the Babylonian armies forced an entrance through a breach which they made in the city wall. The king and his principal officers attempted to escape to the south-east, but were pursued and caught, and brought before Nebuchadrezzar, who had taken up his headquarters in the Syrian city of Riblah. Here stern vengeance was exacted from those who had betrayed their oaths of loyalty to him. The sons of Zedekiah were put to death before their father's eyes, and he himself was then blinded, and taken to Babylon, where he spent the remainder of his life in prison.

Zedekiah was a weak character—as one writer puts it, he 'had a wish-bone where a backbone should have been'[20]—and could not resist his foolish pro-Egyptian counsellors. But in the eyes of the prophets his chief sin was his perjury: after swearing to be loyal to Nebuchadrezzar in the name of Yahweh, he rebelled against him, and brought disgrace upon the crown of David.

> O profane and wicked prince of Israel, whose day has come, whose time of punishment has reached its climax, this is what the Lord Yahweh says: 'Take off the turban, remove the crown. It will not be as it was: The lowly will be exalted and the exalted will be brought low. A ruin! A ruin! I will make it a ruin! It will not be restored until he comes to whom it rightfully belongs; to him I will give it.'[21]

So spoke the prophet Ezekiel; but in the very hour of doom his word of judgment contained a gleam of hope—the hope that one day a worthier king than Zedekiah would receive the crown of David.

A month after the storming of Jerusalem, Nebuzaradan, captain of Nebuchadrezzar's bodyguard, arrived in Jerusalem to carry out that king's vengeance against the city. The temple, the palace-buildings, and all the great houses of Jerusalem were set on fire, and the wall round the city was demolished. The metal work of the temple and the costly sacred vessels were removed to Babylon. A number of the principal citizens, including the chief priests as well as military and civil leaders, were executed. Many members of the upper and middle classes were deported to Babylonia, to swell the numbers of those who had been deported earlier.[22]

More bitter than the vengeance of the Babylonians was the action of the Edomites, Judah's old enemies. They did not try to conceal their joy over the disasters to Judah and Jerusalem, and openly exulted over the fall of the city. The words of Psalm 137:7 express Judah's bitter resentment:

> Remember, Yahweh, what the Edomites did
> on the day Jerusalem fell.
> 'Tear it down,' they cried,
> 'tear it down to its foundations!'

Edom's cruel behaviour to a neighbour was severely rebuked by the prophets, and the memory of it poisoned relations between the two peo-ples. The Edomites did not only rejoice in Judah's misfortune; they overran and occupied the southern part of the territory of Judah. In post-exilic times Edom (or Idumaea, to give it its Graeco-Roman name) is no longer the area between the Dead Sea and Aqaba, but the Negev of Judaea. Possibly the Chaldaeans officially gave the Negev to Edom.

NOTES

[1] It is possible that in Josiah's reign Judah became subject to some Egyptian control. See J. M. Miller and J. H. Hayes, *History of Ancient Israel and Judah* (1986), pp. 388 ff.

[2] Nah. 3:1–3, 18 f.

[3] Jer. 22:15 f.

[4] Jer. 22:10.

[5] Jer. 22:13–17.

[6] Jer. 7:1–20, condensed in Jer. 26:1–6.

[7] Jer. 7:11.

[8] Jer. 26:7–24.

[9] This is probably the setting of Dan. 1:1–6.

[10] Jer. 36:23.

[11] J. Paterson, *The Goodly Fellowship of the Prophets* (1948), p. 152.

[12] Ezek. 19:6–9; for this reconstruction see N. H. Baynes, *Israel amongst the Nations* (1927), pp. 99 f. Ezekiel's allegory of the lions is not easy to interpret (see M. Greenberg, *Ezekiel 1–20* (1983), pp. 354 ff.). Most scholars think these verses refer to Zedekiah rather than Jehoiakim.

[13] This Aramaic document was found at Sakkara in Egypt in 1942. One widely held view is that its author, Adon, was king of Ashkelon, which was captured and destroyed by Nebuchadrezzar at the end of 603 BC (cf. D. J. Wiseman, *Chronicles of Chaldaean Kings* [1956], p. 28; DOTT, pp. 79 f.).

[14] 2 Kgs 24:7.

[15] It was shortly before this that a body of Jewish mercenaries was hired by Psamtek II (595–589 BC) to help to garrison the southern frontier of Egypt, and settled with their families at Syene and Elephantine (see pp.107 ff.).

[16] The Lachish Letters, discovered in 1935 and 1938, illustrate both the boastful patriotism and yet the despair of public opinion in Judah at this time; see the translations by W. F. Albright in ANET, pp. 321 f., and D. W. Thomas in DOTT, pp. 212 ff.

[17] Jer. 37:5 ff.

[18] Jer. 34:8 ff.

[19] Lam. 2:11 f.; 4:4 f., 8 f.

[20] J. Paterson, *The Goodly Fellowship of the Prophets* (1948), p. 152.

[21] Ezek. 21:25–27.

[22] In addition to those deported in 597 BC others were perhaps deported from the cities of Judah at the beginning of the siege of Jerusalem in 588 BC.

Chapter Eleven

The Exile
(587–550 BC)

THE FIRST YEARS OF THE EXILE

After he had punished Judah for its rebellion, Nebuchadrezzar reduced its size and made it a province of his empire. He showed his skill as a statesman by appointing as governor a Jew, Gedaliah, who had been a palace official of Zedekiah and was known to have opposed the pro-Egyptian policy. Gedaliah set up his administration at Mizpah, where one of his supporters was the prophet Jeremiah, who had been released from prison by the Babylonians, and allowed to go where he wished, to Babylonia, to Mizpah, or anywhere else.

Even so, the devastated land was not permitted to enjoy peace. There were still Jews who were determined to resist Babylonian control, and in their eyes Gedaliah and his supporters were traitors to the national cause. One of these groups was led by a member of the royal family named Ishmael, who had taken refuge with the king of Ammon.[1] This group now came to Mizpah and treacherously assassinated Gedaliah and his supporters. But they could not remain in Judah and face Nebuchadrezzar's vengeance after this, so they went to Egypt, compelling the people of Mizpah to accompany them. In Egypt they joined many of their fellow-countrymen who had settled there already. One of those who were forced to go to Egypt with them was the aged prophet Jeremiah. He warned them that they would not escape Nebuchadrezzar by fleeing into Egypt, for Nebuchadrezzar would pitch his military tent in the forecourt of the royal palace of Tahpanhes (Daphnae), the frontier city of Egypt in which the fleeing Jews settled at first. But he was still ignored, just as he had been throughout his forty years' prophetic ministry in Jerusalem. They ought to have admitted that Jeremiah had been right all along, and that all their disasters were due to their rebellion against God. Instead, they insisted that things had never gone right since Josiah's reformation, and blamed him for their troubles. They decided that the best thing they could do was to resume the pagan practices which Josiah had abolished. So, in response to Jeremiah's last appeal to all the Jews in Egypt to turn to the God of their fathers and serve him only, they said:

> We will not listen to the message you have spoken to us in the name of Yahweh. We will certainly do everything we said we would: we will burn incense to the Queen of Heaven and will pour out drink offerings to her just as we and our fathers, our kings and our officials, did in the towns of Judah and in the streets of Jerusalem. At that time we had plenty of food and were well off and suffered no harm. But ever since we stopped burning incense to the Queen of Heaven and pouring out drink offerings to her, we have had nothing and have been perishing by sword and famine.[2]

And that is the last authentic record in the career of Jeremiah.

A further deportation from Judaea which can be dated in the year 582 BC may have been a sequel to the assassination of Gedaliah or may be connected with some further revolt.[3] Probably about this time the whole of Judaea except the Negev (now occupied by the Edomites) was added to the province of Samaria. All political activity in Judaea ceased.

There were other states in western Asia which resisted Nebuchadrezzar's control. An important one was Tyre, which preferred an alliance with Egypt to one with Babylonia, and withstood a thirteen years' siege from 587 to 574 BC. At last Tyre was captured, but the Babylonians gained very little profit or wealth.[4] The siege of Tyre was followed by military operations against Egypt itself. Hophra was defeated, deposed and replaced by Amasis, an Egyptian general. But in 568 BC Amasis revolted against Nebuchadrezzar, who then invaded and occupied part of the Egyptian frontier lands.

THE REIGN OF NABONIDUS

Nebuchadrezzar's empire did not long survive the great king's death. The years that followed were marked by usurpation and civil war in Babylon, and there were threatening forces on the frontiers of the empire.

His son Evil-merodach (Amel-Marduk), who succeeded him in 562 BC, is mentioned in the Biblical record as the king who liberated Jehoiachin from custody and gave him a place of dignity at his court. Jehoiachin appears to have been recognized as the legitimate king of Judah throughout his captivity— especially (we may suppose) after the revolt and deposition of Zedekiah.

But two years after his succession Evil-merodach was assassinated in a palace revolt, and his brother-in-law Nergal-sharezer (Neriglissar in the Greek historians) succeeded him. The principal event of his reign is the campaign which he led in 557–556 BC into Cilicia, which had become tributary to Babylon under Nebuchadrezzar. Not long afterwards Neriglissar died and was succeeded by his infant son Labashi-Marduk. But the time seemed to demand a strong ruler, and a further conspiracy was formed in which Labashi-Marduk was assassinated. The conspirators chose a king from their own group, Nabonidus by name. The fact that they chose Nabonidus to be king at such a time suggests that he was a man of outstanding ability, and not a weakling or mere antiquarian, as has often been supposed. The growing power of the Median empire, to the north of the Babylonian empire, made a strong and wise ruler necessary in Babylonia.

The Medes had begun to encroach on the Babylonian territories in north Syria, so much so that Babylonian control of the usual trade route from the Egyptian frontier to Mesopotamia via Carchemish was in danger. Nabonidus took various measures to counter this threat. One was direct: he campaigned against the Medes in Syria in an endeavour to drive them out of Babylonian territory. Secondly, to strengthen his position against them, he allied himself with the small but growing Indo-European kingdom of Anshan, a former province of Elam, which had extended its territories westwards as a result of the fall of the kingdom of Elam in 645 BC, but was now over-shadowed by the dominant power of Media. This kingdom, known farther west as the kingdom of Persia, was ruled at this time by a young monarch of exceptional military and political ability, Cyrus II, who had succeeded to the throne of his fathers in 559 BC, and was allied by marriage to the royal house of Media.

Thirdly, Nabonidus determined to impose Babylonian control more firmly over the southern part of his empire, between the Persian Gulf and the Egyptian frontier, and to create new trade-routes in that area, in view of the Median threat to those in the north. To do this more effectively, he seized the oasis of Tema in north Arabia, the centre of several important trade-routes, and laid it out almost as a second capital city for his empire. He made Tema his headquarters for some years, while he developed these southern trade-routes. In view of his long absences from Babylon, he appointed his eldest son Belshazzar as viceroy in his absence. Nabonidus's absence from Babylon caused considerable discontent there, especially as for several years he did not trouble to attend the New Year ceremony and play the part which was expected of a Babylonian king. This was one of his functions which a viceroy, even when that viceroy was also crown-prince, could not carry out for him.

His neglect of this ceremony was partly due to his many activities in north Arabia. It is doubtful if he deliberately neglected the worship of Marduk, the chief god of Babylon, but it is certainly true that he showed a special interest in the worship of the moon-god Sin.[5]

Very little is known about the condition of the Jewish exiles in Babylonia during the reign of Nabonidus. Perhaps he used some of them to serve in the garrisons he placed in several cities of northern Arabia.[6] It is at any rate clear that the Jews, in both Babylonia and Palestine, warmly welcomed the end of the Babylonian empire when it fell to Cyrus.

The first hint of the impending fall of Babylon came in 550 BC, when the Median and Persian armies met in decisive battle, and victory went to the Persians. The Median army was more numerous and powerful, but the smaller army of Persia was led by a military genius, Cyrus. The power of Media was overthrown. Cyrus immediately displayed the qualities of a statesman as well as those of a military commander. Instead of treating the Medes as defeated enemies and a subject nation, he had himself installed as king of Media and governed Media and Persia as a dual monarchy, each part of which enjoyed equal rights.[7] The only reason for Babylonia's alliance with Persia, namely their common fear of Media, immediately disappeared. Nabonidus now had along his whole eastern frontier one single powerful neighbour, whose realm extended from the Persian Gulf to the river Halys in central Asia Minor.

NOTES

[1] Ammon had rebelled against Nebuchadrezzar about the same time as Judah, but Nebuchadrezzar decided to conquer Judah first, so that Ammon still remained a centre of anti-Babylonian intrigue (see Ezek. 21:18–23).

[2] Jer. 44:16–18.

[3] Jer. 52:30.

[4] Cf. Ezek. 29:18. See H. J. Katzenstein, *The History of Tyre* (1973), pp. 330 f.

[5] For a description of the reign of Nabonidus, see D. J. Wiseman in CAH, 2nd ed., vol. 3, part 2 (1991), pp. 243–251.

[6] T. C. Mitchell in CAH, 2nd ed., vol. 3, part 2 (1991), pp. 425 f.

[7] Hence the frequent references in the Old Testament literature of the postexilic period to the Medes and Persians as the component nations of this dual monarchy; hence too, the Greek historians' habit of using the names Medes and Persians as synonyms.

Chapter Twelve

When the Lord Turned Again
the Captivity of Zion
(550–465 BC)

THE RISE OF CYRUS

According to the late Dom Gregory Dix:

> The tapestry of history has no point at which you can cut it and leave the design intelligible. Yet the sudden rise to Empire c. 550 BC of Cyrus, the prince of a petty Persian tribe, is almost such a point. Herodotus saw in this event the turning point of all Greek history. That is only a part of the truth. Deutero-Isaiah, who saw in Cyrus God's Shepherd of the nations, the man whose right hand God Himself had held, 'to open the doors before him and the gates shall not be shut,' suggests a wider vision. The life's work of this one man moulded the destiny of three great civilizations and set the main lines upon which universal history would run for more than fifteen hundred years, with consequences that are still potent today.[1]

When Cyrus took control of Media in 550 BC he completely changed the balance of power in western Asia. The alliance between himself and Nabonidus evaporated because Media was no longer their common enemy. Nabonidus allied himself instead with Lydia and Egypt. Instead of ruling over a small territory on the eastern shore of the Persian Gulf, Cyrus was now king of a realm that extended westwards across northern Mesopotamia well into Asia Minor.

Croesus of Lydia now had the Persian Cyrus as his eastern neighbour instead of the Median rulers. He was unsure whether Cyrus would observe the truce which his Median predecessors had made with Lydia in 585 BC, or whether he would continue to expand his territory—by invading Lydia. Herodotus tells us how Croesus, in his perplexity, went to get advice from the renowned oracle of Apollo at Delphi. The oracle returned an ominous response, warning Croesus to take measures for his safety when a mule ruled over the Medes. But how could a mule rule over the Medes?—unless, indeed, the reference was to Cyrus, who was the son of a Persian father and a Median mother. The more Croesus pondered the matter, the more certain he was that Cyrus's rise to power was a serious danger to Lydia. There was only one thing to be done—not to wait for Cyrus to attack him but to take the initiative against Cyrus and attack him first. Such an important decision, however, must await the oracle's advice. Should Croesus, or should he not, lead his armies across the River Halys into Cyrus's territory? 'By crossing the Halys', the oracle replied, 'Croesus will destroy a great empire'. Croesus was satisfied: he thought that the oracle had promised him victory, and so he took his armies across the Halys. But the great empire which perished as a result of this action was not the Medo-Persian but the Lydian. Cyrus drove back the invaders, pursued them back across the Halys into their own land of Lydia, pressed westwards until he stormed and destroyed Croesus's royal city of Sardis and took Croesus himself captive (about 546 BC). All Lydia fell into Cyrus's hands. His empire now extended west to the Aegean Sea; the Greek cities of the Aegean coast of Asia Minor, which had till now paid tribute to Croesus, were compelled to transfer their loyalty and their tribute to Cyrus.

We can imagine the alarm which the apparently irresistible progress of Cyrus produced in the ruling classes of Babylon. But in the hearts of the subject-races of the Babylonian empire, and especially in the hearts of the displaced persons from Palestine and elsewhere, the news of his conquests must have caused excitement and raised great hopes.

THE SERVANT OF THE LORD

This situation forms the background to chapters 40 to 55 of the book of Isaiah. At the beginning of this group of oracles Cyrus's rise to power and conquering progress are described; his conquest of Babylon is foretold. But Cyrus is shown to be one raised up by the God of Israel to fulfil God's purposes without knowing it. Yahweh has anointed Cyrus to be his agent. By defeating Israel's oppressors Cyrus will enable the exiles of Judah and Jerusalem to return home and rebuild their state. But this is not the end of the divine purpose; it is for a much greater purpose than this that Persian dominion has grown so rapidly, allowing Israel's exiles to return home. It is in order that through Israel the knowledge of the true God may be carried to all the nations. For Israel's God is the only real God; all the other so-called gods are mere nonentities. The gods of the nations conquered by Cyrus were unable to give their worshippers wise counsel and powerless to deliver them. Greek historians told how Croesus consulted the most famous oracles of their land, but only received responses which were ambiguous and misleading.

But Israel's God could foretell the future by his wisdom, and by his power he had raised up Cyrus and directed his victorious career, in order to accomplish his own will and to deliver his people from bondage and restore them to their own land, that they might be the messengers of his truth to the ends of the earth.

But Israel's mission, these chapters also tell us, is to be brought to its fulfilment by someone called the Servant of Yahweh, who is closely associated with the Israelite nation and yet is distinguished from it. Like Cyrus, he is raised up to accomplish the purpose of God, but while Cyrus carried out that purpose unconsciously, the Servant fulfils it intelligently and gladly. Nor are his methods those of Cyrus. Instead of making a noise in the world and imposing his will on others by force, he works quietly and unseen, maintaining his obedience to God in spite of unjust judgment, suffering, contempt—and death.[2] But by enduring these things he carries his obedience to God to its appointed end, achieving the divine purpose to bring the knowledge of God and forgiveness of sins to the nations of the earth:

> It is too small a thing for you to be my servant
> to restore the tribes of Jacob
> and bring back those of Israel I have kept.
> I will also make you a light to the Gentiles,
> that you may bring my salvation to the ends of the earth.[3]

CYRUS AND BABYLON

As the prophet foretold, so it came to pass: Cyrus added Babylon to his conquests on October 12, 539 BC, and entered the city on October 29. This was followed quickly by two decrees authorizing the Jewish exiles to return and to rebuild their temple in Jerusalem.

As Cyrus marched through Babylonia, city after city opened its gates to him. Although the crown-prince Belshazzar lost his life in the course of the Persian entry into Babylon, even that city was taken with very little fighting. Such at any rate is the account given by Cyrus himself, and preserved in two inscriptions: the 'Verse Chronicle of Nabonidus' and the 'Cyrus Cylinder'.[4] Cyrus won over the official classes to his side by claiming to be the champion of the gods of the various cities for whom Nabonidus had shown contempt. He sent back to the other cities of Babylonia the images which Nabonidus had brought to Babylon. In Babylon itself he declared that he was the vindicator of the rights of the god Marduk, which had been so shamefully neglected by Nabonidus in favour of the moon-god. He stated that Marduk had for this very reason given him victory. Nabonidus had lost the goodwill of his people in Babylon by omitting the New Year ceremony in which he ought to have taken the hand of Marduk and thus been solemnly reinstalled in his royal office year by year. Cyrus in 537 BC took the hand of Marduk and thus legitimated his status as rightful king of Babylon. This act did not signify any special devotion to Marduk on Cyrus's part, but he was sensible enough to realize that outward respect to the deities of his subject nations cost him nothing and would gain their submission and even their gratitude.

In this respect, as in many others, Cyrus's conception of empire was quite different from that of earlier rulers. The Assyrians, even if they did not usually impose the worship of their chief gods on their subjects, certainly boasted of defeating their subjects' gods. Cyrus, whose personal religious views are not easy to determine, had no intention of offending his subjects' religious feelings by such a policy. On the contrary, he would win them over by playing the part of a worshipper of their various gods. 'The Great King,' as one scholar has remarked, 'had no objection to bowing in the house of Rimmon if there was anything to be picked up on the floor.' There is evidence from other parts of the Persian empire that this policy was not followed in Babylonia only.

CYRUS AND THE JEWS

Against this background we can understand the political motives of Cyrus's action with regard to the Jews. The Assyrian and Babylonian policy of deportation had filled their empires with groups of discontented exiles. It was easy for Cyrus to win the gratitude of these exiles by cancelling his predecessors' edicts of deportation. As a wise administrator, he knew it was easier to control an empire full of contented subjects than discontented ones.

Probably two decrees were issued by Cyrus with regard to the Jews, one authorizing the rebuilding of the temple at Jerusalem and the other authorizing the return to Judaea of a large group of exiles. Both decrees were no doubt written in Aramaic, the common and official administrative language throughout the Persian empire. The edict authorizing the return of a body of Jewish exiles to their homeland is not preserved in its Aramaic form; the sense of it is given in the Hebrew text of 2 Chronicles 36:23 and Ezra 1:2–4. The exiles who returned at this time were led by another descendant of David—Zerubbabel, son or grandson of Jehoiachin's eldest son Shealtiel.

The original Aramaic text of the former decree is preserved in Ezra 6:3–5:

Concerning the temple of God in Jerusalem: Let the temple be rebuilt as a place to present sacrifices and let its foundations be laid. It is to be ninety feet high and ninety feet wide, with three courses of large stones and one of timbers. The costs are to be paid by the royal treasury. Also, the gold and silver articles of the house of God, which Nebuchadnezzar took from the temple in Jerusalem and brought to Babylon, are to be returned to their places in the temple in Jerusalem; they are to be deposited in the house of God.

The task of transporting the temple vessels back to Jerusalem and supervising the work of rebuilding the temple was entrusted to a man named Sheshbazzar, who is given the title 'prince of Judah' (Ezra 1:8). He was perhaps a younger son of King Jehoiachin.[5] The altar of burnt-offering was set up and the sacrificial ritual was re-inaugurated; the foundation of a new temple was laid. Having carried out these tasks, it seems that Sheshbazzar went back to Persia. The small community which remained behind found so many obstacles and discouragements in the way that they did not press on with the work of rebuilding the temple. During the exile some attempt had been made to maintain a centre of worship at the old sanctuary at Bethel, and some people thought that instead of rebuilding the Jerusalem temple it would be best to maintain the sanctuary at Bethel. No doubt they argued that this would have the advantage of uniting the northern Israelites with their southern kinsfolk in Judaea, whereas the northerners would be less attracted to the restored Jerusalem shrine.

However, when it appeared that the returning exiles were determined to rebuild the Jerusalem temple, a deputation of northerners approached Zerubbabel and the chief men of Judaea and offered to co-operate in the rebuilding of the temple and in its worship. They received an unfriendly answer: the royal authorization had been given to the returning exiles and did not extend to the people who had remained in the land, whether in Samaria or in Judaea. Thus the old division between the two parts of the nation was certain to continue; a more co-operative response to the northerners' approach might have helped to heal the breach. Before we blame the returning exiles, however, we must recall that they were a tiny community and would have been swamped by their much more numerous neighbours of the north if they had accepted their offers of help. Besides, the new Jerusalem community preserved certain religious ideals of great value which mighty easily have disappeared if north and south had united.

The northerners were angered by the refusal. The Samaritans regarded the tiny area of Judaea[6] as part of their territory, and they determined to put so many obstacles in the way of the returned exiles that the work of rebuilding the temple was soon halted. For fifteen years or so nothing more was done about it. The returned exiles settled in the neighbourhood of Jerusalem; they built houses for themselves and cultivated their lands. But a succession of droughts and consequent poor harvests brought further misery.

PERSIAN ORGANIZATION

Meanwhile the Persian empire was extending its territories more widely. Cyrus died in battle in 530 BC, and was succeeded by his son Cambyses, who in 525 BC invaded Egypt and added it to his realm. Cambyses's death in 522 BC began a period of civil war, which came to an end when a member of another branch of the royal family took power—Darius the son of Hystaspes. Darius was an able administrator who organized his very large realm as no empire had been organized before. Probably the civil war before he took power gave some of the subject nations cause to hope that the Persian domination would soon disappear and that they would regain their independence; if so, their hopes were quickly dashed.

The empire was divided into great areas, each governed by a viceroy or 'satrap' who was almost a subordinate king with a court and bodyguard of his own. Judaea belonged to the very big satrapy which comprised the territory between the Euphrates and the Mediterranean Sea, and was known in the official Aramaic of the Persian court as Abar-nahara ('Beyond the River')—a name which appears in inscriptions as well as in the book of Ezra (4:10 ff., etc.).[7]

The satrap had supreme control of the provincial troops, of the administration of justice and of financial affairs. There might, however, be special fortresses in his satrapy manned by garrisons whose commanders were appointed by the king and were directly responsible to him. The secretary of state for the satrapy was also directly responsible to the Great King. In addition, there was an elaborate system of imperial inspectors, known as the 'King's Eyes and Ears' who went on annual circuits through the satrapies to investigate the administration and deal with grounds for complaint. There may be an allusion to these in the explanation of the seven lamps which the contemporary prophet Zechariah saw in one of his visions: 'These seven are the eyes of Yahweh, which range throughout the earth.'[8] And the general administration of the empire may be reflected in the same prophet's vision of horsemen described as those 'whom Yahweh has sent to go throughout the earth.'[9] In any case, Darius instituted an elaborate system of checks and counterchecks to prevent disloyalty and to ensure good administration.

REBUILDING THE TEMPLE

Early in the reign of Darius the exiles who had returned to Jerusalem were urged to resume the work of temple rebuilding by the two prophets Haggai and Zechariah. Both of them declared that the building of the temple was essential if the nation was to receive the blessing of God promised by the earlier prophets, a promise until now largely unfulfilled. The recent disorder in the Persian world showed that God was about to act; the droughts and bad harvests which had recently affected the land of Judah would give way to abundant rain and fresh prosperity—if only the people of God would put his interests first, instead of their own. In particular, the prophets spoke encouraging words to Zerubbabel. The hopes of many Jews rested on this prince of the house of David. His grandfather Jehoiachin had been rejected,[10] even though he is described as the signet ring on God's right hand, but Zerubbabel would be restored to that place of honour.[11] He had laid the foundation stone of the new temple, and he would complete the work and enjoy the special favour of God.[12] Jeremiah had spoken of the day when God would raise up a worthy 'branch' or descendant of the line of David; Zerubbabel was hailed by Zechariah as 'the man whose name is the Branch',[13] who will 'build the temple of Yahweh; he shall bear royal honour, and shall sit and rule on his throne. There shall be a priest by his throne, with peaceful understanding between the two of them.'[14] The priest here mentioned was Jeshua, grandson of the last high priest of Solomon's temple; he was to be the first chief priest of Zadok's line in the restored temple.

Encouraged by the two prophets, Zerubbabel and Jeshua took the lead in resuming the work of rebuilding the temple. Their action was quickly reported to Tattenai, satrap of the province of Abar-nahara, and his subordinate governors. It is quite likely that the Samaritans, still resentful that their offer of assistance some years before had been rejected, drew the satrap's attention to the work in the hope that it would be prohibited. Tattenai asked the Jews by what authority they were rebuilding the temple; they replied that they did so in order to obey Cyrus's decree. Tattenai reported the matter to the Persian court, and asked that the Jews' claim should be investigated. The document containing the decree was found among the archives at Ecbatana, the old capital of Media, which was now the summer capital of the Persian kings.[15] So an official reply was sent from the court to Tattenai, telling him not to hinder the Jews in their work, but rather to give them all the assistance mentioned in the original decree of Cyrus. Heartened by this further sign of the favour of God, the Jews pressed on with the work, and the temple was completed and dedicated four years after its resumption, on March 12, 515 BC. The passover and the festival of unleavened bread were celebrated with special rejoicing in the following month. Jerusalem once more had its temple, seventy years after the destruction of the first temple by Nebuchadrezzar. It probably seemed a poor structure by contrast with the magnificent temple which King Solomon had built; yet the prophets assured the people that this poor shrine, as it appeared to them at present, would gain greater glory than had ever graced the temple of Solomon.

After the dedication of the temple Zerubbabel is not mentioned again in the biblical records, but there is no reason to suppose that the Persians became suspicious of his actions and removed him from office. It is probably true that many Jews believed he was the descendant of David who would become king in Jerusalem. It may also be true that the success of the rebuilding of the temple led some Jews to lay plans to rebuild the walls of Jerusalem again—perhaps to guard against a Samaritan assault. Such a plan may be alluded to in a vision of Zechariah in which a young man who is on the point of measuring the length and breadth of Jerusalem is restrained by an angel who assures him that in future Jerusalem will have so many inhabitants that she will far exceed her ancient boundaries. Meanwhile the city can safely remain unwalled because Yahweh, 'a wall of fire around it, and . . . its glory within', will be a more effective protection than any walls could be.[16] In his own time God will shake all nations, remove the 'mighty mountain' that stands in Zerubbabel's path and establish his kingdom.[17] But we may reasonably suppose that, in spite of the ambitions of some of the Jews, Zerubbabel himself acted with caution and prudence, and continued as governor. At any rate, his successor Elnathan seems to have married into the Davidic royal family, so clearly the Persians were not suspicious of the royal family.[18]

The Samaritans had not been able to stop the completion of the temple, but throughout the following decades they seized every opportunity to annoy their Jewish neighbours. They kept careful watch on them and if the Jews seemed to do anything that broke Persian law or seemed to threaten Persian interests, they immediately reported it to the Persian authorities. Darius had shown his good will to the Jews, and the Samaritans were unable to achieve anything so long as he lived, but as soon as he died they sent a message to his son and successor Xerxes[19] (486–465 BC) containing an accusation against the Jews of Judaea. No details of this accusation have been preserved.

NOTES

1. G. Dix, *Jew and Greek* (1953), pp. 14 f. The 'three great civilizations' which he mentions are those of Greece, Syria and Persia.
2. Isa. 42:1–4; 49:1–6; 50:4–9; 52:13–53:12.

3   Isa. 49:6.

4   DOTT, pp. 81 ff., 92 ff.

5   1 Chr. 3:18 names 'Shenazzar' as a son of Jehoiachin. Shenazzar and Sheshbazzar could be variant spellings of the Babylonian Sinabusur, 'May Sin (the moon-god) protect the father', which is best preserved in the Septuagint form Sanabassaros (1 Esdras 2:12, 15).

6   A tiny area indeed, 'stretching less than twenty-five miles in a straight line along the watershed-ridge from north of Jerusalem to south of Beth-zur, with a total population which can scarcely have exceeded 20,000 in 522 BC' (W. F. Albright, BA 9 [1946], p. 8).

7   The NIV translates the name as 'Trans-Euphrates'.

8   Zech. 4:10.

9   Zech. 1:10; cf. 6:1 ff.

10 Jer. 22:24.

11 Hag. 2:20–23.

12 Zech. 4:9.

13 Cf. Jer. 23:5; 33:15. Zerubbabel himself did not fulfil Jeremiah's prophecy; but the fact that after the exile a prince of the house of David was governor of Judah showed that God's promises made to that house had by no means been cancelled.

14 Zech. 6:12 f., NRSV. The NIV understands verse 13 differently.

15 The Persian kings had three capitals. The other two were Susa, the old Elamite capital (now the spring residence), and the rebuilt Persian capital of Pasargadae (the winter residence).

16 Zech. 2:5. 'The young man would represent the cautious Jew of the day, or he may have been acting out of defiance against Persia' (J. G. Baldwin, *Haggai, Zechariah, Malachi* [1972], p. 106).

17 Hag. 2:21 f.; Zech. 4:7.

18 Cf. C. L. and E. M. Meyers, *Haggai, Zechariah 1–8* (1987), pp. 12 ff.

19 The book of Esther describes an attempt in the reign of Xerxes by influential officials at the Persian court to take hostile action against the Jews throughout the Persian empire.

Chapter Thirteen

The People of the Law
(465–400 BC)

NEHEMIAH AT THE PERSIAN COURT

In the reign of the next king, Artaxerxes I (465–424 BC), the Samaritans found an opportunity to make a really serious complaint against the Jews. The returned exiles, at some point early in his reign, began to rebuild the walls of Jerusalem. This was something which could not legally be done without royal authorization, and the officials of the province of Samaria knew that no such authorization had been given. They therefore sent a letter to the court, drawing attention to Jerusalem's rebellious record in the Assyrian and Babylonian periods, and warned the king that this rebuilding of the wall was the first step towards a declaration of independence. If it was allowed to proceed unhindered, they said, Jerusalem would become a centre of unrest and disloyalty in that part of the Persian empire. So an official reply came back from the court ordering that the rebuilding must cease until the king himself might choose to decree otherwise.

Early in Artaxerxes' reign there was a nationalist revolt in Egypt, and it took six years before it was put down (460–454 BC). If it was during this period that the report of the rebuilding of the walls of Jerusalem reached Artaxerxes, we can understand that his suspicions would be aroused, especially if he was aware that the Jewish rebellions of earlier days, of which his informants told him, were regularly undertaken in alliance with Egypt. In any case, his response was received with joy by the Samaritans, and with corresponding dismay by the Judaeans. It is quite likely that the Samaritans, not content with communicating the king's decision to the wall-builders, took the opportunity to demolish the part of the wall that had already been built, knowing that the Persian authorities would take no action against them for this zeal on behalf of the king's interests.

This may explain the situation to which we are introduced in the twentieth year of Artaxerxes (445 BC) when his chief cup-bearer at Susa, a Jewish man named Nehemiah, received a visit from some of his kinsmen from

Judaea. When he enquired about Jerusalem, he was told that the Jewish community there was 'in great trouble and disgrace. The wall of Jerusalem is broken down, and its gates have been burned with fire.'[1] Nehemiah, a man of simple piety and single-minded determination, wrote down his thoughts and actions in his personal journal, parts of which have fortunately been preserved for us in the book of Nehemiah. He tells how he was so distressed by the news which his visitors brought that he could not conceal his sorrow when he entered the king's presence to carry out his normal duties. The king noticed his sadness and asked the cause. The question alarmed Nehemiah because his private grief had no right to intrude into the presence of the king, even though the king had showed him favour. But he spoke out: 'May the king live for ever! Why should my face not look sad when the city where my fathers are buried lies in ruins, and its gates have been destroyed by fire?' The king's response was encouraging: 'What is it you want?' he asked. Then Nehemiah boldly asked the king to send him 'to the city in Judah where my fathers are buried so that I can rebuild it'. Such a request might have enraged the king, but instead he shrewdly asked: 'How long will your journey take, and when will you get back?'[2]

Did the king not realize that the city which Nehemiah wished to fortify was the very one whose unauthorized walls he had banned some years before? No doubt Nehemiah was wise not to mention Jerusalem by name until he saw that the king was favourably disposed to his request. But the king may not have been so ignorant or inconsistent. The political and military situation had changed during the last three or four years. In 448 BC a serious rebellion was raised against the Persian government by Megabyzus, satrap of Abar-nahara. It is possible that the Samaritan officials Rehum and Shimshai (the men who had taken the action against the Jews when they began to build the wall of Jerusalem) were involved in this rebellion. If so, this must have changed the attitude of the Persian court to the status of Jerusalem. The Jews would not have joined a rebellion in which the Samaritans took part. It may well have seemed to the king and his advisers that to give Jerusalem the status of a walled city, instead of being a threat to law and order, might be expected to promote stability in that part of the empire. Rehum and Shimshai disappear from the record; their places are taken by Sanballat as governor of Samaria.

NEHEMIAH'S ACHIEVEMENTS

Nehemiah, then, was sent to Judaea as governor, with a specific commission to rebuild Jerusalem's walls. His commission, and the determination and speed with which he proceeded to carry it out, enraged Sanballat, the new governor of Samaria. His right of supervision over Judaea must have been reduced if not abolished by Nehemiah's appointment. Sanballat had the support of the governors of some smaller neighbouring states—Tobiah of Ammon, Gashmu of Kedar in north-west Arabia, and the governor of the Philistine territory. They tried to hinder Nehemiah by intimidation and deceit, but he would not be turned aside from the task, and he found such hearty and enthusiastic co-operation from all the inhabitants of Judaea that in fifty-two days the wall was erected. Jerusalem was once more a city. The completion of the work was followed by a service of dedication, marked by public thanksgiving and rejoicing and by a solemn procession round the new wall.[3]

But that was only the beginning of Nehemiah's work as governor. It seems that earlier governors of Judaea in the seventy years since Zerubbabel had allowed several serious problems to arise. The situation now required drastic action in various ways. We do not know what answer Nehemiah gave Artaxerxes when the king asked him how long he would be away in Judaea, but in fact his first governorship lasted for twelve years.

The old curse of the land in the days of the great prophets, money-lending, had appeared again. All too often those who had borrowed money became insolvent debtors. Smallholders had not only to maintain themselves by the produce of their land; they had to pay the temple tax and an imperial tax as well, and many of them were driven to mortgage their fields, vineyards and houses to their wealthier neighbours to raise the money. When they were unable to repay the loans, they were forced to sell their children into virtual slavery. Nehemiah called an assembly of the people and publicly attacked such social injustice. He then persuaded the creditors to restore the mortgaged lands free of charge and to cancel the debts owed to them. They may not have done this very willingly, but at least they could not complain that Nehemiah did not set them a good example. For instead of imposing a tax on the people of Judaea in order to maintain his household in lavish style, as earlier governors had done, he himself regularly entertained a hundred and fifty Jews at his table at his own expense. He also did what he could to pay to release Jews who had been sold into slavery to foreigners. His servants, instead of being a charge upon the community, took part in public work such as the building of the wall.

EZRA'S MISSION

But there were other problems which required to be dealt with by an authority which Nehemiah did not and could not hold. The civil governor could not regulate the religious life of the people, and yet their religious life too needed regulation. So, perhaps at the suggestion of Nehemiah (although we have no explicit statement to this effect), another official was sent from the Persian court to Judaea. This was a priest descended from Aaron, Ezra by name, who was described in official documents as 'scribe of the law of the God of heaven'. 'The God of heaven' is a title by which Yahweh is normally designated under the Persian regime, and since 'the law of the God of heaven' constituted the way of life which the Jews followed, it has been suggested that Ezra's title was equivalent to 'Secretary of State for Jewish Affairs' in the imperial civil service. Whatever his official position may have been, Ezra was sent to Judaea by the king and his council 'to enquire about Judah and Jerusalem with regard to the Law of your God, which is in your hand'.[4] He took with him a generous contribution from the king and freewill offerings from the Jews still in Babylonia, to organize the sacrificial ritual in the Jerusalem temple on a more suitable and regular basis. Ezra was also authorized to appoint magistrates and judges who would teach and administer 'the laws of your God' among the Jews in the satrapy of Abar-nahara.[5] The satrap of Abar-nahara was also required to give Ezra further financial support up to a fixed amount, and instructions were given that the temple staff should be exempt from tax and tribute.

Ezra did not set out for Judaea unaccompanied; there went with him nearly two thousand Jews from the province of Babylonia, including a considerable number of priests, Levites and temple attendants.

Ezra's task, in effect, was to regulate the religious life of the Jews in conformity with a written law-book which he took with him. What the scope of this law-book was is a matter of some debate among scholars, but there seems to be no sound reason why it should not have been the completed Pentateuch, more or less in the form familiar to us. Jewish and Christian traditions give Ezra an important place in the history of the formation of the Old Testament canon. The most important feature that emerges from these traditions is that Ezra stands at the end of the history of the Pentateuchal law of the Old Testament as Moses stands at the beginning of it. Not that Ezra was in any sense an author or creative figure such as Moses was; he was not even a legislator, but more probably an editor and codifier, and 'a teacher well versed in the Law of Moses, which Yahweh, the God of Israel, had given'.[6]

The official interest taken by the Persian court in the religious affairs of subject nations is illustrated by the Elephantine documents, of which more will be said later.[7] The details in the letter addressed by Artaxerxes to Ezra do not necessarily imply a personal interest on the king's part; the letter would be issued by the department of state dealing with these affairs, but bore the king's name because it was an official state document.

EZRA'S LAW-BOOK

Ezra's mission had far-reaching results for the life of the Jews. The law-book which he carried became the officially recognized constitution of the community in Judaea and Jerusalem. From the imperial point of view Judaea was formally constituted a hierocracy or temple-state, that is to say, a community the centre of whose life was the temple, and whose constitution was founded on the constitution of the temple. The civil governor of Judaea was the representative of the imperial overlord, but the community enjoyed a considerable measure of freedom in internal matters, raised its own taxes and struck its own coins. In these internal matters the head of the community was the head of the temple organization, the high priest. This form of sacred constitution was not unparalleled in the Persian empire, and the system continued into the Greek and Roman periods.

The law-book was formally accepted by the people as their constitution at a public ceremony, described in the eighth chapter of Nehemiah. At the beginning of the month Tishri, the people of Judaea gathered in Jerusalem, and listened to the public reading of the law-book from dawn to noon. It was read aloud by Ezra from a wooden pulpit erected in 'the square before the Water Gate' and interpreted by his assistants— perhaps for the special benefit of those people who understood Aramaic better than Hebrew. It is improbable that the whole Pentateuch was thus read; probably what was read was the Deuteronomic legislation, for this is the part of the Pentateuchal law which gives instructions about its being publicly read.[8] Later in the same month came an opportunity to put the festal requirements of the law into practice, when the time for the Feast of Tabernacles came round. The people spent the week from the fifteenth to the twenty-second day of the month in the booths or 'tabernacles' from which the feast receives its name—a thing they had not done, we are told, since the time of Joshua[9]— and throughout the week there were further opportunities to learn more of the law-book, for it was read publicly day by day.

Part of the religious policy of Ezra (in which he had the firm support of Nehemiah) was to avoid, as far as possible, all foreign associations, as indicated in Israel's ancient covenant-law. During the years since the return from exile, there had been much trading and other contacts between the people of Judaea and their non-Jewish neighbours. In particular, there had been a good deal of intermarriage. It was plain that, if the people were to live in accordance with the law-book, this tendency must not continue. When the Feast of Booths was over, a solemn assembly was held in which the covenant was reaffirmed by the people, led by Nehemiah and the chief personages in religious and civil life. 'Those of Israelite descent . . . separated themselves from all foreigners. They stood in their places and confessed their sins and the wickedness of their fathers'.[10] In particular, they agreed to refuse intermarriage with Gentiles, to abstain from trade on the sabbath and generally to observe the sacredness of that day and other holy days, to leave their lands uncultivated and give a free release to all their Jewish debtors every seventh year, to pay a third of a shekel of silver each year for the maintenance of the temple service and to contribute tithes, first-fruits, and various freewill offerings for the same purpose. Their leaders set their seal to a confirmatory document in which they bound themselves under oath to keep the divine law.

No doubt Ezra and Nehemiah co-operated fully when both were in Jerusalem. In the matter of intermarriage with Gentiles, however, we find that the two men acted differently. Ezra took no stronger action than persuasion; but Nehemiah took firm steps to annul foreign marriages. The explanation may well be that Ezra's policy dates from the period after Nehemiah had returned to the Persian court at the end of his first term as governor. Then Nehemiah on his return to Jerusalem took more vigorous action. This sequence makes very good sense if Ezra came to Judaea about 438 BC[11] and remained there when Nehemiah returned to the Persian court after his first term of office as governor.

Ezra, then, distressed by the extent of intermarriage between Jews and Gentiles, was able to persuade many of the people who had married foreign wives to divorce them, including a number of priests and Levites. It may be that many of these men had married foreign wives after first divorcing their Jewish wives; at least, this scandalous conduct is rebuked in the prophecy of Malachi which belongs to this period. It is plain that many of the other obligations to which the people bound themselves under covenant were intended to remove other abuses attacked by Malachi, such as the neglect of the temple services.

THE INFLUENCE OF EZRA AND NEHEMIAH

When Nehemiah returned to assume the duties of governor for a second term, he pushed ahead vigorously with the social and civic reforms which Ezra had begun—not least where mixed marriages were concerned. It was particularly irritating to Nehemiah to hear the children of mixed marriages using the speech of their mothers, from the Philistine seaboard and the lands east of Jordan, instead of the Hebrew language. He not only annulled mixed marriages, he also took strong action against those who had created this state of affairs, even against leading men in the community. A grandson of Eliashib the high priest had married the daughter of Nehemiah's old enemy Sanballat; Nehemiah expelled him from the city.[12] Another of

Nehemiah's old enemies, Tobiah, had actually been granted the use of an apartment in the temple buildings by Eliashib, who was related to him. Nehemiah threw Tobiah's furniture out of the room, and restored it to its original purpose, which was to house the frankincense and cereal offerings given to the Levites and other temple servants. This was just one sign of the general neglect of the temple services, and Nehemiah did his best to remedy this. The disregard of the sabbath similarly caused him concern. He ordered the gates of Jerusalem to be kept shut over the sabbath to prevent tradesmen from outside coming in to sell their wares on the sacred day, and he forbade the tradesmen themselves to camp outside the city over the weekend until the sabbath was past.

The combined influence of Ezra and Nehemiah succeeded in making the people of Judaea regard the written law-book as the divinely appointed basis of their way of life, and gave to orthodox Judaism a direction which it has followed ever since.

Josiah's religious reformation in the seventh century BC had been followed by important literary activity, which had produced the Old Testament historical books culminating in the books of Kings. Similarly now the new reform under Ezra resulted in a further rewriting of the history of Israel, preserved in our canonical books of Chronicles, Ezra and Nehemiah. The Chronicler outlines the earlier history, before the reign of David, in skeleton form by means of genealogical tables. The history of a temple-state must lay special emphasis on the temple, and so his history proper begins with the reign of David, who planned to build the temple, and of Solomon, who carried his father's plans into effect. The history of the northern kingdom is for the most part ignored; the writer concentrates on the southern kingdom in which the holy city and the legitimate temple stood, and makes ample use of temple archives. He stresses the role of the Levites in the national life to such an extent that it has been thought he was a Levite himself. In his history of the post-exilic age he has made use of the personal journals of Ezra and Nehemiah, and incorporates much valuable genealogical material. The man (or men) who wrote these historical books[13] drew their inspiration from the work of Ezra. The state of political and religious stability which the community had achieved in the Persian empire through the work of Ezra and Nehemiah is reflected throughout these three Old Testament books.

NOTES

[1] Neh. 1:3.
[2] Neh. 2:1–6.
[3] Nehemiah's eastern wall was built farther west than its predecessor, owing to the collapse

of the platform structures by which the pre-exilic city was extended eastwards. See W. H. Mare, *The Archaeology of the Jerusalem Area* (1987), chapter 6, especially pp. 127 f.

[4] Ezra 7:14.

[5] Ezra 7:25.

[6] Ezra 7:6. 'There seems no adequate reason to deny that it [the Pentateuch] was known in Jerusalem generations before Ezra, but it seems highly probable that it was Ezra who introduced the complete Pentateuch into normative Jewish use and who is largely responsible for the way in which its archaic practices were adjusted to actual ritual usage in the Temple. The latter was alone a major contribution to normative Judaism' (W. F. Albright, BA 9 [1946], pp. 14 f.). See more recently H. G. M. Williamson, *Ezra and Nehemiah* (1987), pp. 90 ff.

[7] See pp.107 ff.

[8] Deut. 31:9–13. H. G. M. Williamson, op. cit., pp. 90 ff., draws attention to some of the relevant passages in Deuteronomy.

[9] Neh. 8:17.

[10] Neh. 9:2.

[11] The date of Ezra's mission is very uncertain. According to Ezra 7:7 f., it was 'in the seventh year of Artaxerxes'; but this might be either Artaxerxes I or Artaxerxes II. If it was Artaxerxes I, then Ezra came to Jerusalem in 458 BC (in advance of Nehemiah, who came to Jerusalem in 445 BC); if Artaxerxes II, Ezra's mission was in 398 BC—long after Nehemiah. The date of 438 BC (preferred by F. F. Bruce) has the advantage of placing Nehemiah's mission first while still allowing the two men to overlap (cf. Neh. 8:9); but it has the disadvantage of requiring a double alteration of the figure 'seventh' to 'twenty-seventh' in Ezra 7:7. Recent scholarly discussion tends to favour 458 BC. See Williamson, op. cit., pp. 55–69, for a concise discussion of the arguments and issues and for a bibliography.

[12] See page 110.

[13] Several recent scholars (including Williamson) doubt whether the author of Chronicles also compiled Ezra and Nehemiah. For a defence of the majority view that the Chronicler was responsible for all three biblical books, see J. Blenkinsopp, *Ezra-Nehemiah: A Commentary* (1988), pp. 47–54.

Chapter Fourteen

The Jews in the Persian Empire (539–331 BC)

JEWS AT ELEPHANTINE

Our information about Judaea and the Jews during the period of the Persian empire is very limited. We know some interesting details about one particular Jewish community in Egypt. We know less about events in Palestine, though there were some important developments and possibly at least one major disaster. A development which affected the citizens of the whole empire, Jews and Gentiles alike, was the influence of Persian religious concepts. We must consider these aspects of the history of the Persian period one by one.

There were Jewish communities in many other parts of the Persian empire than Babylonia and Palestine. Special interest attaches to those in Egypt, and particularly to a Jewish settlement on the southern border of the country. The twenty-sixth dynasty of Egyptian kings, founded by Psamtek I, who won his country's independence from Assyria in 654 BC, seems to have made more use of foreign mercenaries than any Egyptian dynasty had done before. Many of these mercenaries were Greeks, but some were Jews. As we have seen, when a group of Judaeans fled to Egypt after the murder of Gedaliah in about 586 BC and forced Jeremiah to accompany them, they found many other Jews had arrived in Egypt before them. The warning oracle preserved in Jeremiah 44 was addressed to all of them. Among those addressed were some 'in the land of Pathros', or Upper Egypt, and these in fact appear to have been the most numerous. At any rate it was they who rejected Jeremiah's plea and declared their intention to continue to worship the queen of heaven as their fathers had done before Josiah's reformation.

We are well informed about one particular group of Jews who were settled in Upper Egypt because of documents from Syene and Elephantine belonging to the fifth century BC[1], discovered between 1893 and 1908. Psamtek II (595–589 BC) employed a force of Jewish mercenaries in a war against his southern neighbours, the Ethiopians.[2] At the end of the war he settled them on his southern frontier, at the first cataract of the Nile, in the fortresses of Syene (modern Aswan) and Elephantine. Elephantine was a river-island, known to the ancient Egyptians as Yeb. There the colony maintained its separate existence for over 180 years. They built a temple of Yahweh at Elephantine and carried on a sacrificial ritual similar to the one carried on at the Jerusalem temple. No doubt this broke the law of Deuteronomy which prescribes one single sanctuary; but Deuteronomy did not envisage a Jewish community in Egypt. (Indeed, the very idea of Israelites' returning to Egypt would have been totally contrary to the ideals of the Deuteronomic law.) The Jerusalem temple, however, lay in ruins; and besides, the religion of these colonists was of a completely unreformed character, showing very little trace of Josiah's purifying influence. This is shown, for example, by the way in which the names of Canaanite gods and goddesses are freely combined with the name of Yahweh—or Yahu, the form in which that name appears in their documents. We find such compound divine names as Anath-Yahu, Anath-Bethel, Ishum-Bethel, Herem-Bethel. The compounds which contain the name Anath[3] remind us of the reference made by the Jews of Upper Egypt to the worship of the queen of heaven. It is possible that by the fifth century BC these compounds were little more than names for different aspects of Yahweh, but the very use of these Canaanite names in any form would have been condemned by the great prophets.

When Cambyses conquered Egypt in 525 BC, he found the Jewish temple at Elephantine already built, and treated the colony and its temple with goodwill—in fact, he showed less hostility to this Jewish temple than he did to some of the native Egyptian cults. Perhaps his goodwill towards it caused some Egyptian resentment. From time to time the Persian court issued directives to the governors of Egypt authorizing certain celebrations in connection with the temple. For instance, one document contains instructions from King Darius II to the colony, sent through the governor Arsames, with reference to the celebration of the Feast of Unleavened Bread in 419 BC. This letter was written by a Jew named Hananiah, who held some post at the Persian court, possibly in the Department of State for Jewish Affairs; but there is not enough evidence to identify him with Nehemiah's brother Hanani.[4] The official interest taken by the court in such religious details presents a useful parallel to a similar interest reflected in the documents preserved in the book of Ezra.

In 410 BC disaster overtook the temple. The governor Arsames was absent, and his place was taken temporarily by a deputy named Waidrang. Waidrang took no action when an anti-Jewish riot broke out at Elephantine, led by the priests of Khnum, the ram-headed potter-god, and the Jewish temple was destroyed. The Jewish colonists did their best to get their temple rebuilt, but had to write a series of letters to various officials before permission was at last given. It is evident that the Persian government exercised such control over the details of their subject-nations' religious life, as well as civil affairs, that even the repair of a building which had been destroyed could not be undertaken without special licence. First the Elephantine Jews sent a letter to the high priest of the Jerusalem temple, asking him to use his influence on their behalf. This letter was ignored. We can quite well appreciate that the Jerusalem high priest would not be over-eager to promote the interests of a rival temple to his own legitimate shrine in Jerusalem. The Jerusalem high priest at this time was John, one of the sons of Eliashib who had been high priest when Nehemiah entered on his first governorship.[5] After patiently waiting for two years, the Elephantine Jews gave up all hope of an answer from John. They therefore sent a letter to the governor of Judaea, a Persian named Bagoas, and another to Delaiah and Shelemiah, the two sons of Sanballat, governor of Samaria. Sanballat, Nehemiah's old opponent of thirty-five years earlier, was still the governor, but it appears that in his old age these two sons acted as his deputies.

The letter to Bagoas and the sons of Sanballat was more effective than that sent to John. A reply has been preserved in the following terms:

> Memorandum from Bagoas and Delaiah. They said to me: Let it be a memorandum to you in Egypt to speak to Arsames concerning the altar-house of the God of heaven, which was built in the fortress of Yeb formerly, before Cambyses—the altar-house which that reprobate Waidrang destroyed in the 14th year of King Darius—that it be rebuilt in its place as it was before, and that cereal offerings and incense be offered upon that altar as was done formerly.

Here we have the title 'the God of heaven' applied to Yahweh just as is done in the Old Testament documents which belong to the Persian period. The Elephantine Jews had asked permission to offer burnt-offerings as well as incense and cereal offerings. It is interesting that there is no mention of burnt-offerings in this reply. Perhaps the offering of burnt-offerings was not permitted, because the sacrificial slaughter of certain animals would be an offence to the religious sentiments of the Egyptians of that district, and the authorities wisely decided not to give unnecessary cause for further riots.

The temple, then, was rebuilt. But probably it did not stand for long. The death of Darius II in 404 BC was followed by rivalry for the succession between his two sons, Artaxerxes and Cyrus. Civil war broke out when Cyrus invaded his elder brother's territory in 401 BC with an army of ten thousand Greek mercenaries. The Egyptians seized the opportunity to revolt against Persia, under a native ruler called Amyrtaeus (perhaps a grandson of the Amyrtaeus who led the revolt against Artaxerxes I in 460–454 BC). They succeeded in gaining their independence. In 404 BC a dynasty came to power which worshipped the god Khnum, and it is likely that the priests of Khnum at Elephantine made sure that the Jewish cult of 'the God of heaven' was suppressed. They knew that there would be no further Persian interference to defend Jewish rights.

So ends the history of this interesting shrine which, in the words of Isaiah's prophecy, contained 'an altar to Yahweh in the heart of Egypt, and a monument to Yahweh at its border'.[6]

JERUSALEM AND GERIZIM

The names of the governor Bagoas and the high priest John have been mentioned above in connection with the Elephantine temple. We also meet these names in a story told by Josephus[7] about improper conduct in the Jerusalem temple. John had a brother named Jeshua, who enjoyed the good will of Bagoas and had received a promise from him that he should become high priest. As a result a quarrel broke out between the two brothers, and John in violent anger dealt his brother a fatal blow in the sacred temple-courts. Bagoas, despite Jewish religious rules, entered the temple-courts to restore order. He stated that his presence there did not defile their sanctity so much as the presence of the killer, John. He imposed as a penalty a fine of fifty shekels for each lamb offered in the public daily sacrifices. This tax was imposed for seven years.

It was about this time that something happened which created another serious breach between the Jews and Samaritans. Towards the end of his memoirs, Nehemiah tells us how he expelled a grandson of the high priest Eliashib for having married the daughter of Sanballat.[8] Josephus tells us how a governor of Samaria named Sanballat gave his daughter in marriage to Manasseh, a younger son of the high priest John. It is natural to identify Manasseh with the unnamed grandson of Eliashib mentioned by Nehemiah. However, Josephus says that Manasseh's father-in-law, Sanballat, was appointed governor of Samaria by the last king of Persia (Darius III, 336–331 BC), while Nehemiah was writing in the days of Artaxerxes I, some one hundred years earlier. Yet the identification is not impossible, for it should be remembered that Josephus is in general quite confused in his account of the kings of Persia, and could have been further confused by the fact that there were at least two Sanballats who governed Samaria in the period between 450 BC and 330 BC.[9]

In any case, this Manasseh, expelled from the temple because he would not divorce his Samaritan wife, went to his father-in-law, Sanballat, who welcomed him warmly. In due course permission was granted by the Great King to build a temple on the sacred Samaritan hill of Gerizim, near the ancient sanctuary of Shechem. Here Manasseh was installed as high priest. A rival cult was established to that in Jerusalem, and it has survived to this day, based on the same law-book as that recognized by the Jews. It is remarkable that while the name of Ezra is cursed in Samaritan tradition (where he is regularly called 'Ezra ha-'arur, ('Ezra the accursed'), yet the law-book which he brought from Babylon was accepted at Gerizim just as it was in Jerusalem. This suggests that the Samaritans recognized that the authority of this law-book was not that of Ezra but of God himself.

THE REIGN OF ARTAXERXES III

In the reign of Artaxerxes III (359–338 BC) the Jews suffered a calamity of which we know very little.[10] During this reign there were revolts in Phoenicia and Cyprus, which were forcibly suppressed. The revolt in Phoenicia was led by the city of Sidon, and supported by 4000 Greek mercenaries from Egypt. Sidon was besieged, and was at last taken by treachery, but the despairing inhabitants set their fleet and city on fire rather than let them fall into the Persian king's hands. It is said that 40,000 Sidonians perished at this time (345 BC). Some neighbouring areas also took part in the revolt, so it is quite likely that Judaea was involved. Several chroniclers tell us that about this time Artaxerxes III removed a considerable number of Jews and settled them in the district called Hyrcania, south-east of the Caspian Sea.[11] Some scholars have magnified these events to the scale of 'the third of Israel's great captivities', comparable to the deportations under the Assyrians in 732–721 BC and the Babylonians in 597–587 BC, and have found here the historical setting for several passages of Old Testament scripture, such as Psalms 74 and 79 and Isaiah 24–27; 63:7–64:12.[12] But our knowledge is too scanty for such conclusions to be established; moreover, such passages could just as easily refer to the disasters of the sixth century BC.

PERSIAN RELIGIOUS IDEAS

The Jews lived for just over two hundred years under Persian sovereignty (539–331 BC). During that period they were exposed to far-reaching influences from Persia, especially in their religious thought. The official religion of Persia from Darius I onwards was Zoroastrianism, and several features of this religion have left their mark on Judaism, without modifying the essence of the Jewish faith. Zoroastrianism was thoroughly dualistic: over against the good spirit Ahura Mazda (the 'wise lord') with the other six Amesha Spentas ('immortal holy ones') who supported him in the cause of truth and light, were ranged his rival Angra Mainyu (the 'hostile spirit') and the Daevas, his attendant evil spirits.[13] Judaism with its strongly rooted monotheism could not and did not become dualistic, but in later Judaism the angelic attendants of the Supreme God become more definitely individualized. Angels increasingly receive names and have distinct areas of activity assigned to them. On the other hand, the hierarchy of evil powers becomes similarly defined, and their origin is traced back to the account in Genesis 6:4 of the 'sons of God' who fell because of their love for the 'daughters of men'. These concepts find clear expression in such a work as the book of Enoch, a body of apocalyptic writings of the closing century BC and first century AD. Other characteristically Persian concepts are apparent in the book of Tobit (c. 200 BC). There the angel Raphael ('one of the seven angels who stand ready and enter before the glory of the Lord')[14] accompanies young Tobias in human guise under the name Azariah. This probably reflects the Zoroastrian concept of the *fravashi*—the spirit-counterpart or guardian angel.[15] More certain still is the Zoroastrian origin of the evil spirit Asmodeus;[16] he is obviously Aeshma-daeva, the 'angry demon', one of the chief demons who attended Angra Mainyu.

Zoroastrianism also had very specific eschatological ideas, from which later Jewish literature—especially apocalyptic literature—may have derived some of the imagery with which it describes the day of judgment. However, while admitting this possibility, care must be taken not to exaggerate the extent of Zoroastrian influence on Jewish thought (as some scholars have done when they have even related Jesus' teaching to Zoroastrian influence). Zoroastrianism affected only the fringes of the Jewish faith, and not its essence.[17]

One problem in assessing the extent of Persian influence on Judaism is that our detailed information about Zoroastrianism comes from a much later period, so that it is difficult to be sure which features of Zoroastrianism already existed at the time of the Persian empire and which features were later developments.

DEVELOPMENTS IN JUDAEA

In other ways the Persian period was of decisive importance for the Jewish people. Since the civil governors were representatives of the Great King, and were not always Jewish,[18] the importance of the high priest steadily increased. He was not only at the head of the temple ritual; he became in practice head of the Jewish state in all that concerned its internal affairs, especially now that the Jewish state was a temple-state. This status was retained by the high priests, with a few exceptional intervals, throughout the era of the Second Temple.

In this period, too, the religion of Judaea tended to become more and more a religion of law; it was accompanied by a policy of religious and racial exclusiveness. Many modern writers have deplored this tendency—so plainly contrary, as it seems, to the programme of Israel's mission to the nations[19]—but it is reasonable to suggest that it was necessary at the time. Perhaps the vulnerable existence of Israel's reborn faith needed to be protected by these legal barriers until it reached maturity and was able to make its own conquering way in the world in the form of Christianity. When the supreme crisis for Israel's faith arrived in the second century BC, it is difficult to see how it could have survived without the strength of that spirit of exclusive devotion to the divine law which Ezra's reforms had introduced.

It may be in this period, too, or even perhaps as early as the exile, that the institution of the synagogue began. Its origins are shrouded in obscurity, but it was closely connected with the reading and exposition of the sacred law. Probably it arose in places like Babylonia where there were Jewish communities isolated from the temple worship of Jerusalem. Instead of following the example of the Elephantine Jews and building a temple, these Babylonian Jews instituted a community centre where the law could be read and expounded. Here a service of worship could be carried out without offering sacrifices, yet following as closely as possible the order of the sacrificial worship in the Jerusalem temple. As time went on, the importance of synagogues as the centres of Jewish community life steadily increased, in Palestine itself as well as in remoter parts, until the day came when the temple worship came to an end (in AD 70) and the synagogue was left to perpetuate the religion and life of Judaism.

Some scholars have suggested that Jewish sects first developed in the Persian period—rather than later, in the Hellenistic period. No doubt there were divisions and differences of opinion, but it is doubtful whether distinct parties emerged; the evidence is very limited and uncertain.[20]

From the Persian period onwards, Aramaic gradually displaced the closely related Hebrew language as the common tongue of the people.[21] In exile Aramaic had served as the common language among an alien population, and even in Palestine it became more and more the speech of ordinary people. When they came to hear the Scriptures read, they needed an interpretation into the language with which they were more familiar. For several centuries these interpretations or 'targums' existed mainly in oral form,[22] but even then a traditional rendering tended to establish itself. It is thought that this practice is what is meant when we are told that on the day when Ezra's law-book was publicly read, the readers 'read from the Book of the Law of God, making it clear[23] and giving the meaning so that the people could understand what was being read.'[24]

It was not only the language that was subjected to this Aramaic influence, but the writing system too. Previously Hebrew had been written in an alphabet similar to the Phoenician script, in which the letters took various angular shapes. From about 400 BC onwards it came to be written in the Aramaic alphabet. This alphabet derived, like the Phoenician, from the original North Semitic alphabet, but the letters had developed a square shape. The 'square' characters in which Hebrew has usually been written and printed ever since were originally Aramaic and not Hebrew. For certain purposes such as inscriptions on coins, and also to some extent (presumably in more conservative schools) for the copying of sacred scripture, the Phoenician or 'palaeo-Hebrew' script was still used. The Samaritans did not change their script as the Jews did; the Samaritan alphabet is a development of the palaeo-Hebrew script.[25]

NOTES

[1] Cf. A. Cowley, *Aramaic Papyri of the Fifth Century BC* (1923); E. G. Kraeling, *The Brooklyn Museum Aramaic Papyri* (1953); B. Porten and A. Yardeni, *Textbook of Aramaic Documents from Ancient Egypt* (1986).

[2] The 'Ethiopia' of the Old Testament was approximately the region of the Sudan and Nubia.

[3] Anath was a Canaanite goddess, sister and consort of Ba'al.

[4] Neh. 1:2; 7:2.

[5] Neh. 3:1; 12:23.

[6] Isa. 19:19.

[7] Josephus, *Antiquities* xi. 297 ff.

[8] Neh. 13:28.

[9] Cf. H. G. M. Williamson in ABD vol. 5, pp. 973 ff.

[10] See L. L. Grabbe, *Judaism from Cyrus to Hadrian* (1992), pp. 141 f.

[11] Grabbe (pp. 99 f.) lists the ancient writers and briefly analyses the data. It is possible that the book of Judith, despite its historical mistakes, preserves some memory of Persian action about this time; at any rate Holofernes, the general of 'Nebuchadnezzar king of Assyria' is probably Orophernes, who was a general under Artaxerxes III.

[12] See T. K. Cheyne, *Introduction to the Book of Isaiah* (1895), pp. xxvii, pp. 155 ff., 358 ff.

[13] For a brief description of early Zoroastrianism, see T. Ling, *History of Religion East and West* (1968), pp. 75 ff.

[14] Tob. 12:15.

[15] Cf. Peter's 'angel' (Acts 12:15).

[16] Tob. 3:8.

[17] For a brief perspective, see L. L. Grabbe, op. cit., pp. 100 ff.; for more detail, see S. Shaked, CHJ vol. 1, pp. 308–325.

[18] In addition to Zerubbabel and Nehemiah, the names of three other Jewish governors of Judaea under the Persians (Elnathan, Jehoezer and Ahzai) are now known. Cf. H. G. M. Williamson, 'The Governors of Judah under the Persians', *Tyndale Bulletin* 39 (1988), pp. 59–82.

[19] Cf. Isa. 2:2 ff.; 11:10; 19:24 f.; 56:6 f.; 60:3.

[20] Cf. L. L. Grabbe, op. cit., pp. 111 f.

[21] There was a patriotic revival of Hebrew as a result of the Hasmonaean rising in the second century BC, and its use (alongside Aramaic) for ordinary purposes is attested in Judaea as late as the second century AD.

[22] Portions of written Targums have been identified among the Qumran texts. Cf. F. F. Bruce, *The Books and the Parchments* (3rd ed., 1963), pp. 134 f.; R. Le Déaut, CHJ vol. 2, pp. 568 ff.

[23] Heb. *mephorash*, the equivalent of Aramaic *mepharash*, a technical term used when an imperial official read an official document off in the vernacular of the people whom he was addressing.

[24] Neh. 8:8.

[25] A table of these forms of the alphabet is given in P. Joüon, *Grammar of Biblical Hebrew* (trans. and rev. T. Muraoka), vol. 1 (1991), p. 18.

Chapter Fifteen

Rival Greek Empires
(334–200 BC)

ALEXANDER THE GREAT

When Cyrus the Great overthrew Croesus of Lydia in about 546 BC, and added the Lydian kingdom to his own, he brought into his empire a number of Greek settlements in the west of Asia Minor which had previously been under Lydian control. These Greeks had close ties with their kinsmen in Greece itself, who lived in independent city-states. A revolt by the Greek settlements of Ionia against the Persians in 494 BC was supported by some of the states of mainland Greece. When Darius I defeated the Ionian revolt, he determined to bring the states of mainland Greece into his empire as well, and in 490 BC sent an expedition against Athens, which had taken the lead in supporting the Ionian revolt. This expedition was defeated at the battle of Marathon. Ten years later Xerxes himself led a much larger army against Greece, attacking by land and sea, but his forces were routed by the combined states of Greece in the naval battle of Salamis (480 BC) and the land battle of Plataea (479 BC). The Greeks then made an attempt to carry the war into the enemy's territory and liberate the Greek states ruled by Persia. This attempt was not so effective as it might have been, because the city-states which had united to repel the Persian invader failed to remain united when the immediate threat receded. The Persian kings were able to take advantage of the continuing Greek disunity and support one Greek city against another. However, in the middle of the fourth century BC, Philip II, king of Macedonia, completely changed the situation. First he established his mastery over all the territory from Epirus to Thrace. Next he took control over the city-states of Greece, and with the Battle of Chaeronea in 338 BC he completed by force and diplomacy the unification which they had never been able to achieve voluntarily. Once he had unified all Thrace, Macedonia and Greece under his rule, Philip planned to lead a united Greco-Macedonian army against the Persian Empire. He was, however, assassinated in 336 BC before he could achieve his ambition, and his plan was bequeathed to his twenty-year-old son Alexander.

Alexander had some trouble at the outset of his reign because some of the Greeks states took the opportunity to revolt, since Alexander was so youthful. They soon discovered their mistake. Alexander was already a forceful man, and he showed that he had inherited to the full his father's military and political skills. By 334 BC he was undisputed master of his father's empire and was ready to put his father's plan into operation. Leading his armies across the Hellespont into Asia, he paused to visit the site of ancient Troy, drawing inspiration, perhaps, from the place where Achilles, whom he claimed as his ancestor, had fought and died. Alexander had a heroic imagination himself, and had the gift of impressing the imagination of his followers. There, in the neighbourhood of Troy, he won the first of his victories over the enemy, when he defeated a Persian army at the river Granicus. This victory opened up all Asia Minor before him. A second victory won at Issus, on the Gulf of Alexandretta (333 BC), opened his way south into Syria. He marched south through Syria and Phoenicia, but his progress was blocked by the city of Tyre which held out against him during a siege of seven months (January–July, 332 BC). At last he conquered the island fortress by building a causeway to it from the mainland. The savage vengeance which he took on the city which had withstood him so long showed that this man who carried Greek culture into Asia had something of the barbarian in him too. He continued his southward route from Tyre, and the various petty states on the way, including Samaria and Judaea, paid homage to him as he went. Gaza, like Tyre, resisted him, but it was captured after hard fighting, and the way now lay open into Egypt, which fell into the conqueror's hands with little trouble. There, in 331 BC, Alexander founded the great city which bears his name to this day—Alexandria. Alexandria was to play a notable part in the history of Israel for many centuries to come.

Samaria did not oppose Alexander's army, but while he was in Egypt their leaders killed the officer he had appointed to take charge of Syria. On his return he destroyed the city. Many of the leaders fled, but were pursued and massacred in a remote cave north of Jericho.[1]

Having established his dominion over Egypt, Alexander retraced his steps. There remained a large area of the Persian Empire to conquer yet, and the Great King had raised a third army to oppose his advance. So Alexander marched north (destroying Samaria on the way), passed through Syria, and crossed the Euphrates and Tigris. In October, 331 BC, he met the new Persian army at Gaugamela, in the plain of Arbela, east of the Tigris. This army, too, fell before him, and this final defeat effectually brought the Persian empire to an end. Darius III fled east, where he was assassinated by one of his courtiers, but his family and treasures fell into the hands of Alexander. Alexander continued his eastward march, occupying the Persian capitals of Susa, Ecbatana and Persepolis on his way. The burning of Persepolis may have been Alexander's revenge on the Persians for their invasion of Greece and burning of Athens a century and a half before—or so tradition claims. But it is certain that Alexander's policy afterwards was never motivated by thoughts of revenge on Persia.

His advance was not finished with the destruction of Persepolis. He marched farther east, through Afghanistan into India, crossing the Indus and occupying the territory which we now know as Pakistan. By this time, however, his soldiers (not unreasonably) felt that they had marched far enough away from home, and that they and their leader had won sufficient glory. So Alexander began to lead them back, while his admiral Nearchus sailed back from the mouth of the Indus to the Persian Gulf, exploring the uncharted waters of that part of the Indian Ocean.

Alexander died of a fever at Babylon in 323 BC, having conquered most of the known world. He did not live to consolidate the empire he had won, and its political unity did not last after his death. But his conquests created a cultural unity over the whole of the Near and Middle East which was to last for a thousand years.

GREEK CULTURE

Alexander planned to bring about the union of east and west under his control. Once he had conquered Persia in battle and taken limited vengeance by the burning of Persepolis, he did not treat the Persians as second-class subjects or slaves. He married Statira, daughter of the last Persian king, and he encouraged his generals to marry other Persian noblewomen. He had already married Roxana, daughter of a Scythian chief, following Scythian rites. The men who marched behind him, having come from all parts of the Greek-speaking world, began to develop a common Greek speech, not marked by the dialect peculiarities of the various cities from which they had come. This common speech (known as Hellenistic Greek) spread all over the eastern Mediterranean and western Asia throughout the following centuries. But the outstanding feature of the Greek way of life was the Greek city, or 'polis'. The old days when each polis was an independent state had been swept away by Philip's conquest, but the Greek cities retained their internal freedom and provided their citizens with all the means for what they regarded as the 'good life'. There they lived together, talked together in the market place, administered civic affairs and justice, and enjoyed the amenities provided by the temple, the theatre, the gymnasium, the hippodrome (for chariot-races), the stadium (for foot-races), and others too. One of the chief cultural effects of Alexander's conquests was the rise of new cities after the Greek model wherever his armies marched and his veterans settled. Many of these were named after Alexander himself, or after his generals, or after members of their families. Among the many Alexandrias which arose at this time we must include not only the most famous of all, Egyptian Alexandria, but, far to the east, those Alexandrias whose name survives to this day in Kandahar (Afghanistan) and Khojend (Uzbekistan). In those cities Alexander's veterans, traders and many other Greeks, settled and married and brought up children, philosophized and worshipped their gods and pursued their favourite way of life. In the surrounding countryside the native inhabitants pursued their traditional way of life, speaking non-Greek languages—Coptic, Aramaic, and others—and worshipping other deities. Yet they could not remain uninfluenced by the Greek cities in their midst. They had to learn some Greek themselves when they brought their wares to sell in the city market-place and bought products of city industry to take back home with them. It was soon realized that gods as well as men are very much like one another the wide world over, so that Aphrodite was easily identified with Astarte, Athene with Anath. The supreme god Zeus himself, Olympian Zeus, was identified with the deity whom the Syrians worshipped as 'the Lord of heaven', Ba'al Shamen.

RIVAL GREEK RULERS

Alexander's legal heirs were his mentally defective half-brother Philip Arrhidaeus and his child by Roxana, not yet born at the time of his death, who proved to be a boy, and was named Alexander after his father. A council of Alexander's generals appointed one of their number, Perdiccas, as guardian of the two heirs. Meanwhile six other generals administered large areas of Alexander's empire as regents. In particular, Ptolemy the son of Lagus administered Egypt, Seleucus the satrapy of Babylon, and Antigonus the greater part of western Asia. These three, with Antipater, regent of Macedonia and Greece, made an alliance against Perdiccas. They feared that his guardianship of the rightful heirs, added to his alliance with Alexander's mother Olympias and his widow Roxana, made him aim at supreme authority for himself. Perdiccas was assassinated in 321 BC, and Antipater was named as guardian, but Antipater's death in 319 BC was followed by civil war in Macedonia and Greece. Within a few years Philip Arrhidaeus and his wife Eurydice had been put to death by Olympias; Olympias in turn was put to death by Cassander, son of Antipater, who controlled Macedonia and Greece, and later on Cassander also murdered Roxana and her young son Alexander. In this way all Alexander's legitimate heirs were removed, so there was no longer any need to maintain the pretence of guardianship and regency. A power struggle followed. By 275 BC the Macedonian dynasties were reduced to three—Ptolemies in Egypt, Seleucids in Asia and Antigonids in Macedonia.

Of these rulers the two who are important for the history of Israel are Ptolemy in Egypt and Seleucus in Asia. They both founded dynasties, one of which (the Ptolemaic) lasted until 31 BC, the other (the Seleucid) until c. 6 BC. For most of this period the relations between the two dynasties were hostile, even when they were not actually fighting. Judaea, which lay on the frontier between them, was intimately involved in their quarrels, as may be seen from the eleventh chapter of Daniel, where the relations between 'the king of the north' (the Seleucids) and 'the king of the south' (the Ptolemies) are outlined in the rather secretive language of apocalyptic.

PTOLEMY AND SELEUCUS

To begin with, Ptolemy and Seleucus were friends and allies. Indeed, Seleucus was glad to find refuge with Ptolemy and serve as admiral of his Mediterranean fleet when Antigonus drove him out of Babylon in 316 BC and extended his control over all Asia. When Ptolemy and Seleucus, with Lysimachus, the ruler of Thrace, defeated Antigonus at Gaza in 312 BC, Seleucus was able to return to Babylon. It is from the year of his return (312 BC) that the Seleucid dynasty reckoned its official era. Ptolemy, however, profited by his victory by adding to his empire Coelesyria (southern Syria and Phoenicia). Antigonus was again defeated (and killed) at Ipsus in Phrygia in 301 BC, and Seleucus became master of most of western Asia.

Ptolemy's command of the Mediterranean coastland of Asia as far north as the Phoenician ports brought him a great deal of maritime and commercial power, especially as he also controlled Cyprus. His command of the land-bridge between Egypt and Asia gave him further commercial advantages by his control of the trade-routes leading north and east from the Egyptian frontier. His control of Lebanon gave him a plentiful supply of timber for his building projects in Alexandria, for the city built by Alexander was now Ptolemy's capital, and he determined to make it a worthy capital of a great empire. It was towards the end of his reign, for example, that the great lighthouse was erected on the island of Pharos, just off the Alexandrian shore, which speedily became famous as one of the seven wonders of the world.

But from our point of view, the most important feature of Ptolemy's control of Syria and Phoenicia is the fact that he was thus master of Judaea. Josephus tells how Ptolemy entered Jerusalem on a sabbath day in 320 BC, pretending that he wished to offer sacrifice in the temple, and made himself master of the city by force. At that time, too, he deported a considerable number of people from Jerusalem and Judaea, and settled them in Alexandria. There they lived with free status under their own laws, and the attractions of the new city were such that many other Jews soon made their way there voluntarily. Soon one of the five sectors of the city was completely Jewish and they spread into one of the other sectors as well. The Jewish community of Alexandria speedily became one of the most important communities of the Diaspora. They formed the most important section of the city's non-Greek population; they were granted special privileges and had their own constitution as a sort of municipality within a municipality. In Alexandria after one or two generations the Jews gave up the use of their old Semitic tongue and spoke Greek like their neighbours.

It was for the benefit of these Greek-speaking Jews of Alexandria that the first translation of the Bible was made. The legend preserved in the Letter of Aristeas tells how Ptolemy II (282–246 BC), son and successor of the first Ptolemy, wished to complete his great library by the inclusion of the sacred books of the Jews. He sent to the high priest at Jerusalem who supplied him with seventy-two selected scholars who were given accommodation on the island of Pharos and there translated the Pentateuch from Hebrew into Greek in seventy-two days. It is in fact true that some beginning was made with the translation of the Hebrew scriptures into Greek at Alexandria in the third century BC, but the work was carried out in the first instance for the benefit of members of the Jewish community of the city, not for the royal library. In due course a carefully prepared Greek version of the Pentateuch appears to have been given official authorization by the leaders of the Jewish community. The translations of the books of the prophets and the other sacred writings were achieved by private enterprise over a period of 150 years or so.

The Seleucid dynasty also built great cities, prominent among which were Antioch, fifteen miles from the mouth of the Orontes in north Syria, and its seaport of Seleucia. Another Seleucia was built on the Tigris, some miles north of Babylon, and it soon became much more important than Babylon itself. In these cities too Jewish merchants settled and received special privileges from Seleucus and his successors, just as their kinsmen in Alexandria did from the Ptolemies.

As for Jerusalem and Judaea, the Jews there continued to enjoy their temple-constitution under the new Macedonian overlords as they had formerly done under the Persians. Although the Seleucid and Ptolemaic armies marched against each other along the coastal road, Jerusalem and the surrounding territory were not directly affected by these wars until nearly the end of the third century.

WAR BETWEEN EGYPT AND SYRIA

Ptolemy I abdicated in favour of his son in 285 BC, and died two years later. In 281 BC Seleucus was murdered, and his son Antiochus I succeeded him on the throne. (All the male sovereigns of the Ptolemaic dynasty bore the throne-name Ptolemy, but there was a little more variety in the names of the Seleucid monarchs.) War broke out between the two kingdoms. In 276 BC Ptolemy II invaded northern Syria, but he was forced to retreat, and after an indecisive war of three or four years peace was declared. A second outbreak took place in 260 BC, after Antiochus I had been succeeded by Antiochus II. This time it was the Seleucid monarch who attacked, but the result was equally indecisive, and at last peace was concluded in 253 BC. The treaty between the two rulers was confirmed by Antiochus II receiving in marriage Berenice, daughter of Ptolemy II and his sister-queen Arsinoe.[2]

But it was in fact this marriage that led to a third outbreak of hostilities. In order to marry the Alexandrian princess, Antiochus divorced his existing wife Laodice, by whom he already had a son Seleucus. She had Antiochus poisoned in 246 BC, her supporters murdered Berenice and her son, and Laodice's son ascended the throne as Seleucus II. Naturally Ptolemy III, who now reigned at Alexandria in place of his father, was bound to avenge his sister's murder and the insult offered to his family. He invaded Asia, extended his territory as far north as Damascus, and carried immense booty home to Egypt. Peace was again restored in 241 BC. An attempt by Seleucus II to invade Ptolemy's territory was repulsed with heavy losses.

When Seleucus II died in 226 BC, he left his throne to his son Seleucus III, but three years later the new king was poisoned and was succeeded by his younger brother Antiochus III (223–187 BC). This Antiochus has come down in history as 'Antiochus the Great', for he extended his realm both north and south and seemed likely to recover the major part of Alexander's empire for himself, until he found himself checked by a greater power than his own.

In 218–217 BC Antiochus marched south along the coastal road, conquered the cities of Phoenicia and Philistia and reached Raphia on the Egyptian frontier. There he was opposed by Ptolemy IV (221–204 BC) and suffered a disastrous defeat at his hands. He was forced to withdraw to his northern territories, and Ptolemy recovered at his leisure the cities which had transferred their loyalty to Antiochus. A tradition preserved in the Third Book of Maccabees tells how this Ptolemy received an embassy from Jerusalem to congratulate him on his victory and how he visited Jerusalem. This is probable enough, but the further tale of his determination to enter the holy of holies and his attempt to revenge himself on the Jews of Alexandria when he was supernaturally prevented from entering cannot be regarded as historical.[3]

Antiochus III, although defeated in his first attempt to extend his realm southward to the Egyptian border, had no intention of abandoning his plan. After spending some years in restoring order on the eastern frontiers of his empire, he resumed his attack on the Ptolemaic territories in Asia in 202 BC, when Ptolemy IV had been succeeded by his infant son Ptolemy V (204–180 BC). Gaza was besieged and conquered by Antiochus's troops, and in 200 BC he won a decisive victory over Ptolemy's general Scopas at Panion, near the source of the Jordan. As a result of this victory he gained control of all Syria and Palestine as far as the frontier of Egypt. After more than a century under Ptolemaic control, Jerusalem found itself obliged to recognize the Seleucid king as overlord.

At least some of the people of Jerusalem were eager to transfer their loyalty to Antiochus, and helped to expel the Ptolemaic garrison from the citadel. Antiochus, in his turn, confirmed the privileges which Jerusalem and the Jews had enjoyed under the Ptolemies, and granted them some reduction in the tribute which they had been accustomed to pay. He even made some contributions to the temple funds. The Sanhedrin—the council of elders—led a deputation of the citizens to greet him as he approached the city and assured him of their welcome. It looked as if Jerusalem would be at least no worse off under the Seleucids than it had been under the Ptolemies. But the events of the next thirty years were to prove otherwise.

NOTES

[1] More than 200 skeletons were found in 1962–3 in a cave in the Wadi Daliyeh, together with some of the papyrus documents the Samaritan leaders carried with them.

[2] See Dan. 11:6 ('the daughter of the king of the South will go to the king of the North to make an alliance').

[3] 3 Maccabees 1:1 ff. The latter part of the story has apparently been confused with an incident which Josephus, with greater probability, assigns to the reign of Ptolemy VIII (*Against Apion* ii, 52 ff.).

Chapter Sixteen

Oniads and Tobiads
(200–175 BC)

SIMON THE HIGH PRIEST

It was inevitable that under the Ptolemaic and Seleucid regimes the Jews should be exposed to the influence of Hellenistic civilization in various ways. This influence was more obvious among the Jewish communities of the great Hellenistic cities such as Alexandria and Antioch, but even in Jerusalem and Judaea it was visible. On a higher level, the influence of Greek thought may be seen in the wisdom literature of Israel at this time. It has even been thought that a literary relationship may be detected in the similar themes occasionally treated in the pastoral idylls of Theocritus and the pastoral passages in the Hebrew Song of Songs; but this is far from certain.

At the time when Judaea passed under Seleucid control the high priest was Simon II.[1] In the contemporary document called the Wisdom of Jesus the son of Sira (or Ecclesiasticus) there is a long passage in praise of Simon:

> The leader of his brothers and the pride of his people
> was the high priest, Simon son of Onias,
> who in his life repaired the house,
> and in his time fortified the temple.
> He laid the foundations for the high double walls,
> the high retaining walls for the temple enclosure.
> In his days a water cistern was dug,
> a reservoir like the sea in circumference.
> He considered how to save his people from ruin,
> and fortified the city against siege.
> How glorious he was, surrounded by the people,
> as he came out of the house of the curtain.
> Like the morning star among the clouds,
> like the full moon at the festal season;
> like the sun shining upon the temple of the Most High,

like the rainbow gleaming in splendid clouds;
like roses in the day of first fruits,
like lilies by a spring of water,
like a green shoot on Lebanon on a summer day . . .

When he put on his glorious robe
and clothed himself in perfect splendour,
when he went up to the holy altar,
he made the court of the sanctuary glorious.
When he received the portions from the hands of the
    priests,
as he stood by the hearth of the altar
with a garland of brothers around him,
he was like a young cedar on Lebanon
surrounded by the trunks of palm trees.
All the sons of Aaron in their splendour
held the Lord's offering in their hands
before the whole congregation of Israel . . .

Then Simon came down and raised his hands
over the whole congregation of Israelites,
to pronounce the blessing of the Lord with his lips,
and to glory in his name;
and they bowed down in worship a second time,
to receive the blessing from the Most High.[2]

The reference here to the work of rebuilding is probably to be linked with what Josephus tells of the decision of Antiochus III to repair the city of Jerusalem, and to finish the work on the temple area, together with the colonnades, as a reward for the goodwill shown him by the people's representatives when he became their overlord.

Simon's reputation as high priest gave added fame to the family to which he belonged, the family of Zadok, and we do not wonder that in a psalm of praise appended to the Hebrew text of Ecclesiasticus, modelled on the hundred and thirty-sixth psalm, one cause for praise should be mentioned in these words: 'Give thanks to him who has chosen the sons of Zadok to be priests, For his mercy endures for ever'.

THE TOBIAD FAMILY

Simon's immediate family are frequently referred to as the Oniads—Onias being an attempt to Hellenize the Hebrew name Honi, a shortened form of

Yohanan (John). The name Onias was borne by the great-grandfather, father and son of Simon II. The Oniads were specially respected by those in Judaea who deplored the excessive adoption of Greek customs practised by other leading families of Jerusalem. Of these other families one of the most notable was the Tobiad family. In an earlier century Tobiah, the governor of Ammon who had been one of Nehemiah's enemies, had belonged to this family.[3] The fortunes of one branch of the Tobiad family illustrates the sort of career that was possible under the Hellenistic monarchies for Jews who were not unduly concerned to be faithful to the traditional piety of Israel.

The Tobiads were related by marriage to the Oniads. Josephus tells how Joseph, son of Tobiah, and nephew of the high priest Onias II, won the favour of Ptolemy III (246–221 BC), when the latter was angered by the high priest's slowness in paying him the customary tribute of twenty talents. Ptolemy sent one of his courtiers, Athenion by name, as ambassador, demanding payment and threatening that if it was not received strong action would be taken against the temple constitution and the territory of Judaea. Joseph obtained permission from his uncle Onias, who found the responsibilities of his office heavy and distasteful, to act on his behalf. Joseph accordingly welcomed Athenion, entertained him sumptuously, and made sure that he would take back to Ptolemy a very favourable report of the treatment he had received. Joseph journeyed to Egypt a short time after Athenion's return and found (as he expected) that Ptolemy and his queen Cleopatra were already well disposed to him as a result of Athenion's report.

The collection of taxes in the Ptolemaic empire was arranged by selling the right to collect them to the highest bidders; Joseph, using money which he had borrowed from friends in the province of Samaria, made the highest bid for the right of collecting the taxes of the king's Asian provinces. He then returned to Syria, and exercised this right with ruthless severity. He borrowed the services of some of the royal troops, and when at first the citizens of one of the Philistine towns refused to pay what he demanded, he had twenty of the wealthiest of them put to death and their property confiscated. He acted similarly at Scythopolis (Beth-shan). These grim examples effectively discouraged the other cities from withholding what Joseph demanded. He exacted so much money that he not only paid the agreed sum into the royal exchequer, and repaid his creditors with interest, but gave generous presents to the king and queen as well. By this mixture of unscrupulous enterprise and diplomacy he retained the right of collecting the taxes in and around Judah for twenty-two years. Members of his family continued to collect them after his death, and found no great difficulty in transferring their services to Antiochus after his victory in 200 BC.

Joseph's youngest son Hyrcanus, borne to him by his niece, the daughter of his brother Solymius, also won great favour at the Alexandrian court. Later on he was able to create a small independent realm for himself in Transjordan, with a fortress-palace at Araq al-Amir, from which he made constant raids upon the subjects of the Nabataean kingdom, a powerful Arabian state established in the third century BC with Petra as its capital.

THE HASIDIM

There were other members of leading families in Jerusalem who were eager to enjoy in their own city those amenities of Greek city life which were available in places like Alexandria and Antioch. For instance, they wanted Jerusalem too to have its open-air gymnasium and theatre, its hippodrome and stadium. The Seleucid rulers after 200 BC did more than the Ptolemies had done to encourage the Greek way of life, and many Jews responded warmly. However, some of the elements of Greek culture which they adopted were incompatible with the true calling of Israel, because they brought Jews and Greeks together on the wrong basis, by blurring the sharp distinction between Israel's ethical monotheism and Greek paganism. The old-fashioned pious people of Jerusalem deplored these changes, but there was little they could do to prevent them. From these pious people there emerged a definite party—the hasidim (or Hasideans, as they are called in the books of Maccabees). No doubt they were despised as hopelessly old-fashioned by the 'progressive' elements in the population, but the time eventually came when they proved to be the saviours of their people.

THE DEFEAT OF ANTIOCHUS III

The conquests won by Antiochus III on the eastern and southern frontiers of his empire were not enough for his ambition. He set out to expand his dominions in the north and west as well. In the course of his operations against Egypt he made an agreement with Philip V, king of Macedonia, to divide between them Ptolemy's possessions outside Egypt. The Aegean possessions were to go to Philip. Now this Philip had some years previously become involved in war with the Roman Republic, for in 215 BC, when Rome seemed to lie at the mercy of the Carthaginian invaders of Italy, led by Hannibal, Philip made an alliance with Hannibal in order to acquire control of the Adriatic Sea. The Romans did not forget Philip's attack on them at a time when they were fighting for their lives against Hannibal. In 202 BC Rome's second Punic War came to an end, when Hannibal was decisively defeated at the battle of Zama by the Roman general Publius Cornelius Scipio Africanus.

About the same time Philip's efforts to gain control of the Aegean alarmed the Rhodians and the king of Pergamum (whose kingdom had emerged as an independent state some sixty years previously). Both Rhodes and Pergamum sought the help of Rome against Philip, and Rome declared war on him. In order to win the support of the Greek city-states, the Roman general Flamininus proclaimed independence for all the Greeks in 198 BC, and defeated Philip decisively at Cynoscephalae in Thessaly in 197 BC. Philip was restricted to his home-territory of Macedonia, and the Romans withdrew their armies from liberated Greece in 194 BC.

But some of the Greek states, united in the Aetolian League, resented the restrictions which the Roman gift of liberty imposed on them. They invited Antiochus to come over from Asia and 'liberate' Greece from her 'liberators'. In 192 BC Antiochus landed in Greece and made himself master of Euboea and part of Thessaly. Next year, however, the Romans took action against this challenge to their policies for Greece, and routed Antiochus in the historic pass of Thermopylae. They then pursued their war against Antiochus into Asia. In 190 BC Antiochus's fleet was destroyed in a naval battle in the Aegean Sea, and a large Roman army crossed into Asia under the command of Lucius Cornelius Scipio (Asiaticus), brother of the conqueror of Hannibal. The army which Antiochus raised to meet the Roman force was destroyed at the Battle of Magnesia (190 BC), and Antiochus accepted the Roman conditions of peace. By the Peace of Apamea (188 BC) he agreed to evacuate all his territories west of the Taurus mountain range, which were divided between the Rhodians and the Pergamenes, to surrender all his elephants and most of what remained of his fleet, to agree to recruit no soldiers from Greece and the Aegean lands, and to pay an indemnity of 15,000 talents.

These Roman demands placed a heavy burden on Seleucid resources. The indemnity, which was to be paid in instalments over twelve years, was the heaviest known to ancient history. The wealthiest parts of Antiochus's empire, from whose revenues he might have raised a considerable part of the sum, were detached from him by the treaty. On his eastern frontier, too, Armenia, Parthia and Bactria, which had been tributary to him, asserted their complete independence and no longer paid him tribute or acknowledged him as king. The money had to be raised somehow, and the following year Antiochus made an expedition into Susiana (the former territory of Elam) in order to plunder a wealthy temple of Bel ('Elymaean Zeus' to the Greeks). Temples were largely used as banks in antiquity, and some of them housed large stocks of treasure. The greater the wealth that was stored within their walls, the greater became the temptation for some needy ruler or adventurer to ignore the sacred sanctions by which it was protected. While Antiochus was engaged in this sacrilegious enterprise, he was surprised by an attack from the local inhabitants and lost his life (187 BC).

THE RAID ON THE TEMPLE

Antiochus III was succeeded by his elder son Seleucus IV. His younger son, Antiochus, was being brought up at Rome, for he had been sent there in accordance with the Peace of Apamea as a hostage until the war indemnity had been paid in full. Seleucus now inherited the difficult task of finding money to raise the annual instalments. The only way to do it was by increasing the taxes to be paid by his subjects. The inhabitants of Coelesyria, including Judaea, now had reason to regret the fact that the Seleucids had taken over control from the Ptolemies. Even the very heavy taxes exacted by Joseph the Tobiad were not such a burden as the exactions of Seleucus's tax-collectors. This is the only feature of Seleucus's reign which is mentioned in the review of Daniel 11:20, 'His [Antiochus III's] successor will send out a tax collector to maintain the royal splendour.' If in the strenuous quest for money even the sanctity of temples was disregarded, there was no reason why the tax collectors should spare the temple of 'the God of heaven' at Jerusalem. To the Jews, of course, this temple was the only temple in the world where the true God was worshipped; all other shrines were dedicated to the worship of gods that were no gods. But the Seleucid kings and their ministers could not be expected to make any such distinction.

According to the narrative of 2 Maccabees, Apollonius, governor of Coelesyria, had his attention drawn to the wealth that lay stored in the Jerusalem temple. His informant, we are told, was Simon, captain of the temple, probably a son of Joseph the Tobiad. Simon acted in this way because of a quarrel which he had with the high priest Onias III. This may well be a biassed account. In any case, the story continues, Apollonius reported his information to the king, and the king instructed his chancellor Heliodorus to go to Jerusalem and take possession of the gold in the temple. When Heliodorus came to Jerusalem, he was courteously entertained by the high priest. When he asked about the temple treasures, the high priest assured him that they consisted chiefly of deposits made by widows and orphans, and included also money deposited there by Hyrcanus the Tobiad (who at this time had installed himself as an independent chieftain in Transjordan). Heliodorus, however, said he must carry out the royal orders and take possession of this wealth. But when he insisted on doing so despite the protests of the priests, he was attacked by a heavenly apparition and thought himself lucky to have escaped with his life.[4] What basis of truth underlies this story we cannot be sure. Not long afterwards the temple was not only plundered but desecrated, and no supernatural intervention prevented it.

The feud between Onias III and Simon continued, and Simon took every opportunity to poison the minds of the people of Judaea, and that of the king's governor as well, against Onias. At last Onias decided that the only way in which he could put the matter right, and defend himself against the accusations of disloyalty which Simon was continually bringing against him, was to go to Antioch himself and seek an interview with the king. To Antioch, then, he went in 175 BC, and he was there when King Seleucus met his death, assassinated by his chancellor Heliodorus.

NOTES

[1] Perhaps he should be identified with Simon the Just of rabbinical tradition. According to the tractate of the Mishnah called 'The Sayings of the Fathers', Simon the Just was one of the last survivors of the Great Synagogue. He used to say 'Upon three things the world is based: upon Torah, upon the temple service, and upon the practice of charity'.

[2] Ecclus. 50:1–8, 11–13, 20 f. This poem in praise of Simon concludes the section of Ecclesiasticus known as 'The Praise of the Elders' (which begins with 44:1, 'Let us now sing the praises of famous men . . .'). See p. 150, n. 2.

[3] See pp. 101, 105. Cf. B. Mazar, 'The Tobiads', IEJ 7 (1957), pp. 137 ff., 229 ff.; L. L. Grabbe, *Judaism from Cyrus to Hadrian* (1992), pp. 192 ff.

[4] 2 Macc. 3:4 ff.

Chapter Seventeen

An Ambitious Greek King
(175–168 BC)

ANTIOCHUS IV EPIPHANES

The assassinated King Seleucus IV had two young sons, Antiochus and Demetrius. Heliodorus appointed himself regent for the young Antiochus, but there is little doubt that his intention was to assume the kingship. However, his plans were thwarted by the arrival of another Antiochus, who was the brother of the dead king.

Seleucus's brother Antiochus had been absent from Antioch for twelve years, kept as a hostage in Rome to guarantee payment of the indemnity imposed by the Treaty of Apamaea. Shortly before his assassination, Seleucus IV had arranged for his younger son, Demetrius, to replace Antiochus as hostage. Antiochus had left Rome. and travelled to Athens, where he spent some time as a very popular visitor. He so won the affection of the people of Athens by his democratic ways and by the generosity which he displayed in adorning their city (as he did other cities) with gifts of temples and other buildings that they made him an honorary citizen and bestowed on him the office of Master of the Mint. His years of exile in Rome had made him a warm admirer of Roman power and institutions, but he was also a passionate champion of the Hellenistic way of life in all its aspects.

Antiochus was still at Athens when news reached him that Heliodorus had murdered his brother Seleucus. As both the sons of Seleucus were still young, Antiochus was lawful regent of the kingdom. He borrowed troops from King Eumenes II of Pergamum, and with their aid was able to remove Heliodorus from power. He received a warm welcome at Antioch. Once he had defeated the usurping Heliodorus, Antiochus took the status not of regent but of king. His nephew Antiochus was nominal joint-king until his death some years later. (This nephew ought by rights to be known as Antiochus IV, but in fact that title has always been given to his uncle.) Antiochus's action in taking the position of joint-king with his nephew, the rightful heir, was in fact quite usual in the Hellenistic world. Indeed, the

Pergamene king took it for granted that he would assume royal status, for when he lent him an army to achieve his purpose, he also presented him with some royal objects, including a crown.

Many tales were told about Antiochus's friendly and democratic ways, his fondness for practical jokes, his proneness for roaming the streets of his capital by night in disguise, his unpredictable fits of generosity. Some of his subjects called him Epimanes, the 'madman'—probably a punning reference to the title which he himself adopted later in his reign (c. 169 BC), Epiphanes. (The full title was Theos Epiphanes, 'God Manifest'—even if he did not identify himself with Olympian Zeus, the chief Greek god.) But he proved himself a good soldier and wise administrator. He saw the dangerous state to which his kingdom had been reduced by the Peace of Apamea, and planned to keep on good terms with Rome. At the same time he sought ways to compensate for the financial losses suffered by the terms of that Peace—in particular from Egypt and from the eastern territories of his kingdom. For our purposes, however, we have to pay special consideration to his relations with the Jews. In these he does not appear in such a good light as he does in some of the other affairs of his kingdom.

JASON BECOMES HIGH PRIEST

When Antiochus established himself as king, the high priest Onias III was visiting Antioch; he had gone there to persuade Seleucus IV that the accusations of the Tobiads were false. But now another rival to Onias made his appearance at Antioch—none other than his own brother Jason.[1] Jason was able to persuade King Antiochus that if he were made high priest in his brother's place, he would promote the cause of Hellenism in Jerusalem, and would pay a large sum into the royal treasury. Antiochus listened to him, and appointed him high priest instead of his brother Onias. Jason accordingly instituted a gymnasium at Jerusalem, and enrolled several of the young men of noble families in an order of *epheboi*, an athletic corporation such as was common in Greek cities. It shocked the pious party in Jerusalem to see these young men walking through the streets of Jerusalem wearing the broad-brimmed hat or *petasos*, the badge of the *epheboi*; it also shocked them to see the same young men engage in athletic exercises in the gymnasium—wrestling and discus-throwing—completely naked. Worse still, some of these Jewish athletes took steps to obscure the fact that they were circumcised. Even among the priestly families this enthusiasm for Greek ways was spreading. Some of the priests hurried through their sacrificial duties in the temple so as to attend the sports in the gymnasium as quickly as possible.

The old temple constitution of Jerusalem still continued, but now those citizens of Jerusalem who wished to do so could be enrolled as citizens of Antioch. This was a privilege which Jason bought from the king for 150 talents at the same time as he bought the high priesthood for himself. These 'Antiochenes of Jerusalem' probably formed a distinct group with special rights in Jerusalem, enjoying the privileges normally granted to a free Greek city. It has sometimes been thought that Jerusalem itself was given the constitution of a Greek city and had its name changed to Antioch. This would be in accord with Antiochus's practice in many other parts of his kingdom, for he founded many new cities or gave Greek civic constitutions to old cities (such as Tarsus), and many of these new foundations received the name Antioch in honour of their founder. But there is no real evidence to support the view that Jerusalem was actually given a civic constitution under the name Antioch. No doubt the granting of Antiochene citizenship to the new corporation in Jerusalem, without at this stage removing the old temple-constitution, was regarded as a first step towards granting Jerusalem full status as a Greek city. But there were special features in the situation of Jerusalem which Antiochus completely failed to understand. These effectively prevented him from achieving this goal.

Further offence was given to the pious Jews in 174 BC when the quinquennial games were held at Tyre in honour of the city and its patron deity Heracles.[2] Jason sent a deputation of 'Antiochenes of Jerusalem' as sacred envoys to this festival, bearing a gift of 300 talents. Other Greek cities and corporations dedicated their gifts to Heracles himself; Jason's gift, however, was not dedicated to the pagan deity, but donated directly to the king's fleet. Even a Hellenizing high priest of Jerusalem dared not openly recognize a pagan divinity! Even so, Jason's action was condemned as gross impiety by the hasidim. The hasidim, however, were unable by themselves to stop the Hellenistic trends which they disliked so heartily. But in another part of the Hellenistic world events were taking place at this time which were to have a very profound effect on the situation in Jerusalem.

ANTIOCHUS VISITS JERUSALEM

Ptolemy V, king of Egypt, died in 181 BC. His heir, Ptolemy VI, was only a child, and Cleopatra, the boy-king's mother, acted as regent for him. Cleopatra was a sister of Antiochus IV.[3] She died in 176 BC, and two members of the Egyptian court became joint regents in her place. The new regents began to make plans to recover Coelesyria (including Judaea) for the Ptolemaic kingdom.

In 174 BC Apollonius, an experienced statesman and a former governor

of Coelesyria under Seleucus IV, was sent to Alexandria to act as Antiochus's representative at a royal celebration (perhaps the young king's
marriage, according to Egyptian established custom, with his sister Cleopatra). There Apollonius heard rumours of the plot, and reported it to
Antiochus on his return. Antiochus himself went to inspect the province of
Coelesyria, in order to take what steps were necessary to defend it against
any Egyptian invasion. He paid a visit to Judaea, in which (as was quite
well known) there were many people who would prefer Ptolemaic to
Seleucid rule. This was partly because they felt the weight of the increased
taxation since 187 BC. Also, the pious elements in the population felt that
the Ptolemies were less likely to interfere in support of Hellenizing developments than the Seleucids were. The Hellenizers,[4] on the other hand, had
begun to learn that they could count on Seleucid support. When Antiochus
visited Jerusalem (his first visit to the city, probably, since his accession),
he was welcomed by Jason and his party with a torchlight procession. No
doubt he got the impression that the city as a whole was well disposed both
to his own person and to the Hellenizing cause.

Next year (173 BC) Apollonius was sent on a more distant mission; he
went to Rome to present the final instalment of the indemnity due under
the Peace of Apamea, and to try to renew a treaty of friendship between the
Seleucid kingdom and the Roman Republic. Antiochus had major military
ambitions, but he was wise enough to know that it was essential to avoid
giving offence to the Romans. No doubt he hoped to win their approval for
his future plans.

MENELAUS BECOMES HIGH PRIEST

In 171 BC Jason sent his usual payment to the king, and appointed as
tribute-bearer Menelaus,[5] brother of that Simon whom we have already
met as captain of the temple in the reign of Seleucus IV. But when
Menelaus came to Antioch, he took his own opportunity to make a bid
for the high-priesthood, promising to pay Antiochus 300 talents more
than Jason did. Antiochus unwisely allowed himself to be persuaded by
Menelaus, and appointed him high priest. The appointment of Jason three
years earlier had been arrogant and improper, because his elder brother
Onias was alive and in office; but at least Jason belonged to the legitimate
high-priestly family. Menelaus, however, certainly did not belong to the
house of Zadok, and we cannot be sure that he belonged to any priestly
family.

Menelaus discovered that it was more difficult than he had expected to
keep his promise, and he failed to provide the additional 300 talents which

he had offered as the price of the high-priesthood. Even Sostratus, military governor of the district, found it impossible to extract the sum from him. Both Sostratus and Menelaus were therefore summoned to the royal court, where some sort of agreement was reached and Menelaus was confirmed in the high-priesthood.

But Menelaus knew that he had no right at all in Jewish religious law to the office which he had secured by bribery. He knew that those in Judaea who had some respect for that law would continue to regard the members of the house of Zadok as true high priests. It would therefore be necessary to eliminate them. Jason recognized this danger, and escaped to Transjordan. Onias, who still lived at Antioch, was less fortunate. The king had to make an expedition into Cilicia to deal with disturbances there, and in his absence left a minister Andronicus in charge in Antioch. Menelaus bribed Andronicus with some of the temple treasures to have Onias murdered, and this he did, although Onias had sought sanctuary in the sacred temple courts at Daphne, five miles from Antioch. The news of this assassination filled the pious Jews with horror, since they still regarded him as their legitimate high priest. When Antiochus returned to Antioch he punished Andronicus by degrading him from his high rank and having him executed on the very spot where the murder had taken place. So it is clear that at this stage Antiochus had no wish at all to offend the religious beliefs of the Jews.

Menelaus himself was placed in danger, for serious complaints were brought against him before the king. When he and Sostratus had been summoned to Antioch he had left his brother Lysimachus as his deputy in Jerusalem. Lysimachus's acts of sacrilege against the temple, when he took some of the sacred vessels, provoked serious riots. Three members of the Sanhedrin were deputed to go to Tyre when the king was there to present the accusations against Menelaus. But Menelaus once again paid bribes to achieve his aims; he was acquitted, and the three senators were sentenced to death. They were treated as the representatives of the party blamed for the rioting. Most of their fellow-Jews viewed them as martyrs who laid down their lives for the sanctity of the temple. Even in Tyre they had sympathizers, who provided them with an honourable burial in that city.

WAR WITH EGYPT

Some time in the winter of 170–169 BC the Egyptian government declared war on Antiochus.[6] This was an act of great folly, because it gave Antiochus the excuse and opportunity to attack Egypt. In spite of the restrictive clauses

of the Peace of Apamea, he had in the first five years of his reign built up
his military strength to very impressive proportions. The situation in Egypt,
where his nephew, the reigning Ptolemy, was a child, promised to develop
favourably for him, if he acted wisely—especially if he achieved his aim of
establishing control over Egypt without incurring the disapproval of Rome.
Rome at the moment was involved in another war against Macedonia, the
Third Macedonian War (171–168 BC). Rome's ally, Eumenes of Pergamum,
had lodged complaints at Rome against the Macedonian king Perseus
(178–168 BC) and war had broken out when Perseus rejected Rome's ulti-
matum ordering him to disarm.

The Egyptian forces were about to invade Coelesyria, with the aim of
bringing it once more under Ptolemaic sovereignty, when Antiochus struck
first. Crossing the frontier with his army, he defeated them so thoroughly
near Pelusium that the way into the heart of Egypt lay open before him. He
advanced to Memphis, and there his nephew came to him with an embassy
to discuss terms of peace. Antiochus imposed terms which confirmed
Ptolemy VI as having the title of king of Egypt, but gave himself the real
control over the land. In this way he hoped to build a position of strength
in the south which would compensate for his father's losses in the north,
and yet to do so in such a way as not to violate the terms of his treaty with
the Romans. That treaty forbade him to attack a friend or ally of Rome, such
as Egypt was, but did not prevent him from resisting aggression such as
Egypt had initiated. He wished to be welcomed by the Egyptians as a friend
and protector, and as the champion of their royal house. The unity of Syria
and Egypt would not only promote the cause of Hellenistic culture in
general but also strengthen the Hellenistic world against the growing
menace of the Parthians to the east. When Antiochus and Ptolemy concluded their treaty at Memphis in 169 BC, it looked as if these aims were
very likely to be achieved.

But when the terms of the treaty became known in Alexandria, trouble
broke out. The Alexandrians would not tolerate the idea of Seleucid overlordship, no matter how mildly the terms of that overlordship might be
expressed. They rejected the Egyptian king who had made this agreement
with Antiochus, together with his counsellors, and proclaimed his younger
brother king in his place as Ptolemy VIII.[7] He was given the official surname
Euergetes ('Benefactor'), but was commonly known as Ptolemy Physcon
('Pot-belly'). Alexandria prepared itself to withstand the assault which they
were sure Antiochus would make against it. So successful were its preparations that when the assault was launched (in the late summer of 169 BC)
it was repulsed. Antiochus withdrew, determined to besiege Alexandria
more successfully in the next campaigning season.

THE RAID ON THE TEMPLE

The military operations of this summer, and the operations he planned for the following year, demanded very heavy expenditure, especially as Antiochus's army was a very large one. But his diplomatic policy towards Egypt made it impossible for him to demand money on a large scale from what was officially a friendly country. The Alexandrian revolt had, in a way, strengthened his position; he was now the ally of Egypt's rightful king, Ptolemy VI, against his rebellious subjects. But the Egyptians would soon cease to regard him as a friend if he plundered their land.

The revenue must therefore be raised elsewhere, in his own Seleucid kingdom. The ordinary tribute, heavy as it was, was inadequate to finance large-scale military expeditions of this sort; he must somehow find money elsewhere. And it was well known that treasure was available in many of the temples of the kingdom, including the temple of Jerusalem. Antiochus accordingly called at Jerusalem on his way back to Antioch. Something had happened to prevent the attempt to raid the temple treasures in the time of Antiochus's elder brother, but Antiochus had no such difficulty. Onias III had then obstructed Heliodorus; but now Menelaus actually escorted Antiochus in person into the sanctuary (where no Jewish layman was allowed to penetrate, and certainly not a pagan king), and helped him to take the sacred vessels and costly dedications and ornaments, to the sum of 1800 talents.

From the viewpoint of royal policy, the robbing of a temple was not particularly serious. From the viewpoint of the custodians of any particular temple, and of the people who worshipped there, such an act was a dreadful sacrilege. What he did to other temples did not much matter to them, but pious Jews believed that their temple was totally different from other temples. To Antiochus the act was simply one forced on him by financial necessity; at this stage he was no more hostile towards the Jewish religion than towards the cults associated with any of the other temples which he robbed. But to the Jews, especially in the light of later events, this act of sacrilege was one of the first steps in Antiochus's attacks on their faith and practice. The religious narrator of 2 Maccabees explains that Antiochus was able to accomplish his impious deed unhindered because God was angry with his people's sins and had therefore temporarily turned away his face from his sanctuary (otherwise, it is implied, Antiochus would have been supernaturally repulsed even as Heliodorus had been).[8] The more secular author of 1 Maccabees records in poetry how

Israel mourned deeply in every community,
rulers and elders groaned,

young women and young men became faint,
the beauty of the women faded.
Every bridegroom took up the lament;
she who sat in the bridal chamber was mourning.
Even the land trembled for its inhabitants,
and all the house of Jacob was clothed with shame.[9]

It must be remembered that when we are dealing with the history of Israel Antiochus inevitably creates a different impression from that which we find in the record of the wider Hellenistic world. From the wider point of view Judaea was a minor province of his empire; from Judaea's point of view Antiochus was the devil in human form.

ANTIOCHUS AND THE ROMANS

Antiochus made a second expedition against Egypt in 168 BC, but the situation was not so favourable to him as it had appeared to be when he left Egypt the previous year.[10] The two Ptolemies had come to an agreement with each other, and were now reigning as joint sovereigns together with their sister Cleopatra, who was also the wife of the older brother. Antiochus could no longer pose as the defender of the rightful king against a usurper. If he invaded Egypt now, it would be difficult to avoid the accusation of aggression. But the Romans were still engaged in the Third Macedonian War; they might be too busy to interfere at the moment. He hoped that by the time they were free to take an interest in Egyptian affairs, he would have achieved his aims and it would be too late for them to stop him.

Early in the year he attacked Cyprus, which belonged to the Ptolemies; the governor surrendered to him. In the spring his army invaded the Egyptian mainland and began the siege of Alexandria. Antiochus himself remained in Memphis, the ancient capital of Lower Egypt, and there he had himself crowned king of Egypt according to the traditional rites by the priests of Ptah. He no longer pretended to be the ally and protector of the Egyptian king. In the previous year he had carefully refrained from offending the population by plunder and extortion, but now he looted the temples of Egypt as thoroughly as he had the temples of Asia.

From Memphis Antiochus set out to join his besieging army at Alexandria. But now his ambitions in Egypt met a sudden obstacle. About a week before (June 22), Rome had brought the Third Macedonian War to a victorious conclusion by the battle of Pydna. Rome had been well aware of Antiochus's activity in Egypt, but took no action until the Macedonian War was over. A Roman envoy was waiting in the Aegean Sea, ready to sail for Alexandria as soon as victory was won. This envoy was Lucius Popillius

Laenas, with whom Antiochus had formed a friendship in the days of his exile at Rome. The meeting of the two men outside Alexandria is one of the famous scenes of history. Laenas, instead of accepting the friendly right hand which Antiochus held out to greet an old friend, put into it a copy of the decree of the Roman senate ordering Antiochus to leave Egypt at once, and told him of the Roman triumph at Pydna. Antiochus said he must consult with his advisers; Laenas drew a circle round the king in the sand and told him to give his answer before he stepped out of the circle. Antiochus had no choice; he submitted to the commands of Rome. It was little consolation for him that Laenas then consented to shake hands with him on the basis of their old friendship! The power of Rome, which had been important in the east since Magnesia, was now supreme: within a week she had conquered Macedonia, taken Egypt under her protection, and forced the Seleucid king to submit to her orders. These three kingdoms, which had been the chief heirs of Alexander's empire, now had to acknowledge a new and superior power.

NOTES

[1] A Hellenized form of Joshua.

[2] Heracles was the name which the Greeks gave to Melqart, the chief deity of Tyre; see p. 33.

[3] She is the 'daughter' in Dan. 11:17 ('he [Antiochus III] will give him [Ptolemy V] a daughter in marriage in order to overthrow the kingdom').

[4] It is convenient to call those Jews who opposed the hasidim and the Maccabees 'Hellenizers', though no doubt they had a variety of beliefs and motives. It is at least certain that Greek culture appealed to them more strongly than to devout Jews.

[5] Hellenized form of Menahem.

[6] Diodorus, *History* xxx, 15.

[7] Ptolemy VI's son briefly claimed the throne and can therefore be listed as Ptolemy VII. However, the attempt was so unsuccessful that many historians ignore him and call Euergetes Ptolemy VII rather than VIII.

[8] 2 Macc. 5:15–20.

[9] 1 Macc. 1:25–28.

[10] 1 Maccabees (1:16–19) records only Antiochus's first invasion of Egypt, making no reference to the second; 2 Maccabees (5:1) records only the second, but calls it the second; Daniel records both the first (11:25–27) and the second (11:29 f.).

Chapter Eighteen

The Abomination of Desolation
(168–167 BC)

THE ATTACK ON JERUSALEM

The Romans compelled Antiochus to abandon his ambitions in Egypt; but took no action to compel the Ptolemaic rulers to abandon their ambitions in Asia. Antiochus therefore needed to guard against any Ptolemaic attempt to take over Coelesyria. And news which reached him suggested that such an attempt was already being plotted inside Coelesyria. He heard that Jerusalem was in revolt against him, supporting the Ptolemies' claims.

News of the rebuff which Antiochus received from the Romans had spread quickly, before he could get back to his own kingdom, and in some places, including Jerusalem, was exaggerated into news of his death. This distorted rumour reached the former high priest Jason in his place of refuge in Transjordan. Immediately he decided that the opportunity had come for him to regain his high priesthood and to expel the illegitimate high priest whom Antiochus had appointed, Menelaus. So he gathered a band of a thousand men and led them against Jerusalem, seizing the city and temple, with the exception of the citadel, in which Menelaus was forced to take refuge. Although Jason himself had originally obtained the high priesthood by bribery and usurpation, and was known to favour Hellenistic ways, at least he belonged to the legitimate high-priestly family, and was for this reason far more acceptable to the pious people of Jerusalem than Menelaus could ever have been. In addition, Onias, whom Jason had displaced in the first instance, was now dead. On the other hand, the pious party could not approve of Jason's violent methods, which involved the death of Jewish people—or so they reasoned when his attempts failed and he had to flee from the country.

For his attempt was certain to fail. Antiochus was not dead, but on his way back from Egypt, angered at the rebuff he had suffered. And as he was on his way back, news came to him of the fighting at Jerusalem. To him, naturally, the events in Jerusalem looked like a revolt against his authority—doubtless, he supposed, a revolt in favour of the Ptolemies. There seemed to be more rebels in Jerusalem than he had imagined; otherwise it would not have been so easy for Jason to seize the city with so little trouble. He therefore sent part of his army against Jerusalem with instructions to crush the revolt, punish the rebels, and reinstate Menelaus as high priest. The soldiers treated Jerusalem as a rebellious city, and taking it by force of arms they killed many people, not only among the military defenders but among the civil population as well. Many of the inhabitants were seized and sold into slavery. Menelaus was forcibly reimposed upon them as high priest, and was more unpopular than ever. In addition, a garrison was stationed in the city under the command of a native of Phrygia named Philip, and the citizens were placed under martial law.

These actions were intended to punish the city for having revolted. But other measures were considered necessary to prevent any further rebellion. The changed situation made it doubly necessary for Antiochus to guard the parts of his kingdom close to the Egyptian frontier. He could not afford to ignore a city like Jerusalem with a population most of whom supported the Ptolemies. So he decided to abolish Judaea's former constitution as a temple-state, and to establish a Greek city-state in its place, controlled by men whom Antiochus could trust. The carrying out of this plan was entrusted to Apollonius, who was now governor of Samaria and Judaea. He began his operations on a sabbath day, after speaking peaceably to the people. The walls were demolished (as regularly happened to a city which had revolted), a new citadel, the Acra, was erected to dominate the temple area,[1] and a garrison was stationed in it. This citadel was also to serve as the centre for the new civic body of Jerusalem, in which the Hellenizing members of the population were enrolled as citizens, 'Antiochenes of Jerusalem.' Apollonius's actions inevitably caused some loss of life; probably there was some attempt at resistance when he began to demolish the walls, and he repressed this resistance without much care to distinguish combatants from non-combatants.

The members of the garrison in the Acra were probably given some lands around Jerusalem. The former walled city was now reduced to the status of an unwalled village which it had had before Nehemiah's time.

THE ATTACK ON JEWISH RELIGION

But Antiochus was not content with this radical revision of Jerusalem's political status. Its religious organization must be revised as well. And revised it was, quite probably with the co-operation of Menelaus, the Hellenizing high priest. For reasons which are not fully clear to us,

Antiochus had come to believe that the traditional Jewish faith was the cause of Jewish rebelliousness.[2] The Jews' religion was of an exclusive kind, unlike the religion of the other subject-nations of the kingdom, including the various temple-states. There was therefore no need to take steps against the religion of these other peoples such as were now taken against the Jewish religion. And the steps taken against the Jewish religion were drastic in the extreme. Orders were given that the temple ritual.must be suspended, the sacred scriptures be destroyed, the sabbath and other festival days be no longer observed, the strict food laws be abolished, and the rite of circumcision (to the Jews the sign of the covenant made by God with their ancestor Abraham) be discontinued. These steps were taken towards the end of 167 BC. The culminating attack on Jewish worship came in December of that year, when a new and smaller altar was erected upon the altar of burnt offering in the temple court, and solemnly dedicated to the worship of Olympian Zeus. Among the Syrian subjects of the king Olympian Zeus had already been identified with the god whom they knew as Ba'al Shamen, 'the lord of heaven'; and it was by this name (or by the corresponding Hebrew Ba'al Shamayim) that he was now worshipped in the Jerusalem temple. Probably the more liberal people[3] among the Jerusalem Jews were content to regard Olympian Zeus or Ba'al Shamayim as the equivalent of Yahweh, just as in the Persian period Yahweh had been commonly known as 'the God of heaven' But 'the lord of heaven' to whom the new altar was erected in the temple was worshipped with pagan rituals; his cult was solemnly inaugurated with the sacrifice of animals considered unclean by the Jewish law. The more pious Jews refused to take upon their lips the name of the pagan divinity: for centuries they had been accustomed to regard the name Baal as a *shiqqus*, an abomination, and they transformed the name Ba'al Shamayim to *shiqqus shomem*, 'the Appalling Horror' as Moffatt aptly translates it; 'the abomination of desolation' is the traditional rendering of the phrase.

About the same time the worship of Yahweh in the Samaritan temple on Gerizim was transformed into the cult of Zeus Xenios, Zeus the Protector of Strangers.[4]

The author of 1 Maccabees describes Antiochus's action against the Jewish religion as part of a policy designed to make all his subject nations practise one religion and one way of life.[5] No doubt such a policy might have promoted the cultural unity of his kingdom; but in fact there was no need for such a policy. The gradual blending of Syrian and Hellenistic culture was developing throughout his kingdom in any case, except among the pious worshippers of the God of Israel. The primary target of the king's attack on the Jews was not their resistance to religious and cultural assimilation; his first aim was to render them politically harmless and powerless.

He was so ill-advised as to think he could achieve this aim by abolishing their religion. He had been seriously misinformed about the strength and intensity of Jewish religious devotion, as he soon discovered.

The idea of centralization of worship was abolished along with the other distinctive features of the old order; altars in honour of 'the lord of heaven' were now set up throughout Judaea—in the market place of Jerusalem and in every town and village throughout the territory. The inhabitants of each place were compelled to sacrifice at these local altars, and severe penalties were imposed on those who refused, as also on those who persisted in observing those Jewish practices which the king had banned. What followed was in effect a thoroughgoing campaign of persecution on religious grounds—perhaps the first campaign of this kind in history. To circumcise one's children, to be found in possession of a scroll of the sacred law, to refuse to eat pork or the meat of animals offered on these pagan altars, were offences punishable by death.

NOTES

[1] The exact site of the Acra in Jerusalem remains uncertain, but it was probably situated to the south of the temple area, although no certain trace of it has yet been discovered.

[2] Various theories have been advanced to explain Antiochus's attack on the Jewish religion. See L. L. Grabbe, *Judaism from Cyrus to Hadrian* (1992), pp. 247–256, for an outline of theories and his own summary. It should be noted that Grabbe (pp. 264 ff.) dates the desecration of the temple in 168 BC and its rededication in 165 BC.

[3] No doubt these 'liberal' Jews were Hellenizers, but the cult instituted by Antiochus at Jerusalem seems to have owed more to Syrian and Canaanite customs than to Greek religion. Menelaus himself was more concerned with personal power than with religious ideals.

[4] 2 Macc. 6:2.

[5] 1 Macc. 1:41 f.

Chapter Nineteen

The Hasmonaean Resistance
(167–164 BC)

JEWISH MARTYRS

In spite of the royal decree and the severe penalties for disobedience, many Jews refused to submit, choosing to remain loyal to the God of Israel and his holy laws and accept the consequences. Some traditions of their sufferings have been preserved—e.g. in the narratives recorded in 2 Maccabees 6 and 7 about the aged scribe Eleazar and about the mother with her seven sons, all of whom preferred death rather than consent to eat the abominable food urged upon them. Their memory has been preserved not merely in Jewish but also in Christian lists of martyrs; the first day of August has a place in the Church Calendar as the festival of the 'martyrdom of the holy Maccabees'. (The name Maccabees has been attached to them simply because the story of their martyrdom is told in the books of Maccabees.)[1]

One important consequence of this campaign of persecution was the stimulus which it gave to the resurrection hope. The Old Testament has little to say about the future life. Long life in the land which Yahweh their God gave them was more important in the eyes of most pious Israelites during the main Old Testament period than the life of the world to come. As late as the time of Ben Sira (c. 190 BC), posterity's remembrance of a good man's virtues is the kind of immortality most worth desiring.[2] But when the persecution broke out under Antiochus, the fear of the Lord was more likely to lead to an early martyrdom than to length of days. The martyrs had faith to realize that their loyalty to God could not lead only to death and the gloom of Sheol. The hope of resurrection blazed up and burned brightly before their eyes, giving them added courage to endure their torments. Those confessors whose sufferings are recorded in 2 Maccabees died in the confident expectation that they would rise again in the identical bodies that were being tortured and killed, and that their mutilated limbs would then be restored to them in wholeness. It is probably these and others like them who are referred to by the author of the Epistle to the Hebrews in the New Testament. Towards the end of his list of Old Testament characters who were distinguished by their faith, he adds: 'Others were tortured and refused to be released [which they might have won by apostasy], so that they might gain a better resurrection'.[3] From this time onwards the doctrine of resurrection came to be held as an essential article of Jewish belief (except among the Sadducees). As Jesus was later to point out, the doctrine was implied by God's word from as far back as the patriarchal period. For the God who made himself known to Moses as the God of Abraham and Isaac and Jacob[4] 'is not the God of the dead, but of the living, for to him all are alive'.[5] But the doctrine did not win general recognition until the period with which we are now dealing. From now on it came to be also generally accepted that one of the titles under which God received his people's praise in their liturgy was 'The Raiser of the Dead'.[6]

The prohibition of their holy religion, the defilement of the sanctuary, and the apostasy of so many other Jews proved unspeakably bitter to the hasidim, but it also stirred the patriotic indignation of many Jews who had not previously been reckoned among the pious.

The reaction of the hasidim is illustrated by the story of a thousand of them (including wives and children) who fled from the intolerable conditions in Jerusalem to live in caves in the wilderness of Judaea. When the king's officers learned where they were, they sent an expedition against them, and offered to pardon them if they would leave their caves. But this offer was made on the sabbath day, and therefore it was rejected; the law was plain on the matter: 'Everyone is to stay where he is on the seventh day'.[7] They were therefore attacked and all of them slaughtered; they would not violate the sabbath law by resisting their assailants.[8]

These were the true hasidim, showing the purest spirit of uncompromising loyalty to the divine law—a loyalty which despised mere considerations of personal safety. But if every pious Jew had taken this attitude of passive resistance, even though we can admire it, all hope of regaining religious freedom would have died with them.

JEWISH REBELS

Other Jews were sure that such passive resistance was the wrong policy in this crisis. Among them the lead was taken by a priest called Mattathiah and his sons, who lived in the town of Modin, in western Judaea. In this town, as in others, a pagan altar was set up, and the inhabitants were summoned to offer sacrifice on it. The king's officer, who was present to supervise and enforce participation, asked Mattathiah to offer sacrifice first, as he was a leading citizen of the place, and promised him royal favour if he would do so. But Mattathiah loudly and contemptuously refused the request, proclaiming that he and his family would maintain the ancestral covenant even if everyone else broke that covenant. Then, when a less pious citizen came up to the altar to offer sacrifice, Mattathiah ran forward and killed him and then killed the officer who stood by. The altar was then pulled down, and Mattathiah uttered his war-cry: 'Let everyone who is zealous for the law and supports the covenant come out with me !'[9] Then with his five sons and others who joined him he left Modin and made his headquarters in the hill country of Judaea. There they heard the distressing news of the massacre of the non-resistant hasidim on the sabbath, and they made the decision that they themselves, if attacked on that day, would resist. This was a breach of the sabbath law, but they were sure it was necessary if any of those who refused to obey the king's decrees were to survive. There, then, at the headquarters of Mattathiah and his sons, a band of rebels gathered. Most of them opposed the king's decree for patriotic reasons rather than because of the ideals of the hasidim. But it added greatly to the moral prestige as well as to the strength of these men when many of the hasidim joined them, recognizing that, whatever their religious differences might be at other times, now at any rate they were all agreed that they must oppose the king's decrees and must fight for their religious freedom. A powerful guerrilla force was thus built up. Groups of them appeared suddenly in the towns of Judaea, where they demolished idolatrous altars, killed Hellenizing Jews, circumcised boys whose parents, through fear of the authorities, had neglected to do so—and then disappeared as suddenly as they came. It became clear throughout Judaea that there were men in the country who were determined not to let the royal policy triumph if they could stop it.

Yet it must have seemed a hopeless cause. It was not difficult to organize sudden raids on the small towns of Judaea and attacks on small detachments of troops; but the royal policy was backed by powerful armies. How powerful the military forces of Antiochus were was publicly shown in a great parade which was held at Daphne near Antioch in 166 BC.[10] In this parade, according to Polybius, there took part 30,000 heavy-armed infantry, 6,000 light-armed infantry, 9,500 cavalry and 5,000 archers, slingers and similar auxiliary troops. Antiochus himself was a skilful military commander, but fortunately for the Jewish rebels, the presence of his armies was required in other parts of his kingdom. His expulsion from Egypt made it more necessary for him to strengthen the eastern areas of his kingdom, where it was being menaced by the increasing power of Parthia. It was, no doubt, largely as a preliminary step to his eastern expedition that he held the review of his armies at Daphne, although he claimed that he did it to celebrate his Egyptian victory before the Romans intervened.

About this time Mattathiah died, urging his sons with his last breath to persist in the good work which they had begun, putting their trust in God. He instructed them to make Judas their commander-in-chief but to consult Simon, the eldest of the five, for wise counsel. The careers of these two men show how sound the old man's judgment was.

JUDAS MACCABAEUS

Judas bore the surname Maccabaeus, a word which has been variously explained, but probably means 'the Hammer'. From it the term 'Maccabees' has popularly been extended to his brothers, and their descendants, and even to the martyrs who suffered in the persecution. The family, however, is more accurately described as the Hasmonaean family, from Hashmon, an ancestor of Mattathiah. Judas quickly showed himself to be a talented guerrilla chief operating in an area which was ideal for guerrilla tactics, not only in raids on small towns and isolated detachments of the king's soldiers, but in ambushing strong military groups too. In 166 BC he showed his military skill by routing two armies which were making their way against him on the hill-roads leading into Judaea. The first of these was led by Apollonius, governor of Samaria and Judaea, who was killed in the engagement. The second, led by Seron, commander-in-chief of the royal forces in Coelesyria, was attacked in the pass of Beth-horon, which leads from the coastal plain to Jerusalem, and it too was scattered.

These successes brought Judas and his followers great prestige, and won them the support of many Jews who had in the past sympathized with the rebels but thought it unwise to give them public support. Judas's victories also made it clear to Antiochus that the Judaean resistance was much stronger than he had been led to expect. He himself was about to lead the main body of his armies eastwards to recover his lost provinces beyond the Tigris; his kingdom desperately needed the revenues from them. But he left an army of some size under the command of Lysias, who was given charge of the territory west of the Euphrates during the king's absence, with orders that he must suppress the revolt in Judaea, deport the Jewish population and divide up the land among settlers from other parts of his kingdom.

Accordingly, in the summer of next year (165 BC) Lysias sent a larger army than those led by Apollonius and Seron, including cavalry as well as infantry, to crush the revolt once for all. They encamped at Emmaus, in the western lowlands of Judaea, to make their preparations for action against the rebels. Slave-traders from far and wide congregated in the vicinity, ready to buy the huge haul of Jewish captives that (they believed) would be taken in the approaching battle and afterwards. Meanwhile Judas and his followers saw that the danger this time was far greater than it had been the previous year. Ordinary weapons and guerrilla skills were not enough; they must have God's help above all. Accordingly, with prayer and fasting, they solemnly renewed the ancient ritual of the holy war.[11] For this purpose they gathered at Mizpah, where Samuel centuries before had called the people of Israel to repentance and rededication for a holy war against the Philistines.[12] There Judas and his followers consecrated themselves, fulfilling as far as they could the regulations laid down in the ancient law. Having then made every preparation to fight the next day, they committed the course of their endeavour to God.

That night Gorgias, one of the commanders of the Seleucid army, separated a contingent of infantry and cavalry from the main army and (guided by some of the Hellenizing Jews in the Acra) led it against the Jewish forces, to attack them in the morning. But Judas moved his men by night, and in the morning they suddenly attacked the remainder of the king's army, still encamped at Emmaus, and threw them into confusion by the suddenness and violence of their assault. The king's men fled from their assailants to the security of the cities of the Philistine seaboard. And when the troops under Gorgias, returning from their vain quest for the army of Judas, saw the smoke from their burning camp at Emmaus, and the army of Judas drawn up in battle order in the plain, they too took fright and fled to the Greek cities.

We must give Judas as a military leader all the more credit when we recall that over four hundred years had passed since the Jews had taken part in any real fighting. Yet in spite of their complete lack of experience Judas's inspiring genius led them to one victory after another.

Lysias, the viceroy, had failed completely to carry out his commission against the rebels. But another attempt must be made, and in the autumn of the same year (165 BC) he himself marched south with an even bigger army of infantry and cavalry. This time he decided to attack Judas from the south, and not from the west; accordingly he encamped at Beth-zur, on the border of Judaea and Idumaea, four miles north of Hebron. Judas's recent success had attracted more men into his army, but even so they were far fewer than Lysias's army. In spite of this, a surprise attack was again launched against the royal army, and once more the Greek soldiers were dispersed with much loss of life. Lysias returned to Antioch.

PEACE NEGOTIATIONS

It was clear that direct attacks on Judas were ineffective. Instead, Lysias opened peace negotiations with him, with the consent of King Antiochus.

No more soldiers could be spared, because so many were required for the king's eastern expedition. Judas was invited to send ambassadors to Antioch to discuss terms of peace, and he sent two of his lieutenants named John and Absalom. The Hasmonaean demands included a complete removal of the ban on Jewish worship. As this would involve a reversal of the royal decree, it was referred to the king. But early in 164 BC a Roman embassy made its way from Alexandria to Antioch, to investigate rumours of anti-Roman activity by the Seleucids, in violation of the Peace of Apamea.[13] The leaders of this embassy consented very readily to press the Jewish claims at the court of Antioch; any opportunity of weakening the Seleucid power a little further by encouraging an independent attitude in its subjects was welcome to them. At a conference held in Antioch, between the Seleucid government and the Roman ambassadors, to which Antiochus himself returned from the east, both Jewish parties were represented, the Hellenizers by Menelaus and the rebels by John and Absalom. It was clear by this time to Antiochus that the policy of banning the Jewish religion was proving disastrous to his own cause. Instead of promoting peace and order in the south-western parts of his kingdom it had actually produced the opposite effect. Accordingly the ban was withdrawn: the persecution decree was rescinded; the Jews were free once more to practise their religion according to the tradition received from their fathers. However, Menelaus was probably confirmed in the high-priesthood and the king insisted that he must retain control of the temple.[14]

THE CLEANSING OF THE TEMPLE

Although they wanted peace, neither the nationalists nor the pious people among Judas's supporters could be content to leave the temple under the control of one whom they hated as a traitor and an apostate. The withdrawal of the Syrian armies left two military forces in Judaea, the garrison in the Acra and Judas's guerrilla band. All that the garrison could do was to provide protection to those Hellenizing Jews who sought refuge among them from the vengeance of Judas and his men. They were impregnable in their fortress but were not strong enough to take any military initiative against such experienced soldiers as Judas commanded.

Judas now determined to occupy the temple area and cleanse it of its defilement. He sent a detachment to distract the attention of the garrison in the Acra, so that the work of cleansing the temple might be carried out without hindrance. The idol altar and other pagan installations were carried away and dumped in an 'unclean place'[15] (possibly in the Valley of Hinnom). The altar of burnt offering had been defiled by the erection of 'the abomination of desolation' upon it and by the blood and fat of abominable sacrifices which had dripped down on to it; it was therefore dismantled. Without receiving some special revelation, they did not know what the proper procedure was for this altar in its defiled state, so they stored the stones of which it was composed in a convenient place in the temple area until a prophet should appear to give a divine response concerning this matter. A new altar of unhewn stones was set up in place of the polluted altar; the holy place and holy of holies were repaired, the sacred furniture was renewed and placed in the proper position; the seven lamps were lit, incense was burned on the incense-altar, show-bread was placed on the holy table, the curtains were hung in due order before the holy place and between it and the holy of holies. Then, on the 25th day of Kislev, the third anniversary of the day when the abominable sacrifice was offered on the altar of Olympian Zeus, the daily burnt offering was resumed on the new altar in the temple court. By this the temple was formally rededicated to the service of the God of Israel according to the holy law. The dedication festival was prolonged, amid great rejoicing, throughout eight days, in imitation of the feast of Tabernacles which fell two months and ten days earlier.

Since that day the dedication of the temple by Judas has been commemorated year by year in the eight-days' festival of Hanukkah, commonly known as the 'Feast of Lights' because of the Jewish custom of lighting candles or lamps in their houses during the festival.[16]

At the same time the temple hill was fortified to serve as a counter-citadel to the Acra, and Beth-zur was also fortified as a frontier outpost against attacks from Idumaea.

NOTES

[1] For the name Maccabees see below, p. 147.
[2] This is the point of the best known passage in Ben Sira's work, beginning 'Let us now praise famous men . . .' (Ecclus. 44:1 ff). See p. 130, n. 2.
[3] Heb. 11:35.
[4] Ex. 3:6.
[5] Luke 20:38.
[6] E.g. in the words 'Blessed art Thou, O Lord, the Raiser of the Dead', at the end of the second benediction of the Shemoneh 'Esreh (cf. S. Singer, *Authorised Daily Prayer Book*, pp. 44 f.).
[7] Ex. 16:29.
[8] 1 Macc. 2:29–38.
[9] 1 Macc. 2:27.
[10] Polybius, *History* xxx, 25.
[11] Cf. Deut. 20:1–9.
[12] See p. 13.
[13] Polybius, *History* xxxi.,1:6.

[14] Some informative documents relating to these negotiations are preserved in 2 Macc. 11:16–38.

[15] 1 Macc. 4:43.

[16] This feature of the festival is admittedly older than the rededication of the temple. 2 Macc. 1:18 ff. explains it as a commemoration of the alleged recovery in Nehemiah's time of the sacred altar-fire which fell from heaven at the dedication of Solomon's temple; but it probably goes back to an ancient celebration of the winter solstice. No doubt we have here an example of a very common phenomenon in religious history—the adaptation to a new purpose (e.g. to the commemoration of an important historic event) of a festival already in existence. When such a development takes place, many of the former features will survive, but take on a new significance. It is the new significance and not the original derivation that is the important thing, as a consideration of the festivals of the Christian year will show.

Chapter Twenty

Judas Maccabaeus
(164–160 BC)

CAMPAIGNS BY JUDAS

The Seleucid authorities might have been willing to allow the rededication of the Jewish temple, even though they had not agreed to it in advance. But the fortification of the temple hill, in opposition to the Acra, indicated that Judas and his followers were not content with the restoration of religious freedom, or even with the restoration of the temple to its former ritual. So at the end of 164 BC a new phase of the struggle began. The struggle had first started because the religious heritage of Judaea was attacked. Judas and his supporters had succeeded in defending and preserving that heritage. But the struggle now continued in order to win a greater degree of political freedom as well. The successes won by Judas's army over much bigger and better equipped enemy forces suggested to the patriots that further successes might be gained and further aims achieved if they continued to fight. The hasidim, who had joined the militant patriots because they could see no other way of regaining their religious liberty, tended to be satisfied when that goal had been reached; but the Hasmonaeans were not satisfied.

In other parts of Palestine and in Transjordan there were Jewish communities which felt threatened. Some of them were minorities living in the middle of non-Jewish and hostile populations. In 163 BC Judas determined to help these Jewish minorities by bringing them under armed guard from the exposed positions in which they lived and settling them in Judaea, in territory under the control of Judas and his armies. This policy would not only be beneficial to the Jewish communities rescued in this way, it would also strengthen Judas's position in Judaea, because Jews who owed their security to his efforts would be likely to support him in other causes.

In particular, attacks on the Jewish communities of Transjordan and Galilee led to appeals for help by these communities to Judas. Judas and his brother Jonathan made an expedition to Transjordan, in the course of which they attacked several Greek cities and rescued many Jews and brought them under escort to Judaea. While these two brothers were thus busy in Transjordan, Simon, the eldest of the brothers, led a similar campaign in Galilee. Meanwhile the leaders who had been left in command of the forces in Judaea made an attempt to attack Jamnia, in western Palestine, but were repulsed with much loss of life. The author of 1 Maccabees claims that this attack failed because its leaders were not Hasmonaeans: 'They did not belong to the family of those men through whom deliverance was given to Israel'.[1]

Judas and his brothers, on their return, led raids into Idumaean and Philistine territory to demonstrate the strength of Jewish armies. At Marisa, in Idumaea, they clashed with a small force under the governor of that region, and defeated it. But it became known that even among the followers of Judas there were some whose religious practice was idolatrous; among the garments of those Jews who fell at Marisa were found pagan amulets from Jamnia. (This, says the writer of 2 Maccabees complacently, was why they fell in battle; but of course he could not know how many of the survivors possessed similar idolatrous objects.[2]) Judas was deeply shocked, and had a special sin-offering presented in the temple on behalf of those who had died, so that their sin might be forgiven, in order that they might not miss the resurrection of the righteous.

JUDAS DEFEATED

While the Hasmonaeans were engaged in these expeditions outside the Judaean frontiers, Antiochus's expedition in the eastern part of his kingdom, which he was conducting with a skill that brought good hope of success, was brought to an end by his death at Gabae (the modern Isfahan) in May, 163 BC.[3] Before his death (which may have been due to tuberculosis) he sent a letter to the people of Antioch[4] nominating his nine-year-old son Antiochus as his successor. This was a change of policy, for it had been generally expected that his nephew Demetrius, son of Seleucus IV, would succeed to the throne. Demetrius might have been content to be heir to his uncle, but if the boy Antiochus was to be his father's successor, then Demetrius's chances of ever becoming king were non-existent—unless he did something about it. Not only so, but Antiochus nominated as guardian and regent during his son's childhood a high court official named Philip, a member of the Order of Kinsmen, who was with the king at the time. But the young Antiochus had been left in Antioch, under the guardianship of the viceroy Lysias, and Lysias had no intention of losing his twofold authority. The dying king's arrangements therefore created disunity within his kingdom, as the events of the following years made plain. This disunity in the Seleucid state greatly aided the success of the Hasmonaean cause.

When news of the king's death came to Antioch, Lysias ignored the nomination of Philip as guardian and regent, and proclaimed the younger Antiochus king—Antiochus V (Eupator)—with himself as regent. The news of the king's death also reached Jerusalem, and encouraged Judas to besiege the Acra, with its Seleucid garrison, which was the fortress of the Hellenizing party. Menelaus and his friends sent word to Antioch, and Lysias led an army south. The dedication of the temple and fortification of its courts, even though they were not included in the terms of the truce of 164 BC, might be accepted; but a direct attack on a royal fortress must be repelled. At Beth-zechariah, six miles north of Beth-zur, Judas, having raised the siege of the Acra, met the royal army. This time it was Judas who was defeated. For the first time in a battle in Judaea the royal army used elephants. Eleazar, Judas's brother, saw the rich ornamentation on the howdah on one of these elephants and thought that it carried the young king himself. So he gave the elephant a mortal thrust from beneath and was crushed to death when it fell on him—all to no purpose, for it was not the king's elephant after all.

ALCIMUS BECOMES HIGH PRIEST

The Hasmonaean fortress at Beth-zur was surrendered to the king's forces, who put a garrison in it. The fortified temple hill was then besieged and would soon have surrendered because of famine. But news came to Lysias that Philip, the legal regent, had returned from the east, and had occupied Antioch. Lysias therefore offered the Hasmonaeans easy terms of surrender, which were accepted. These terms included a confirmation of the grant of religious freedom made by Antiochus IV in the agreement of the preceding year and the restoration of the temple to the Jews in accordance with their ancient practice. Probably pardon was given for the Hasmonaean breaches of that agreement. Thus the Hasmonaean rededication of the temple was in effect legalized. But Lysias insisted that the temple must be used only as a temple, not as a fortress; so the fortifications recently erected by the Hasmonaeans were now demolished. Lysias made yet another concession: he realized that Menelaus was completely unacceptable as high priest, and that no stable peace could be hoped for so long as he remained in office. He therefore deposed him, and appointed as his successor a priest named Alcimus, who was at least a descendant of Aaron although he did not belong to the Oniad family. The Hasmonaeans presumably agreed to recognize Alcimus, and in general to follow a policy of 'live and let live' with the Hellenizers. Peace was concluded on these terms, and sacrifice was offered for Lysias in the temple when he departed.

Lysias then returned to Antioch and ejected Philip, who escaped to Egypt and was given refuge by Ptolemy VI.

Philip was not the only important person from Asia to seek refuge in Egypt about this time. Another was Onias, son of the murdered high priest Onias III. This younger Onias, as the eldest son of Onias III, was the rightful high priest of Jerusalem, but his claims had been ignored in favour of Lysias's nominee Alcimus. He therefore went to Egypt and obtained permission from Ptolemy VI to build a Jewish temple at Leontopolis, on the pattern of the Jerusalem temple. There the same rituals as in the Jerusalem temple were instituted, and there the legitimate Zadokite high priesthood was continued by Onias IV and his successors for two hundred and thirty years.

DEMETRIUS I BECOMES KING

Demetrius, son of Seleucus IV, had been in Rome since 176 BC. He had gone there to replace his uncle Antiochus as a hostage for the payment of the indemnity of Apamea, and remained there after the indemnity was paid. Now that Antiochus IV was dead, Demetrius asked the Roman senate to allow him to return and reclaim his rightful heritage. But the senate refused; in their opinion the Seleucid kingdom would be weaker and more divided if ruled by the boy-king Antiochus Eupator than it would be under an able ruler like Demetrius. They could see that Demetrius, who was now twenty-three, was likely to be an able ruler if the opportunity offered.

The Roman senate intended to take advantage of the weakness of the Seleucid kingdom. The Treaty of Apamea had forbidden the Seleucids to possess a navy or employ a force of elephants in their army. These terms had not been strictly kept, but till now the Romans had ignored the situation. But in 162 BC three officials from Rome arrived in Syria to inspect the affairs of the Seleucid kingdom, and they enforced the destruction of the navy and the hamstringing of the army elephants. When Lysias protested, they threatened to send Demetrius back to Antioch. But the populace were enraged by this Roman action, and in the naval port of Laodicea one of the three officials, Octavius, was murdered by a Syrian. Lysias sent an embassy to Rome to persuade the senate that he was not responsible for the murder.

When news of this reached him in Rome, Demetrius realized that his opportunity had come. The senate still refused to let him go, but he escaped on board a ship of Carthage bound for Tyre, largely by the aid of his friend the historian Polybius, who was himself resident as a hostage at Rome, and who tells the story of the escape. With sixteen companions Demetrius landed at Tripolis in Syria, and the army immediately chose to support him. The loss of the fleet and the elephants had completely alienated them from Lysias. They offered to hand over Lysias and the young Antiochus to Demetrius, but he wished to avoid all direct responsibility for putting them to death. 'Do not let me see their faces!', he said.[5] So the army took the hint, and killed them.

Demetrius I was now established in the kingdom. In the north-eastern part of his empire Timarchus, satrap of Media, proclaimed himself independent ruler: but elsewhere for the time being Demetrius appeared to have no rival.

The Hellenizers in Jerusalem sent an embassy to him, led by the new high priest Alcimus, complaining of the hostility of Judas Maccabaeus and his followers, who were preventing Alcimus from carrying out his high-priestly duties in the temple. The king sent Bacchides, whom he had made governor of the lands west of the Euphrates, to Jerusalem with soldiers to install Alcimus by force if necessary.

JUDAS'S SUCCESSES

The Hasmonaean party, more than anyone else, were opposed to Alcimus's functioning as high priest. Perhaps they were already planning to secure the high priesthood for the Hasmonaean family. Perhaps, however, they were simply opposed to the idea of accepting a high priest appointed by the Seleucids, even though he was a descendant of Aaron. But the hasidim were content to accept him. Religious freedom had already been recovered, and in their opinion the Hasmonaean actions might endanger that freedom. They were accordingly prepared to welcome Alcimus. But the Seleucid authorities made no distinction between the Maccabaean rebels and the hasidim who had previously supported the rebels. The result was that when a delegation of scribes (who were by now a recognized profession in Judaea) went to Alcimus, he received them with apparent friendliness and promised to do no harm to them or the hasidim in general; but when the Seleucid authorities installed Alcimus in office, they seized and killed sixty hasidim. Bacchides succeeded in imposing Alcimus on the people, but with so much brutality that Alcimus's position was fatally undermined even in the eyes of those who had been inclined to accept him. Bacchides not only attacked Judas's supporters, but he even put to death a number of deserters from Judas's ranks who had gone over to him. Leaving part of his troops in Jerusalem as a bodyguard for Alcimus, Bacchides returned to Antioch.

Bacchides's ruthlessness had the effect of strengthening Judas's position. Judas continued to make raids on the towns of Judaea and to attack members of the Hellenizing party, together with those who deserted from his ranks desiring to lead a quiet life. At last Alcimus went to Antioch and asked for further help. Demetrius had just left for Media, to attack Timarchus. Bacchides, who was left in charge in the west (as Lysias had been when Antiochus IV went east), had few troops to spare. He instructed Nicanor, commander in Judaea, to do what he could, but to try to avoid a battle. Nicanor should rather enter into negotiations with Judas and try to keep him inactive until the king came back with his army from the east.

Nicanor, who had previously had experience of Judas's military ability, entered into negotiations with him and a warm personal friendship sprang up between the two men. They appeared together in public, and Nicanor persuaded Judas that it was time for him to settle down, marry, and bring up a family. Alcimus, however, was angry at this development, and he made a further complaint at Antioch, protesting that Nicanor was showing friendship to the enemy leader instead of attacking him. Orders therefore were sent to Nicanor to take Judas alive. Judas learned of Nicanor's new orders and escaped. Nicanor, exasperated by this, went to the priests and threatened to demolish the temple and replace it with a temple in honour of Dionysus unless they handed over Judas to him or gave information leading to his arrest.

Hearing that Judas was in the region of Samaria, Nicanor went out to attack him. At Adasa, in the same pass of Beth-horon where an earlier Seleucid army had met defeat, the army of Nicanor was defeated and he himself died in battle. The head and right hand of Nicanor were struck off and brought back to Jerusalem, and nailed up in full view of the temple which he had threatened to destroy. Alcimus fled to Antioch (161 BC).

The anniversary of the victory of Adasa was kept as a festival, under the name Nicanor's Day. It fell on Adar 13 (March 9), the day before the festival of Purim. It was indeed an important victory; but it was Judas's last victory.

At this point in the story, the narrative of I Maccabees mentions a treaty between Judas and the Romans.[6] A delegation had been sent by Judas to Rome (probably in 161 BC) and the Roman senate consented to enter into treaty-relations with Judaea. The Romans were always glad to help to weaken the Seleucid power. They had assured Timarchus that they had no objections when he proclaimed himself an independent king in Media; they now encouraged Judas and his followers in their ambitions for independence. Neither Timarchus nor Judas could expect to get any practical support from Rome; but a treaty with Rome greatly increased their prestige in the eyes of their fellow-countrymen and neighbours.

DEATH OF JUDAS

Demetrius was completely successful in his campaign against Timarchus; Timarchus himself was captured and executed (161/160 BC). Demetrius therefore was able to return home, and in the late spring of 160 BC he could spare a strong body of soldiers to march into Judaea and avenge the defeat and death of Nicanor. Another battle was fought in the Pass of Beth-horon, and in this battle the Judaeans were crushed and Judas himself was killed.

Judas had proved himself a guerrilla genius, an inspiring leader of men, and a man of immense personal courage and daring. He lacked the qualities of statesmanship which his brothers showed; but it is unlikely that they would ever have had the opportunity of exploiting their diplomatic qualities if Judas had not first shown his military qualities so effectively. It is not surprising that when he fell in battle 'All Israel' said: 'How is the mighty fallen, the saviour of Israel !'[7] For it seemed at first that all the work he had achieved was undone. Alcimus was reinstated in the temple as high priest, and the Hellenizing party was established in power. Those who had been known as partisans of Judas were sought out and punished, although here it must be admitted that they were simply receiving the treatment that Judas had shown to the Hellenizers when opportunity offered. But in fact the most important of Judas's achievements still remained: the temple had been rededicated to the ancient form of worship, religious freedom had been restored to the Jewish people, and the policy of religious persecution of Antiochus Epiphanes would never be attempted again.

NOTES

[1] 1 Macc. 5:62.
[2] 2 Macc. 12:40.
[3] On the death of Antiochus IV Epiphanes, see J. A. Goldstein, *I. Maccabees* (1976), pp. 307 f.
[4] 2 Macc. 9:19 ff., omitting 'Jews' in verse 19.
[5] 1 Macc. 7:3.
[6] 1 Macc. 8:1 ff.
[7] 1 Macc. 9:21.

Chapter Twenty-One

Independence Won
(160–129 BC)

JONATHAN'S FIRST SUCCESSES

With the death of Judas the cause which he had led seemed lost. True, the temple had been restored to its proper use as the shrine of Yahweh, and the pious Jews were free to practise their ancestral religion. It looked as if the situation would now revert to what it had been before Antiochus IV began his unwise interference in the religious life of Judaea; but two factors brought about new developments. The first factor was the refusal of many of the Hasmonaean supporters to accept the existing state of affairs. The second factor was the constant scheming by men who made claims to the Seleucid throne. Unrest and division in Syria gave advantages to the Jewish nationalists.

Judas's brother Jonathan was invited to take his place as leader of the Jewish rebels. Jonathan was not such a military genius as Judas, but he had greater prudence and diplomatic ability. He was not the man to lead a small army against superior numbers when there was no prospect but certain defeat. He succeeded in reviving the dejected spirits of his followers, in avoiding the attempts of Bacchides to take him by surprise, and in taking military action against a hostile tribe in Transjordan, who had captured and killed his brother John.

West of the Jordan, Bacchides imposed a strict military control over the land by fortifying several strategic points and manning them with garrisons. He also took steps to ensure the good behaviour of the leading citizens of Judaea—especially those of Hasmonaean sympathies—by holding their sons as hostages in the Acra in Jerusalem.

Alcimus's arrogant behaviour as high priest in Jerusalem caused increasing resentment among the Jews, but a measure of tranquillity followed his death in 159 BC. He was the victim of a paralytic stroke which occurred while he was engaged in dismantling the wall around the inner court of the temple, and the author of 1 Maccabees readily discerned a direct divine judgment on this high priest.[1] We are told by Josephus that the position of high priest was unfilled for seven years (159–152 BC).[2] If so, it is probable that Demetrius, after the hostile reception received by Alcimus, decided that there was a better chance of peace in Judaea if no successor was appointed to him. On the other hand, there is a real possibility that a man (his name is unknown) held the high priesthood during this period, but was deposed when Jonathan became high priest; he then became the founder and revered leader of the Qumran sect.[3]

As the situation now appeared quieter, Bacchides returned to Antioch. Two years later (157 BC), Jonathan felt strong enough to strengthen his position in Judaea. Bacchides was then summoned by the Hellenizers to deal with him, but he came off worst in a military clash with Jonathan and his followers east of Bethlehem. So he agreed to a truce with Jonathan; prisoners were returned by both sides, and (probably under the terms of the same agreement) Jonathan was allowed to set up his headquarters at Michmash. For the next five years there was peace in Judaea.

JONATHAN BECOMES HIGH PRIEST

But a disturbing element was introduced into the Syrian scene in 152 BC. A young man, commonly known as Balas, landed at the port of Ptolemais,[4] claiming to be Alexander Epiphanes, the younger son of Antiochus IV. It is very difficult to decide whether his claim was genuine. His coins show a clear facial resemblance to Antiochus IV—but were his features on the coins modified to give support to his claim? On the other hand the family of Demetrius and its supporters declared that he was a mere pretender, a low-born adventurer from Ephesus. But he secured the recognition and support of Ptolemy VI of Egypt, who resented Demetrius's interference with his domains in Cyprus. Ptolemy also saw here an opportunity to gain a position of power in the Seleucid realm, and promised Balas one of his daughters in marriage.

Balas, however, had the support of a greater power than Egypt. The rulers of Cappadocia and Pergamum, annoyed by Demetrius's interference in the affairs of Asia Minor, decided to support Balas in opposition to him, and to win Rome's support for their venture. They succeeded by careful intrigue in obtaining from the Roman senate a decree which authorized Balas to secure the throne, and it was with this backing that Balas landed in Syria in 152 BC.

Balas saw that he could strengthen his position considerably if he could win Jonathan and his veteran guerrilla soldiers over to his side. He therefore came to an understanding with Jonathan. In return for Jonathan's support, he not only permitted him to maintain an independent military force in Judaea, and enrolled him in the order of the 'King's Friends', but actually undertook to recognize him as high priest of the Jews, and presented him with the golden tiara and purple robe which went with this semi-royal dignity.

But we can see how the earlier Hasmonaean ideals have been forgotten! Antiochus IV had begun his policy of interference in Jewish religious affairs, which ultimately led to the Hasmonaean rising, by deposing and appointing Jewish high priests. Now Jonathan, a Hasmonaean, was prepared to accept the high priesthood from a man whose authority (if any) to give it was based on his claim to be the son and successor of that same Antiochus.

RIVAL SELEUCID KINGS

Demetrius had attempted to gain Jonathan's co-operation as soon as Balas landed at Ptolemais, but Balas, having little to lose and much to gain, could afford to make a much higher bid than Demetrius, so Jonathan decided to support Balas. At the same time, he profited by Demetrius's offers too, for the Hellenizers in the Acra, seeing that both sides were eager for Jonathan's support, surrendered to him the hostages whom they held. They then could do nothing to prevent him when he began to rebuild the temple wall, demolished by Lysias in 163 BC, and the city wall, demolished by Apollonius in 168 BC. The garrisons which Bacchides had placed throughout Judaea evacuated their citadels, and only the Jerusalem Acra and Beth-zur remained in the hands of Syrian troops.

Finding that Jonathan had accepted Balas's terms, Demetrius appealed to the whole Jewish nation, Hasmonaean sympathizers and Hellenizers alike, offering them extraordinary privileges, increases of territory and remissions of tax and tribute, if they would support him. But he was too late: Jonathan and his friends, now holding a position of unrivalled strength in Judaea, remained loyal to their treaty with Balas.

Balas and Demetrius met in battle in 150 BC; Demetrius was defeated and lost his life. Ptolemy VI then came to Ptolemais to greet his victorious vassal (for that was more or less what Balas was), and to give him his daughter Cleopatra in marriage. Jonathan was now summoned to Ptolemais to attend the court of the two kings (150 BC). Balas raised him to the higher rank of 'First Friend' and appointed him governor of the province of Judaea. In this way the civil strife in the Seleucid realm speedily turned out to the advantage of Jonathan, who now held the chief religious, military and civil power in Judaea. The Hellenizing party made complaints against this gift of royal favour to the Hasmonaean leader, but their protests went un-heeded.

Balas appears to have been as friendly and popular as Antiochus IV (his father?) had been; but unlike him he took no care to defend the eastern frontiers of his kingdom against the Parthians. This possibly was one reason why he lost his subjects' goodwill.

When Demetrius died in battle against Balas, he left two sons, Demetrius and Antiochus, on the island of Cnidus. In 147 BC the younger Demetrius arrived in the land of his fathers with the backing of a body of Cretan mercenary troops led by Lasthenes. He established control over a good part of Phoenicia and Syria, but when his governor Apollonius demanded the submission of Balas's friend Jonathan, Jonathan attacked him in battle near Ashdod and defeated him. As a result of this action Joppa and a number of the cities of the Philistine seaboard fell into Jonathan's hands, and he received further rewards from Balas, including probably the governorship of all Coelesyria.

Ptolemy VI, however, watched from Egypt this fresh outbreak of civil war in Syria, confident that this progressive weakening of Seleucid power could only work to his own advantage. When he judged the situation ready for intervention, he took an army into Asia, pretending that he meant to aid his son-in-law Balas against Demetrius II. Jonathan, as governor of Coelesyria, escorted him as far as the northern boundary of that territory, but when Ptolemy crossed the frontier he seized the coastal cities of northern Syria and transferred his support—and his daughter—from Balas to Demetrius, on condition that Coelesyria should be restored to the Ptolemaic empire, to which it had belonged before the Battle of Panion fifty years before. Demetrius could not refuse Ptolemy's offer, although it involved the loss of an important part of his ancestral kingdom; and in effect he had to acknowledge Ptolemy as his overlord. But when Ptolemy and Demetrius joined battle with Balas in the plain of Antioch and defeated him, Ptolemy was mortally wounded. Balas sought safety in flight, but he was assassinated, and his head was sent to the victors. Ptolemy lived long enough to see this grisly trophy; but he gained no advantage from it, for he died a few days later.

DEMETRIUS II SUPPORTS JONATHAN

Demetrius II thus got rid of his rival Balas and his overlord Ptolemy in the same battle and reigned as undisputed ruler over the Seleucid realm (145 BC) without having to surrender Coelesyria to Egypt.

Now the Hellenizing party in Judaea, who had resented the favours

which Balas had given to Jonathan, hoped for better things from Demetrius
II. They thought they had a good opportunity to make accusations against
Jonathan, because while the fighting was going on in north Syria, Jonathan
had attacked and tried to capture the Jerusalem citadel, with its Seleucid
garrison. So Demetrius summoned Jonathan to Ptolemais, but Jonathan
was able to gain from him a continuation of the privileges which he and his
followers had received from Balas. He was confirmed in the dual office of
high priest and governor of Judaea, and was enrolled among Demetrius's
'First Friends', as he had formerly been enrolled among Balas's. However,
he had to agree to abandon his siege of the Acra, and consent to the
continuance of Seleucid garrisons there and at Beth-zur. Clearly Demetrius
was wise enough to recognize that Jonathan could be of great value as a
supporter, whereas he could be a powerful and dangerous enemy.

But Demetrius was not able to enjoy his new-won power for long without
interference. He took the unwise step of dismissing the mercenary soldiers
who had helped him gain power, and these disbanded troops were only
too ready to follow a new commander.

This was not the only step taken by the new king—or rather by his
commander-in-chief and adviser the Cretan Lasthenes—which speedily
made him very unpopular. In Antioch itself he lost the sympathies of a large
section of the civic population by his severe measures against the supporters of Balas. A revolt broke out in the capital, and to crush it Demetrius
called on Jonathan for help. Jonathan sent 3,000 men, who co-operated with
the king's Cretan mercenaries and created such destruction in the city with
fire and sword that the rebels soon laid down their arms and hoped for the
mercy of the king.

Once the revolt was quelled, however, Jonathan did not receive from
Demetrius the further rewards which he thought he deserved for his timely
help. Accordingly, when a new claimant to the Seleucid throne appeared,
Jonathan was ready to transfer his support to the newcomer.

DEATH OF JONATHAN

When Balas was assassinated, after his defeat by the forces of Ptolemy VI
and Demetrius II, he left his infant son Antiochus in the care of an Arabian
chief. A former officer of Balas, named Trypho, saw that he could profit
from the resentment of the Syrian mercenaries whom Demetrius had
disbanded after they had secured the kingdom for him. He therefore
persuaded the Arabians to transfer the infant Antiochus to his care and
proclaimed him king as Antiochus VI (Epiphanes Dionysus). Acting in the
infant king's name, Trypho was able to gather the disbanded troops

together with an elephant-force, which Ptolemy VI had left behind him when he died of his wounds, and to seize Antioch and many other cities (145 BC).

Demetrius retained control of Cilicia, one or two coastal cities, and the eastern part of the Empire. But Trypho gained the support of Jonathan when he confirmed him in his previous privileges, increased his territory as governor of Judaea and made his brother Simon military commander of the coastal area from the Egyptian border to the 'Ladder of Tyre'. Jonathan and Simon both took part in military operations in support of Trypho. Simon captured the fortress of Joppa, which had been occupied by a garrison of troops supporting Demetrius. Jonathan, however, suffered a heavy defeat at the hand of Demetrius's forces in Galilee. His other operations in Coelesyria in 144 BC were also unsuccessful, but he was able to enrich himself by a raid on an Arab tribe.

Jonathan and Simon only supported Trypho in order to strengthen their own cause, and Trypho recognized this very well, especially when the two brothers strengthened the fortifications of Jerusalem and other districts which they held. Trypho found it convenient to make use of them for a time, until their independent action threatened his plans. For Trypho, too, had ambitions of his own. So long as it was convenient to act in the name of the infant king, Trypho was content with the status of regent, but his ambition was to secure the royal title and the royal power for himself.

He was unable to invade Judaea and attack the Hasmonaeans with any hope of success, so he resorted to treachery instead of force. He invited Jonathan to Ptolemais, and arrested him there. He gained no advantage from this action, however, because Jonathan's followers immediately acclaimed Simon, the oldest (and only survivor) of the Maccabaean brothers, as Jonathan's deputy.

So when Trypho invaded Judaea, Simon confronted him with a force which made Trypho decide to negotiate rather than to fight. He pretended that Jonathan was being held as hostage for the payment of money, but when the ransom-money was paid over, Jonathan was not set free but shortly afterwards put to death. His body was then handed over and he was buried in the family sepulchre at Modin, where a splendid monument was erected for the brothers and their parents.

During his seventeen years' career as leader (160–143 BC), Jonathan showed neither the the military genius of Judas nor the wise statesmanship of Simon. His successes were due mainly to the skill with which he negotiated with the rival claimants to the Seleucid throne, and to the unscrupulous way in which he transferred his support to one claimant after another. His readiness to accept honours, and above all the high-priestly dignity itself, from the Syrian rulers marked a sad departure from the ideals of the earlier days of the struggle for liberty. His wider diplomacy brought at least honour and prestige to the Jews: he renewed the alliance with Rome, and made a treaty with Sparta (it was claimed that the Spartans too were descended from Abraham!).

However, these actions brought more prestige than any effective increase of strength to his people's cause. So long as the Seleucid kingdom remained united, he achieved little against it. It was only when its period of internal division began with the arrival of Alexander Balas in 152 BC that he was able to achieve greater power and freedom by exploiting the Seleucid difficulties.

SIMON'S LEADERSHIP

In view of Trypho's hostility, Simon, who was now undisputed leader of the Jews, entered into negotiations with Demetrius. Demetrius was only too glad now to have the Jews as allies in his fight against Trypho, and agreed that they should no longer have to pay tribute to the Seleucid king. The royal letter which made this decision official dates from May, 142 BC and was in effect a charter of Jewish independence. What Judas had fought for, and Jonathan had partially achieved by diplomacy, Simon now secured: 'In the 170th year [of the Seleucid era] the yoke of the Gentiles was removed from Israel.'[5]

In the same year (142 BC) Simon renewed the alliance with Rome and Sparta. The Roman senate wrote to Demetrius, to Ptolemy VIII of Egypt, and to other eastern Mediterranean rulers, announcing that it recognized Judaea's independence under Simon and forbidding them to make war against him or to collaborate with his enemies.

Perhaps Demetrius did not intend to keep the terms of his agreement with Simon for very long. But Simon, having secured the agreement, showed himself as effective in action as in negotiation. Later in 142 BC he overpowered the Seleucid fortress of Gazara (the ancient Gezer), and then the Jerusalem Acra, which had been continuously held by Seleucid troops since Apollonius fortified it in 167 BC. Both citadels were now garrisoned by Simon with his own followers. But apparently he took no action against the Hellenizing Jews who for many years had enjoyed the protection of the Acra. His brother Judas had always punished severely any Jewish opponents; but Simon was wiser and planned to unite the Jewish nation under his leadership. Old quarrels could be forgotten.

The last trace of Seleucid control was thus removed from Judaea. Demetrius could do nothing to prevent Simon's action, because in 141 BC he was forced to take his armies east against the Parthians, who had been steadily encroaching on Seleucid territory in Mesopotamia. Probably he hoped also, by strengthening his position in the east, to act more effectively in due course against Trypho in the west.

But in about 139 BC Demetrius was taken prisoner by the Parthians, who kept him in honourable captivity for ten years. Trypho now abandoned all pretence of being merely the regent for the infant king Antiochus VI. He had himself proclaimed king by his soldiers, and not long afterwards had the boy-king killed. The boy had been useful to him for a time, but had now served Trypho's purpose sufficiently.

Trypho, however, did not enjoy his undeserved authority for long. Demetrius II had a brother, Antiochus, who had lived for several years in Asia Minor. Antiochus, hearing that his brother had been captured, collected a mercenary force and marched against Trypho. Trypho's troops deserted, preferring to support Antiochus and his new wife Cleopatra. She was previously the wife of Demetrius II, and she now invited Antiochus to marry her[6] and reign in his captive brother's place as Antiochus VII (Sidetes). Trypho was chased from one refuge to another until at last he was captured and compelled to commit suicide.

Meanwhile Simon received great honours from his grateful people for the independence and peace which he had won for them. At a meeting of the popular assembly of the Jews in September, 140 BC, it was decreed, because of the patriotic achievements of Simon and his brothers, that he should be formally appointed commander-in-chief of the army, ethnarch or governor of the nation, and high priest. Simon had taken over from Jonathan, along with the chief civil and military functions, the high-priesthood which Jonathan had first received from Alexander Balas. But it was wrong that the high priest of an independent nation should hold his sacred office as the gift of a foreign monarch, and so it was now bestowed on Simon by popular vote. It was true that he did not belong to the ancient Zadokite family, but it was no longer a practical possibility to reinstate the Zadokites in the high priesthood. So Simon was made hereditary high priest ('high priest for ever') until such time as the will of God might be declared in the matter by the mouth of 'a trustworthy prophet'.[7] At the time it was believed that prophecy had ceased in Israel.

Simon thus held the supreme civil, military, and religious dignities. Of all the members of the Hasmonaean family, none deserved the triple honour so much as he did. As ruler of an independent state he had the right to mint his own coinage. If he did not avail himself of this right, as his successors certainly did, it was perhaps because there were no facilities for minting money in his territory.[8]

When Antiochus VII arrived in Syria in 139 BC to fight against the usurper Trypho he was glad to ask for the aid of Simon. But as Trypho's cause weakened, Antiochus adopted a more arrogant attitude towards Simon. At last (early in 138 BC) he sent a message to him demanding either the surrender of the strongholds he had taken—Joppa, Gazara, and the Jerusalem Acra—or else a monetary payment to compensate for the financial loss which Simon's control of them had caused. Simon denied the king's right to make any such demands in respect of Judaean territory, but offered 100 talents for his occupation of Joppa and Gazara. Antiochus treated this offer as an insult, and sent one of his captains, Cendebaeus, military commander of the coastal territories, to attack Judaea. Cendebaeus took up his headquarters at Jamnia and from there he invaded Simon's territory and built a forward military base near Azotus (the ancient Ashdod).

Simon's son, John Hyrcanus, who had been placed in command of Gezer, reported the situation to his father. Simon appointed John and his brother Judas to take the necessary measures against Cendebaeus. They inflicted such a heavy defeat on him in the plain of Azotus that Judaea had no more trouble from the Seleucids for three or four years.

In 135 BC Simon was assassinated at a family banquet by his son-in-law Ptolemy son of Abubus, whom he had appointed commander of Jericho. Ptolemy's motive seems to have been a desire for personal power; he hoped to take Simon's place as ruler of the nation. To do this, of course, he had also to remove Simon's sons. He seized two who were with their father at the time of his assassination and kept them in custody in the fortress of Dok, near Jericho, and sent messengers to Gazara to seize John Hyrcanus. But news of the murder reached John before Ptolemy's messengers arrived; he was ready for them when they came and killed them on their arrival. Then he led troops east to Ptolemy's fortress of Dok and besieged it. Ptolemy, seeing that his cause was hopeless, killed John's brothers and mother, whom he had held captive in the fortress, and escaped to Cappadocia.

JOHN HYRCANUS GAINS INDEPENDENCE

John Hyrcanus was now acclaimed by the people as his father's successor in all his offices. But the first six years of his rule were troubled. The disorder which followed Simon's untimely death gave Antiochus VII an opportunity to invade Judaea and besiege Jerusalem. John resisted for a year, but in the end was compelled to ask for terms. The terms imposed included the repayment of tribute, as well as arrears of tribute for the years of independence, the demolition of the walls of Jerusalem, and the surrender of hostages (133 BC).

For a few years, then, Judaea was once more subject to a Seleucid overlord. But in 129 BC Antiochus VII went on a campaign against the

Parthians, and was killed in battle with them. Demetrius II, his brother, who had been held in Parthian captivity for ten years, was set free and came home to reoccupy the throne in Antioch. But the Seleucid power was by this time so thoroughly weakened that Judaea was able to regain complete independence without fear of further interference from Syria.

NOTES

[1] 1 Macc. 9:55 f.

[2] *Antiquities* xx. 237

[3] The Dead Sea Scrolls refer to the founder of the sect as 'the Teacher of Righteousness', who was persecuted by 'the Wicked Priest'. Various theories for dating and identifying these two men have been proposed, and there can be no certainty; but Jonathan is the most likely identification for the 'Wicked Priest'. Cf. A. R. C. Leaney, *The Jewish and Christian World 200 BC to AD 200* (1984), pp. 178 f.; G. Vermes, *The Dead Sea Scrolls in English* (4th ed., 1995), pp. 34–40.

[4] The Greek foundation on the site of the ancient Acco.

[5] 1 Macc. 13:41.

[6] He thus became her third husband. She had first been married to Balas.

[7] 1 Macc. 14:41.

[8] Coins bearing the inscription 'Simeon prince of Israel' and celebrating the 'liberation of Israel' formerly assigned to this period, are now known to date from the second Jewish revolt against Rome, under Simeon ben Kosebah (AD 132–135).

Chapter Twenty-Two

The Hasmonaean Dynasty
(128–65 BC)

JOHN HYRCANUS AND HIS OPPONENTS

In the seventh year of John Hyrcanus, then, the independent state of Judaea was securely established. Forty years had gone by since Antiochus Epiphanes had abolished the old constitution of Jerusalem and the surrounding territory as an independent temple-state within his empire. The self-sacrifice and devotion of the hasidim, the strategic genius of Judas and the statesmanship of Simon—combined, it is true, with the increasing dividedness and weakness of the Seleucid imperial power—had won for the Jewish people more (to all outward appearance) than they had lost at the hands of Antiochus. No wonder, then, that the early years of independence and security under John Hyrcanus, before the Judaean state was divided by inner conflict, seemed to be a miniature golden age in the eyes of later generations. The ancient and honoured offices of prophet and priest and king seemed to be combined in him. 'He was esteemed by God worthy of the three greatest privileges', says Josephus,[1] 'the government of his nation, the dignity of the high priesthood, and the gift of prophecy, for God was with him and enabled him to know and foretell the future.' He celebrated his nation's regaining of independence by issuing bronze coins inscribed 'John the high priest and the commonwealth of the Jews.'

But the hasidim, or some of them at least, continued their dislike of the power and influence of the Hasmonaean family. According to Josephus,[2] an open breach came between John and these people at a banquet to which he invited them. At the banquet he assured them that he honoured their principles and desired to please God in everything, which he knew to be their desire too. So if they ever saw him unintentionally break God's law in any point, he begged that they would point it out. At this one of the guests, Eleazar by name, told him that if he wished to do the will of God perfectly, he should give up the high priesthood and content himself with the civil and military leadership of the nation. The reasoning behind this demand was a rumour that not long before John's birth, in the reign of Antiochus Epiphanes, his mother (the wife of Simon) had been held captive for a time by the king's officials. Under these circumstances John's legitimacy, it was suggested, could not be certain; and since legitimacy of birth was an essential requirement for the priestly office,[3] John was urged to relinquish his position as high priest. There is no reason to suppose that the rumour had any truth in it. John himself interpreted Eleazar's action as an attempt to undermine his position, and he broke off relations with the party to which Eleazar belonged. This marks the emergence of the Pharisaic party[4] as an opposition group to the Hasmonaean dynasty—a position which they retained for half a century. As the Hasmonaeans later became less popular, so the popularity of the Pharisees increased. On the other hand, John received the support of another group in the national senate or Sanhedrin, the group whom we know under the name of the Sadducees. Whatever the origin of the name may be—probably they claimed a link with Zadok, the high priest of David's time[5]—it came to be explained as derived from the Hebrew word meaning 'righteous'. For the next fifty years, then, the Sadducees retained control of the Sanhedrin, which acted as the council of the rulers of the Hasmonaean dynasty, and gave their support to the dynasty.

JOHN'S CONQUESTS

John Hyrcanus profited by the constant quarrels and power-seeking which progressively weakened the Seleucid power, and was able to extend his own power. It is clear that his ambition was to restore the kingdom of Judaea to the full extent of David's kingdom, back in the great days of the united Israelite monarchy. In the south he fought against the Idumaeans, who had been so troublesome to the Judaeans since the dark days of the Babylonian exile. He conquered them, and compelled them to accept circumcision and so be formally incorporated as members of the Jewish nation. One result of his action was that the members of one important Idumaean family were to become even more troublesome to the Jews than any Idumaeans had ever been before.

In Transjordan John conquered the Greek city of Medeba. To the north of his own realm he took hostile action against the Samaritans. The Jews were now in a position to take ample vengeance on them for all the irritations the Samaritans had caused them since the return from exile. Shechem was captured (c. 128 BC), and it is said that he destroyed the hated rival shrine on Gerizim, though this is uncertain.

The city of Samaria, now a Greek foundation, made use of its strong position to resist a siege for a long time, as it had done against the

Aramaeans and Assyrians in the days of the monarchy, but after a year John stormed it and destroyed it, enslaving the population. The Seleucid king Antiochus IX (Cyzicenus), son of Antiochus VII, tried to intervene and to defend Samaria, but had to stop on the orders of the Romans. This was because John had renewed the agreement with Rome made in the time of his father.

John was not content with the destruction of Samaria, but continued his campaign northwards as far as Scythopolis (the ancient Beth-shan), which he also took. John had forced the Idumaeans to become Jews, but this judaization could not be repeated with Samaritans. The Samaritans were circumcised Israelites already, and they were very conscious of their ancient quarrels with the Jews. John's conquest of Samaria did not lead to better relations between the two groups; on the contrary, it embittered the Samaritans still more. Even if John destroyed their temple, he could not deprive Mount Gerizim of its sacred character, and it continued to be the Samaritans' holy place. For two generations the Samaritans had to endure the Hasmonaean domination, until at last the Roman conquest of Palestine freed them from the Jewish yoke.

ARISTOBULUS I

The work of conquest which John had achieved so well was continued by his son and successor Aristobulus (104–103 BC) who in the course of a short reign of one year took control of much of Galilee and forcibly judaized some of the Gentile groups living there as well as the Ituraeans in the foothills of Lebanon. No doubt there were several Israelite areas in Galilee, remaining there from the days when the region had become an Assyrian province in 732 BC. They must be distinguished from the Jewish colonists in Galilee whom Judas Maccabaeus brought back to Judaea in 163 BC.[6] Perhaps in the postexilic age these Israelite communities had been influenced by Jerusalem in matters of religious belief and practice. At any rate Galilee, after its conquest by the Hasmonaeans, did not feel any such opposition to Judaea as Samaria did, and in fact in the Roman period the Galilaeans tended to be even more zealous Jewish patriots than the Judaeans themselves were. The part which Galilee plays in the gospel narrative gives the conquest and judaization of that region a special interest.

The fact that Aristobulus is commonly known by this Greek name is significant. The Hasmonaean dynasty, which had risen to power in a patriotic reaction against Hellenistic domination, now increasingly adopted the external and material features of Hellenism, especially its less attractive aspects. At the same time they destroyed the better elements of

Hellenistic culture in the regions which they had recently conquered. A new example of the adoption of Hellenistic practices is the fact that Aristobulus was the first member of the Hasmonaean family to take the title 'king'(Greek *basileus*) instead of 'ethnarch', the title which his father and grandfather had accepted; and he chose to wear the royal diadem. This was no doubt intended to increase his prestige among his Gentile neighbours. Among Jews he called himself by his Jewish name Judah, as is shown by the coins of his reign, which bear the Hebrew words: 'Judah the high priest and the commonwealth of the Jews'.

At the start of his reign, Aristobulus imprisoned his step-mother and half-brothers. He showed brotherly love only to his full brother Antigonus, but as a result of a plot against Antigonus, Aristobulus unintentionally gave orders for his death. This is said to have so preyed upon his mind that it hastened his death (which appears to have been due to tuberculosis).

ALEXANDER JANNAEUS AND HIS CONQUESTS

Aristobulus's widow bore the double name of Salome[7] Alexandra: like other members of the family, she had both a Greek name and a Jewish one. She is the most outstanding woman in the history of the Hasmonaean dynasty. When her husband died, she released his half-brothers from prison, and then married one of them, Alexander Jannaeus, whom she also enabled to take his late brother's place as king and high priest. (As she had borne no children to Aristobulus, her marriage to his brother conformed with Jewish law.[8]) This new king and high-priest had the usual combination of Hellenistic and Jewish names; alongside his Greek name Alexander he bore the Jewish name Jannaeus. This is a slightly Hellenized form of Hebrew Yannai, an abridged form of Jonathan, the name he bears on his coins. Some of his coins have the wording 'Jonathan the high priest and the commonwealth of the Jews'; others have more simply 'King Jonathan' in Hebrew and 'King Alexander' in Greek.

A more unsuitable person to be high priest than Jannaeus could hardly be imagined. The chief ambition of his whole reign was military conquest and territorial expansion. Although this policy involved him in many setbacks, he achieved many of his ambitions—but at a ruinous cost to all that was worthwhile in the spiritual heritage of his people.

Shortly after his accession to power (103 BC) he besieged the ancient seaport of Ptolemais, in the north-west of Palestine. The inhabitants turned for help to Ptolemy Lathyrus, a member of the royal family of Egypt, who was at this time ruler of Cyprus. His aid was effective, for Jannaeus was forced to abandon the siege and make a truce with Lathyrus. But at the same time he plotted against Lathyrus by making an agreement with Lathyrus's mother Cleopatra III (Thea), who had driven her son from the Egyptian throne in order to enjoy supreme power herself. Alexander asked for her aid against Lathyrus. When Lathyrus heard of Jannaeus's deceit, he invaded Jannaeus's kingdom, inflicted an annihilating defeat on the Jewish army in a battle on the Jordan, and then marched rapidly down the coastal road into Egypt. By this time, however, his mother Cleopatra had gathered the reinforcements she had promised to send to Jannaeus's assistance. Her troops drove back Lathyrus's army from Egyptian soil and drove it into Gaza. Then they went on and occupied the whole of Jannaeus's realm. If Cleopatra had chosen, she could have once more incorporated Palestine in the Ptolemaic empire as it had been before 200 BC: Jannaeus's rashness had brought his kingdom to this desperate situation. Fortunately for him, Cleopatra ignored those of her advisers who urged her to annex Palestine. Instead she followed the advice of her Jewish commander-in-chief, Ananias, who advised her that it would be better to make a treaty with Jannaeus. Lathyrus withdrew his army to Cyprus again, Cleopatra's forces returned to Egypt, and Jannaeus's kingdom was under his control once more.

He now turned to Transjordan and conquered two Greek cities in that area—Gadara and Amathus. Then he marched west to the Philistine seaboard and took the cities of Raphia (near the Egyptian frontier), Anthedon, and Gaza. Gaza, as usual, resisted the besieging army for a long time, but was at last captured in 96 BC, after a year's resistance, and was completely destroyed. No doubt when he was fighting in this region Alexander felt that the nearness of his Egyptian ally was a safeguard against interference from Cyprus or anywhere else.

But his urge to conquer and destroy was still strong. He crossed the Jordan once again and tried to conquer the southern part of Transjordan— the territory formerly occupied by the Ammonites and Moabites. Here, however, he ran into fresh trouble. The Nabataean Arabs[9] had interests in the territories which Jannaeus was now attacking. They were already, in fact, suspicious of Jannaeus's intentions. Before the fall of Gaza they had thought of sending help to the besieged city, but did not send it in time. Now that Jannaeus's army was near their own borders they ambushed it and practically destroyed it. Jannaeus himself barely escaped with his life and fled home to Jerusalem.

ALEXANDER JANNAEUS AND HIS OPPONENTS

During the ten years or so which had passed since he began to reign, he had become thoroughly unpopular with many of his subjects. Even though

he was a member of a Jewish dynasty, his rule was more oppressive than
the rule of many of their Hellenistic overlords had been. The opposition of
the Pharisees to the dynasty was hardening, and the Pharisees influenced
many of the common people. The first occasion on which something like
open rebellion broke out against him, according to Josephus,[10] was at the
Feast of Tabernacles, when as high priest he was officiating in the temple
court. As he was about to offer sacrifice, the people began to pelt him with
the citrons which they carried as part of the ritual, adding insulting words
to their action. Alexander sent mercenary troops among them, and 600 were
slaughtered. Further information about this incident is given by a tradition
preserved in the Talmud,[11] which tells how an unnamed Sadducee poured
out the customary libation of water on the ground and not (as the Pharisees
preferred) on the altar, and was pelted with citrons by the people in
consequence.

The spectacle of the king hurrying home to Jerusalem in order to escape
from the Nabataeans suggested to his opponents at home that their opportunity had come. They raised a rebellion against him, and for six years
(94–88 BC) Jannaeus was compelled to fight against his own subjects using
mercenary troops from the Hellenistic territories around: an ironic situation
for a descendant of the Maccabees! When his opponents felt their cause
weakening, they too called in Hellenistic aid; they invited the Seleucid king,
Demetrius III (Eukairos), to help them. With his aid they defeated Alexander in battle near Shechem; his mercenaries were dispersed, and he himself
had to seek refuge in the hill country. But this was the turning point in his
military fortunes. The sight of a Jewish king driven to wander as a fugitive
in the mountains after defeat at the hands of Seleucid forces roused the
patriotism of many of his subjects, including some six thousand of those
who had originally rebelled against him. Now regretting their revolt, they
put themselves under Alexander's command, and with this new army he
drove out the Seleucid forces from his country and defeated the remaining
rebels.

Having thus re-established his control over his kingdom, he returned to
his capital, taking the rebel leaders with him as captives. There he took a
grim revenge. Eight hundred of them were crucified in full view of the royal
palace, where the king and his concubines feasted their eyes on their
torments; and while they were still alive on their crosses, their wives and
children were brought out and slaughtered before their eyes. This cruelty
was effective; the remainder of his opponents in Jerusalem and Judaea were
so appalled by his actions that eight thousand of them fled to be out of his
reach.[12]

HIS LAST YEARS

It is not surprising that his subjects were quiet and submissive for the rest of his reign. But the Seleucids and Nabataeans still gave him some major difficulties. In 86 BC the last effective Seleucid king, Antiochus XII (Dionysus), led an army against the Nabataean king Aretas II, and passed through Judaea on his way, in spite of Jannaeus's attempt to bar his way. Aretas, however, defeated and killed Antiochus, and profited by his victory to extend his own territory as far north as Coelesyria and Damascus. The remainder of the Seleucid kingdom was overrun and annexed by Tigranes, king of Armenia. The Nabataean kingdom thus became the strongest and most dangerous power in the neighbourhood of Alexander's realm. Aretas followed up his success against the Seleucids by an attack on Jannaeus; he invaded Judaea and defeated him at Adida, near the road from Jerusalem to Joppa. Jannaeus was compelled to seek for peace, and had to make concessions to persuade Aretas to withdraw from Judaean soil. All this, however, did not deter him from further military adventures, and in the following years he campaigned in northern Transjordan and conquered several of the Greek cities of the Decapolis—Pella, Dium, Gerasa, Gaulana, Seleucia and Gamala.

In the closing years of his reign he suffered from ill-health, but even this failed to stop his military activities. When at last he died in 76 BC, he had won control of a realm west and east of the Jordan which was almost identical to the territory claimed in earlier days by the twelve tribes of Israel. But he had won it at too great a cost. He had treated with contempt the ideals which had been so important and so valued in the early days of the Hasmonaean revolt against Antiochus. The spectacle of a high priest who spent most of his time as a military adventurer was unpleasant and a betrayal of Israel's highest traditions. Many Jews were horrified that a Hasmonaean king should use pagan mercenaries against his own Jewish subjects. When his own subjects requested the aid of a Seleucid ruler against the Hasmonean ruler, it was after he had set them this bad example. His way of life was based on that of the least attractive Hellenistic minor rulers of western Asia. But he ignored the really valuable elements in Greek civilization, as was shown by the ruthless vandalism displayed in the destruction of the Hellenistic cities which he besieged and took one after another.

SALOME ALEXANDRA

When he died, he bequeathed his kingdom not to one of his sons but to his wife Salome Alexandra, from whom he had in fact gained it in the first instance. She was now sixty-four years old, but proved herself an able and prudent ruler for the nine years of her reign. According to Josephus,[13] Jannaeus on his deathbed advised her to make peace with the Pharisees. Whether he did so or not, she certainly brought the Pharisees into her council and paid careful heed to their advice, so much so that rabbinical tradition pictures her reign as a golden age. According to tradition, she was the sister of Simeon ben Shetach, a notable Pharisaic teacher of the period, though this is uncertain. The Pharisees wanted some revenge for the persecution they had endured under Alexander Jannaeus. In particular, they were successful in bringing about the execution of several of the men who were believed to have advised Alexander to crucify his eight hundred Jewish captives in 88 BC. But the Sadducean party became anxious that their opponents would take their revenge too far and destroy the old aristocracy of Judaea (which had close links with the Sadducees). So they approached the queen, using her younger son Aristobulus as an intermediary, and the Pharisees' plans for further vengeance were checked.

In its foreign relations, Judaea was relatively quiet during Alexandra's reign. By diplomatic approaches she was able to prevent a threatened invasion by the Armenian king Tigranes, when he came south to besiege Ptolemais in 69 BC. Her younger son Aristobulus led an expedition against Damascus, but it was quite unsuccessful.

HYRCANUS II AND ARISTOBULUS II

Alexandra had borne two sons to Jannaeus—Hyrcanus and Aristobulus. Hyrcanus, the elder brother, was a quiet and perhaps unambitious man, but his brother had a similar character to that of his father and his uncle, Aristobulus I, whose name he bore. When Alexandra became queen at her husband's death, she could not (being a woman) succeed him in the high-priesthood, and she appointed her elder son Hyrcanus to this office. She probably knew that with his peaceful character he would not exploit his position as high priest and undermine his mother's queenly authority. Her younger son Aristobulus she entrusted with a military command.

But Aristobulus, with the support of the Sadducees, waited for an opportunity to gratify his ambitions and gain the power he lacked so long as his mother reigned. When she died in 67 BC his plans were ready for immediate action. The legitimate successor to the throne was Hyrcanus, who was already high priest. But Aristobulus gathered an army and attacked Hyrcanus. There was a battle near Jericho, and so many of Hyrcanus's followers deserted to Aristobulus that Hyrcanus had to flee for safety to Jerusalem. There he surrendered to his brother, conceding to him not only the kingly power but the high-priesthood as well. His only condition was that he might continue to live unmolested as a private citizen in possession of his personal estate.

It is unclear whether Hyrcanus was an ambitious man or not, but in any case he was not allowed to enjoy his retirement undisturbed. There was a very ambitious man in the country, who saw that he could make good use of Hyrcanus to achieve his own ambitions. This man was Antipater, an Idumaean by birth,[14] whose father (also called Antipater) had been governor of Idumaea under Alexander Jannaeus and Alexandra. Possibly he himself had also held this position. At any rate, Antipater was one of those men who are clever enough to realize that it is much more important to have the reality of power than any titles. His scheme was that Hyrcanus should regain the titles of power in order that he himself, as the power behind Hyrcanus's throne, should enjoy the substance.

Antipater therefore set out to win the friendship and confidence of Hyrcanus, and at the same time to persuade many in Judaea to support the claims of the rightful heir against the 'usurper' Aristobulus. He also found a useful ally in Aretas III, the Nabataean king. Then he began to rouse Hyrcanus's fears by repeatedly insisting that, in spite of his promise to Aristobulus to be content with a private life, his brother would not feel safe as long as he was alive. At first Hyrcanus was not inclined to listen to him, and would not believe that his life was in such danger. At last, however, Antipater's urgent warnings had their effect, and Hyrcanus was persuaded to leave Jerusalem secretly and accept the hospitality offered by Aretas at his capital, Petra.

Aretas promised to support Hyrcanus in recovering the throne of Judaea. In return he was promised twelve cities on the Nabataean border which Alexander Jannaeus had captured. Aretas sent a large army with Hyrcanus and Antipater against Aristobulus, and heavily defeated him. Many of Aristobulus's followers immediately deserted to Hyrcanus's side, and Aristobulus had to flee to Jerusalem and fortify himself in the temple area (65 BC). There he was besieged by the army of Hyrcanus and his Nabataean allies.

But the whole of western Asia was at this moment undergoing a swift and radical change, and as a result the control of affairs in Judaea would no longer remain in Hasmonaean hands.

NOTES

[1] *Antiquities* xii. 299.

[2] *Antiquities* xiii. 289 ff.

[3] This is implied in Lev. 21:7, 13 f. TB *Qiddushin* 66a (cf. Josephus, *Antiquities* xiii. 372) puts the incident in the reign of Alexander Jannaeus (103–76 BC).

[4] The word 'Pharisee' derives from Heb. *parash*, 'separate'; i.e. they were 'separatists', presumably from uncleanness, as they defined it. See Schürer, *History of the Jewish People* (rev.ed.), vol. 2, pp. 395 ff.

[5] See Schürer, op. cit., pp. 404 ff.

[6] See pp. 152 f.

[7] In a Qumran text her Jewish name appears in the fuller form Shelom-sion ('peace of Zion').

[8] For the 'levirate' marriage see Deut. 25:5 ff. Cf. p. 198

[9] See p. 127.

[10] *Antiquities* xiii. 372 f.

[11] TB *Sukkah* 48b.

[12] This incident is probably referred to in the Nahum commentary found in Cave 4 at Qumran, which interprets Nahum 2 :11 f. of 'the raging lion, who . . . took vengeance on the 'seekers after smooth things' [Pharisees?] by hanging them up alive, which was never done in Israel before' (F. F. Bruce, *Second Thoughts on the Dead Sea Scrolls* [3rd ed.,1969], pp. 78 f.).

[13] *Antiquities* xiii. 401.

[14] The Idumaean ancestry of Antipater (and therefore of Herod the Great) seems probable, but has been questioned. See L. L. Grabbe, *Judaism from Cyrus to Hadrian* (1992), pp. 322 f.

Chapter Twenty-Three

The Roman Conquest
(200–37 BC)

THE ROMANS IN GREECE AND ASIA MINOR

By 200 BC the city of Rome, after becoming the dominant power in Italy, had also emerged victorious from a life-and-death struggle with Carthage, on the opposite shore of the Mediterranean Sea. By defeating Hannibal the Romans became the strongest state in the western Mediterranean. They then imposed their power over the Macedonian king, who had given support to Hannibal, and claimed to act as the protectors of the city-states of Greece. When Antiochus III of Syria intervened in the affairs of Greece in 192 BC, the Romans, as protectors of Greece, made war against him, and defeated him decisively at Magnesia in Asia Minor two years later. Antiochus had to withdraw from western Asia Minor, and the greater part of that territory was added to the kingdom of Pergamum, which was closely allied to Rome. The growing reputation of Rome is clearly seen in the incident of 168 BC, when the demand of a Roman official, Popillius Laenas, was sufficient to turn Antiochus Epiphanes back from his planned assault on Alexandria.[1] It was natural, too, that when Judas Maccabaeus revolted against Antiochus Epiphanes he should enter into diplomatic relations with Rome; so too did his successors Jonathan, Simon and John Hyrcanus.

In 146 BC Carthage was finally destroyed by the Romans and the former Carthaginian territory became the Roman province of 'Africa'. In the same year a rebellion in Greece was crushed by the Romans, who then reduced the southern part of the Balkan Peninsula to the status of two Roman provinces—Macedonia in the north and Achaia in the south. Thirteen years later, Attalus III, the last king of Pergamum, died, and bequeathed his kingdom to the Roman senate and people. They decided to accept this inheritance, and the realm of the Attalids now received a new status as the Roman province of 'Asia'—the first Roman possession on the continent of Asia.

To the north-east of this province, however, there arose an ambitious king whose aim was to found a new empire for himself in Asia Minor and surrounding territories. This was Mithridates VI, last and greatest ruler of the Arsacid dynasty which had dominated Pontus, in northern Asia Minor, since about 300 BC. His ambition brought him into collision with the Romans, who now controlled the province of Asia, and who were bound by treaty to those neighbours of Mithridates who had most cause to fear his ambitions. In 88 BC he launched an attack on the Roman administrators and settlers in the province. The natives of the province had found the taxation and extortion of the Roman governors intolerably oppressive, and many of them supported Mithridates.

The Romans at once sent armies against him, but the war between them dragged on for twenty-five years. This was due partly to the Pontic king's skill, and partly because the Romans were distracted by civil war in Rome itself.[2] At last, in 66 BC, the Roman general Pompey was given command of operations against Mithridates, and he drove the king out of Asia Minor in a single campaign. Mithridates fled to the northern shore of the Black Sea and took his own life in 63 BC. Having conquered Mithridates, the Romans were now faced with the necessity of reorganizing the whole political structure of western Asia. Tigranes, king of Armenia, Mithridates' son-in-law, who had annexed a large part of the former Seleucid territory, submitted to Rome in 66 BC. The Romans agreed that he should control his own kingdom and part of the territory he had conquered in western Mesopotamia. Pompey sent his senior officer Scaurus into Syria to settle the affairs of that area. By now the last remnants of Seleucid rule had collapsed altogether.

THE ROMANS IN SYRIA AND JUDAEA

When Scaurus arrived in Damascus, he received news of the civil war raging in Judaea, and made his way there to see if the matter could be exploited to the advantage of Rome. Both parties sought his favour, offering him large sums of money, by way of persuasion. Scaurus decided to support Aristobulus's cause, and ordered Aretas to abandon the siege. Aretas knew that he could not afford to ignore a Roman order, and withdrew. Scaurus returned to Syria, and Aristobulus profited by the new situation to pursue Aretas on his homeward march and launch a surprise attack on his army. Six thousand Nabataean troops were killed, according to Josephus.[3] Among them was a brother of Antipater, Phallion by name.

Aristobulus determined to achieve everything possible in the changed situation, and to win Pompey's favour as well as that of Scaurus. He sent the great general a golden vine, which was in due course dedicated at Rome in the temple of Jupiter on the Capitoline hill. In 63 BC, Pompey, having conquered the northern parts of Syria, came to Damascus. There he was approached by both Aristobulus and Hyrcanus, pleading their rival causes, and also by a deputation from the Jewish people, who asked him to abolish the Hasmonaean monarchy and restore the old temple-constitution. Pompey listened to these claims and requests, and told the petitioners to be patient until he imposed a settlement. First he intended to send an army against the Nabataeans, to teach them the lesson he thought they needed.

Aristobulus, however, whose cause was at first favoured, incurred Pompey's suspicion by his behaviour on his return to Judaea. He accompanied Pompey at the start of his expedition against the Nabataeans, but then left him and fortified himself in the citadel of Alexandrion, in the Jordan valley. Pompey decided to postpone his Nabataean venture and turned back to deal with Aristobulus. Aristobulus was compelled to hand over to Pompey the fortress of Alexandrion, but went to Jerusalem to prepare resistance there. When Pompey arrived outside Jerusalem, Aristobulus wisely changed his mind and gave himself up. But Aristobulus's supporters in the city were determined to resist the Romans. Hyrcanus's followers, on the other hand, viewed the Romans as allies, and they were able to get control of the city and opened its gates to Pompey's army (April–May). But the resistance party established themselves in the temple area, which occupied a naturally strong position and was separately fortified. Here they held out for three months against the Roman besiegers. At last the Romans succeeded in forcing an entrance from the north side of the temple area, and many Jews were killed as the whole area fell into Roman hands. It is recorded as a remarkable fact that the priests in the temple court went on with their sacrificial duties, ignoring what was happening, and were killed in great numbers. The capture of the temple took place on a sabbath day in July or August (rather than—as Josephus says[4]—on the Day of Atonement, in October).[5]

Pompey visited the captured area and inspected it all thoroughly. He even insisted on entering the holy of holies, despite the horrified protests of the priests, for only the high priest was permitted to enter this innermost shrine, and that only once a year, on the Day of Atonement, bearing the blood of the special sacrifice offered on that day. But their attempts to prevent Pompey from going in made him all the more determined to see what it was they were trying to hide from him; for there were curious rumours among the Gentiles about what was kept in the Jewish holy of holies—among them grotesque and sinister rumours. When Pompey went in, however, he found exactly nothing—it was empty. But the Jews never forgot his gross sacrilege, as it was in their eyes.

Those responsible for the resistance were severely punished. Judaea had to give up the Greek cities in the coastal plain, Samaria and Transjordan which had been annexed by the Hasmonaean rulers; her control was also removed from the Samaritan community of Shechem and its neighbour-hood. Reduced in this way to a purely Jewish state, Judaea was made to pay tribute to Rome. Hyrcanus was confirmed in the high-priesthood and in the leadership of the nation, but he was not allowed to have the title of king. He was placed under the general supervision of Scaurus, now ap-pointed governor of Syria. Aristobulus and his family, together with many other Jews, were taken to Rome to march in humiliation in Pompey's triumphal procession in 61 BC. Many Jews who were taken to Rome as slaves at this time were later given their freedom, and formed the main nucleus of the rapidly expanding Jewish colony in Rome.

Roman intervention in Syria would have meant the loss of Judaea's independence in any case. But she might have retained a much larger measure of autonomy if it had not been for the folly of civil war, which led to so much Roman interference. Now, however, the freedom so laboriously won by the earlier Hasmonaeans, and the empire built up by their succes-sors, vanished almost overnight. The Jews found themselves under the domination of more powerful and ruthless masters than most of their Hellenistic overlords had ever been.

HYRCANUS AND HIS ENEMIES

Roman rule did bring some benefits to Judaea. It brought a few years of peace after the civil strife between Hyrcanus and Aristobulus. The people had to pay heavy tribute, but at least they were spared the dangers of aggressive campaigns such as those into which Alexander Jannaeus had led them. Nor was it really a bad thing that the Greek cities and other non-Jewish areas which they had conquered should be withdrawn from their control.

Now that Hyrcanus was confirmed in the high priesthood, his sponsor Antipater continued to support him, and decided to exploit this new situation to his own advantage, and also (it must be admitted) to the advantage of Judaea. From the time of the Roman conquest onwards, it was the consistent policy of Antipater and his family to support the Roman power in western Asia. The Roman generals who held that power changed from time to time, but Antipater's support was not given to them as individuals but to the empire which they represented.

Scaurus, governor of Syria, followed up the campaign against the Nabataeans which Pompey had abandoned in order to besiege Jerusalem. Antipater seized the opportunity to help him by sending provisions for his army. Then Antipater offered his services as mediator between Aretas and

Scaurus. When Scaurus agreed to withdraw if Aretas paid an indemnity of three hundred talents, Antipater gave his own guarantee that the money would be paid.

Hyrcanus's brother Aristobulus II, who was forced to take part in Pompey's triumph in Rome in 61 BC, was liberated afterwards, but had to live in Rome with his family. Both Aristobulus and his two sons, Alexander and Antigonus, caused considerable trouble in Judaea for several years to come. In 57 BC one of the two young princes, Alexander, who had escaped when his father and other members of his family were taken to Rome, organized a revolt in Judaea. He gained control of three Hasmonaean citadels west and east of Jordan. But Aulus Gabinius, newly appointed proconsul of Syria, put down the rising and captured Alexander. Alexander's mother pleaded with Gabinius for her son's release, which was granted when the fortresses held by Alexander were yielded up to the Romans.

Gabinius now reorganized the administration of Judaea. Hyrcanus was deprived of all political authority and left with nothing but the high-priesthood. Judaea was divided into five administrative areas, based respectively on Jerusalem, Gazara, Amathus (east of Jordan), Jericho, and Sepphoris (in Galilee). These five areas were placed more directly under the jurisdiction of the governor of Syria.

If the purpose of this reconstruction was to discourage further revolts, it was a failure. In the following year (56 BC) Aristobulus himself, having escaped from his 'free custody' in Rome with his other son Antigonus, arrived in Judaea and tried to raise another revolt. This was immediately crushed. Aristobulus fled to the fortress of Machaerus east of Jordan, where he resisted for some time. At last he was taken, and sent back to Rome, but his family were given their freedom. Alexander and Antigonus therefore remained in Palestine, and there, in spite of the failure of the two previous attempts, Alexander staged another revolt in 55 BC. This time he thought he had a favourable opportunity, for Gabinius, instead of carrying out the wishes of the senate in Rome and marching against the Parthians farther east, abandoned his Parthian campaign almost as soon as it was begun in order to help the Egyptian ruler Ptolemy XII (Auletes) to regain his throne, from which he had been driven by a popular revolt. His change of plan was due partly to orders received from Pompey (who was at this time in conflict with the senate) and partly to a large bribe offered him by Ptolemy. Gabinius did in fact restore the deposed monarch to his throne, and on this campaign received aid from Hyrcanus and Antipater in the form of grain, money and men. Alexander's attempted revolt was quickly defeated in a battle near Mount Tabor. But Gabinius's disobedience to the senate led to his recall and impeachment for treason. He was succeeded as proconsul of Syria in 54 BC by Marcus Licinius Crassus.

JULIUS CAESAR TRIUMPHANT

Crassus was at this time one of the three most powerful men in the Roman world. Indeed, it is noteworthy from 63 BC onwards how many of the names most famous in general Roman history figure in the history of Judaea and the neighbouring territories. Syria and Judaea lay on the eastern frontier of Roman power, and not far to the east the powerful Parthian empire was established on the Euphrates. The later Seleucids had fought against the Parthians, with little success. Now the Romans had taken the place of the Seleucids as the imperial power in western Asia, and the senate thought it necessary at the outset to teach the Parthians a lesson that would discourage them from any plans to interfere in the new Roman sphere of influence. Gabinius had not carried out this senatorial policy against the Parthians, but Crassus came determined to lead an army against them.

In 56 BC, Pompey, Crassus and Julius Caesar, who had strengthened their position in the Roman world four years earlier by forming the coalition known as the First Triumvirate, renewed their coalition despite strong senatorial opposition. They agreed that Pompey and Crassus should share the consulship, the chief political position at Rome, for 55 BC. (Caesar, who had been governor (proconsul) of Gaul since the end of his tenure of the consulship in 59 BC, had his proconsulship prolonged for five years more.) When their consular year expired, Pompey chose Spain as his proconsular province (but administered it by deputy and stayed in Rome himself), while Crassus chose Syria, and went to that province in the hope of winning military glory for himself. Both his partners in the triumvirate had already won great fame.

Crassus spent the winter of 54–53 BC in his province collecting money for a campaign against the Parthians planned for the following year. He raided several temples in Syria, including the Jewish temple at Jerusalem. In 53 BC he led an army of 35,000 men across the Euphrates, but at Carrhae (the Harran of the Old Testament) his legions were caught at a disadvantage by the Parthian cavalry and archers, and totally defeated. Crassus himself was killed.

The news of his defeat and death was soon followed by a fresh revolt in Judaea, led this time by a man named Pitholaus. But it was quickly crushed by the new governor of Syria, a staff-officer of Crassus named Cassius. Pitholaus himself was killed and a large number of his followers were sold into slavery. Cassius also, in 51 BC, prevented the Parthians from following up their victory at Carrhae and invading Syria.

The death of Crassus had serious consequences for the triumvirate of which he had been a member. Before long the two survivors, Pompey and Caesar, became increasingly linked with opposing parties in the Roman state. The senate had foolishly caused offence to Pompey after his return from the east, which had led him to make common cause with Caesar and Crassus. Now the senate found itself forced to look to Pompey for protection. In 49 BC civil war broke out between the two sides. Caesar gained control of Rome and Pompey left Italy and crossed the Adriatic Sea. Caesar released Aristobulus from custody in order that he might take a lead in anti-Pompeian activity in Syria, where Pompey's party was in power, but before Aristobulus could leave Rome on this mission he was poisoned by Pompey's supporters. About the same time his son Alexander was also put to death at Antioch by orders of Metellus Scipio, proconsul of Syria from 49 to 48 BC. Metellus was Pompey's father-in-law[6] and acted on Pompey's instructions.

The whole situation was changed, however, by Caesar's victory over Pompey at the battle of Pharsalus in Thessaly early in 48 BC. Pompey fled to Egypt, seeking the hospitality of the young king Ptolemy XIII. But a defeated statesman is sometimes an embarrassing guest, especially when his conqueror is approaching, and Ptolemy's ministers got rid of the embarrassment by assassinating Pompey as soon as he landed. When the news of Pompey's death reached Judaea, many people there remembered how fifteen years before he had captured the temple area and forced his way into the holy of holies, and they considered his death a well-deserved act of divine judgment, delayed but none the less certain.

Caesar was now the dominant power in the Roman world. Antipater, whose consistent policy was to support the representatives of Roman power in the east, soon found an opportunity to win the favour of Caesar, just as he had previously assisted Pompey's officers.

Caesar followed Pompey to Egypt hoping to take him alive and probably to display his generosity towards him. But he arrived too late for this. There were, however, a few matters in Alexandria which needed his attention. In particular, there was a dispute between the boy-king Ptolemy XIII and his sister-queen Cleopatra which Caesar settled in a manner which aroused the resentment of Ptolemy's ministers. They attacked Caesar and blockaded him and his army of three thousand men in the palace quarter of Alexandria throughout the winter of 48–47 BC.

Two men acted to bring assistance to Caesar's besieged army. One was a Pergamene named Mithridates, who quickly organized an army to go to Caesar's help. The other was Antipater, who organized supplies for Caesar and his men. Thus helped and reinforced, Caesar fought and won a pitched battle against the followers of Ptolemy XIII. The young king himself was killed; his brother was put on the throne with the title of Ptolemy XIV, but from now on the chief power in Egypt was exercised by his sister Cleopatra, with whom Caesar had established close personal relations.

ANTIPATER'S RULE

Caesar now returned to Rome by way of Judaea, Syria and Asia Minor. He rewarded Antipater's timely aid (which had been sent in the name of Hyrcanus) by making him a tax-free Roman citizen with the title of procurator of Judaea. Hyrcanus was confirmed in the high-priesthood and given the title ethnarch of the Jews, despite the plea of Antigonus, the surviving son of Aristobulus, that this twofold dignity belonged by right to himself as the lawful Hasmonaean successor. Hyrcanus was allowed to rebuild the walls of Jerusalem, which Pompey had dismantled, and numerous other concessions were made to the Jews, including a reduction in tribute. Gabinius's constitution imposed on Judaea in 57 BC was thus superseded by one which allowed the Jews a considerable measure of independence.

Antipater now had an established position for himself in the Jewish state. He celebrated it by appointing two of his sons, Phasael and Herod, military prefects of Judaea and Galilee respectively. Galilee was at this time severely troubled by brigands, and Herod, who was twenty-five years old, displayed remarkable energy in tackling the problem. But when he captured a brigand chief named Hezekiah and immediately executed him, he caused offence to the Sanhedrin in Jerusalem, since they alone had the authority to inflict such a penalty. Herod was summoned to appear before the Sanhedrin and stand trial for this illegal act. He appeared, accompanied by some troops in the hope of intimidating the Sanhedrin. Hyrcanus, who as high priest was president of the court, wisely adjourned proceedings indefinitely. The majority of the court seemed determined to condemn Herod, regardless of the consequences, and Hyrcanus knew that the consequences could only involve bloodshed and civil warfare.

So Herod was able to depart, without condemnation or penalty. Soon his power was increased, because the proconsul of Syria, Sextus Caesar, who was impressed by Herod's success in Galilee, appointed him also military prefect of Coelesyria.

Sextus Caesar, however, was assassinated in 46 BC at the instigation of a supporter of Pompey, Caecilius Bassus, who made himself master of Syria with Parthian help. Julius Caesar sent an army to Syria, which drove Bassus into Apamea and besieged him there. But the siege was still going on when the assassination of Caesar himself on the Ides of March in 44 BC threw the Roman world into political chaos once again.

The assassination of Caesar led to a fresh outbreak of civil war between the party which supported the leading assassins, Brutus and Cassius, and the partisans of Caesar, led by Caesar's former chief officer Mark Antony and Caesar's great-nephew and adopted son Octavian.

Cassius had already been nominated proconsul of Syria by Caesar and he now proceeded to go there. He had already had experience of the province as an officer in the ill-fated army of Crassus. It was he, as we have seen, who had prevented a Parthian invasion of Roman territory after the disaster of Carrhae in 53 BC. Now the rival Roman forces in Syria abandoned their quarrel and joined Cassius.

The death of Caesar was a great blow to the Jews, who had received extraordinary favours from him, and no doubt hoped for more. The conduct of Cassius was very different from Caesar's, for he was determined to raise a huge sum of money to pay for the campaign he planned against Antony and Octavian; and Judaea had to make its contribution. Some cities which did not raise sufficient funds were treated with great severity: as an example to others their inhabitants were sold as slaves. But even so, Antipater recognized that Cassius was the appointed Roman governor in the area, and therefore supported him, as was his consistent policy. He raised seven hundred talents towards his campaign. Cassius was grateful; he renewed Herod's appointment as military prefect of Coelesyria which had previously been conferred by Sextus Caesar.

In 43 BC Antipater was assassinated. A man named Malichus, who planned to gain control of Judaea, bribed the butler of Hyrcanus II to poison Antipater as he was dining with Hyrcanus. Herod seized an early opportunity of avenging his father's death.

ANTONY IN THE EAST

Next year the rival Roman armies met in battle at Philippi in Macedonia. Victory went to Antony and Octavian, and Brutus and Cassius both committed suicide in the hour of defeat.

After Cassius's departure for the war a state of anarchy broke out in Judaea. The ruler of Tyre grabbed some Galilaean territory. There was a further attempt by Antigonus, the surviving son of Aristobulus, to seize power, but Herod was able to prevent this.

The immediate result of the battle of Philippi was that all the Roman lands in the east came into the control of Antony. The sons of Antipater, Phasael and Herod, were in some danger, since they had supported Cassius. More than one deputation from the Jewish aristocracy accused them of hostility to Antony. But Antony knew well enough that Antipater and his family had not supported Cassius for any other reason than his position as the legal representative of Rome. Antony remembered his friendly relations with Antipater when he had been on Gabinius's staff in Syria fifteen years before, and he knew that he could rely on the loyalty of

Phasael and Herod. He could also control Judaea more effectively through them than in any other way. He therefore appointed them joint tetrarchs[7] of Judaea (41 BC). This appointment brought to an end the political authority of Hyrcanus; but Hyrcanus's political authority had never been significant. He was now content with the prestige of the high-priesthood.

Antony tried to win the favour of the Jews by giving freedom to those of them who had been sold into slavery by Cassius, and also by forcing the Tyrians to hand back the territory they had seized after Cassius's departure. But in fact Antony proved an oppressive overlord. Judaea, in common with the other eastern provinces which he controlled, had to pay enormous taxes to maintain his extravagant standard of living.

Antony spent the winter of 41–40 BC in Egypt as the guest of Cleopatra; he was far more attracted to her than Julius Caesar had ever allowed himself to be. From there he went to Italy and made a truce with Octavian. By now the rivalry between the two victors of Philippi had reached a point where a fresh outbreak of civil war seemed inevitable.

During his absence Syria was invaded by the Parthians under their king Orodes and his son Pacorus, with the support of a Roman officer who had turned traitor, Labienus by name. He had gone to the Parthian court as ambassador of Brutus and Cassius, and remained there after their death. Labienus was able to win over most of the Roman troops in Syria. As for Judaea, Antigonus was at last able to wear the crown of his Hasmonaean ancestors, for he had allied himself with Parthia when he saw no hope of receiving satisfaction from Rome. He imprisoned his uncle Hyrcanus and had his ears mutilated to prevent him from ever again becoming high priest (since nobody with bodily defects could serve as a priest). Phasael committed suicide in prison; Herod escaped to Rome.

HEROD BECOMES KING

For three years (40–37 BC) Antigonus governed Judaea as king and high priest. In 39 BC Ventidius Bassus, whom Antony had sent to take charge of the situation, defeated Labienus and his troops and drove the Parthians from Syria. When they tried to return next year they suffered a crushing defeat at his hands. The crown-prince Pacorus was among those who died in battle. But Ventidius did not interfere with Antigonus; he left him at peace in Judaea on condition that he paid tribute. Ventidius returned to Rome to receive a triumphal welcome.

But in Rome something else had taken place which was to change the whole political situation in Judaea. Herod arrived in Rome late in the year 40 BC, and met Antony and Octavian. They both recognized the services which Herod could give to the Roman cause in the east if he were restored to a position of power, and on their advice the Roman senate declared Herod king of the Jews. A week later he left Rome for the east, in order to gain control of his kingdom—otherwise his title of king would be meaningless.

The reconquest of his kingdom was not an easy task, and the Roman forces in the area gave him little help at first. He took Joppa and relieved Masada, a fortress on the south-west shore of the Dead Sea, where his family had been living under siege conditions for a year. In 38 BC he conquered Galilee, and left it in charge of his brother Joseph while he went to have a further interview with Antony, who had now returned to Syria and was at present at Samosata. During his absence his supporters in Galilee were attacked and defeated by Antigonus, and Joseph was killed. Galilee revolted from Herod, and had to be reconquered. Then a defeat inflicted by Herod upon part of the army of Antigonus in Samaria brought all Palestine except Jerusalem under his control.

In 37 BC he proceeded to besiege Jerusalem, in which he had the support of Sosius, one of Antony's generals, who came with a large army. The siege and gradual capture of Jerusalem took nearly three months, till the whole city was in Herod's hands. He sent Antigonus to Antony in chains. Herod had great difficulty in preventing his Roman allies from unrestrained looting and massacre in his newly-won capital. Only when he paid them a large bribe could they be persuaded to depart. Sosius took Antigonus in chains to Antioch, and there Antony, at Herod's desire, ordered him to be beheaded. It was the first occasion, it was said, on which the Romans had inflicted capital punishment on a king.

NOTES

[1] See pp. 138 f.

[2] During those years Mithridates engaged in vigorous anti-Roman propaganda throughout western Asia (cf. Sallust, *History*, fragment iv. 69. 1–23). Echoes of this can be recognized in the portrayal of the 'Kittim' in the Qumran commentary on Habakkuk (see F. F. Bruce, *Second Thoughts on the Dead Sea Scrolls* [2nd ed., 1961], pp. 71 ff.).

[3] *Antiquities* xiv. 33. As so often with Josephus's numbers, the 6,000 can be considerably reduced.

[4] *Antiquities* xiv. 66.

[5] See M. B. Dagut,' The Habakkuk Scroll and Pompey's capture of Jerusalem,' *Biblica* 32 (1951), pp. 542 ff.

[6] In 60 BC Pompey had married Caesar's young daughter Julia; her untimely death in 54 BC did much to weaken the relationship between the two men.

[7] Originally a Macedonian title, denoting a ruler of a fourth part of a kingdom, 'tetrarch' was used in Roman times to denote the ruler of any part of a province; it was an inferior title to 'ethnarch'.

Chapter Twenty-Four

The Reign of Herod
(37–4 BC)

HEROD'S WIVES

For thirty-three years Herod reigned as king of the Jews, displaying unusual political genius throughout. Josephus has preserved for us a detailed account of these years, derived largely from the work of Herod's court historian, Nicolas of Damascus, and partly from other sources less friendly to Herod.

Herod's kingdom covered all Palestine and a large part of Transjordan. He governed this territory with the official Latin title of *rex socius*. In theory he was an independent king, enjoying an alliance with the Roman state. In fact, he was bound to respect and carry out the will of the Roman people in all his policies; otherwise he might soon have found himself dethroned. But he recognized clearly what the sensible course for a ruler in his position was, and he made it his fixed policy (as it had been his father's before him) to support whichever party or individual represented Roman power in the Near East at any one time. Octavian recognized that Herod could be as useful to his interests in those parts as he had been to Antony's. It was greatly to the Roman advantage to control a difficult strategic territory like Judaea indirectly through a loyal allied king; they gained many benefits from this arrangement. The inevitable hatred many Jews felt towards the regime focussed on Herod rather than on the Romans.

Herod started off with two great disadvantages in his relations with his subjects. Firstly, he was not of pure Israelite lineage, but a descendant of the hated Edomites, although he and his family were Jewish by religion. Secondly, he had acquired his power at the expense of the native Hasmonaean dynasty. He had, in fact, become king by means of the overthrow and execution of a Hasmonaean king. The later Hasmonaeans had been very oppressive, but now that they had fallen from power, their misrule was largely forgotten and people remembered only that they had won independence for the Jews and ruled them as a native line of kings.

In order to gain a little legitimacy for his kingship, at the start of his reign Herod married Princess Mariamne, who was a Hasmonaean on both sides; her father was Alexander, elder son of Aristobulus II, while her mother, Alexandra, was the daughter of Hyrcanus II. Her father had died by poison in 48 BC, at the outbreak of the civil war between Pompey and Caesar; but her mother was not only alive but energetic too! She had a powerful desire to get revenge on Herod for the harm he had caused her family. She also had strong ambitions for her children. In fact, she overreached herself and brought them disaster instead of the power she planned to gain for them.

Before marrying Mariamne, Herod divorced his former wife Doris, by whom he had a son called Antipater, named after his father. His marriage with Mariamne, however, was not merely a political marriage on his side; he appears to have cherished a passionate affection for her. She, however, cherished a continual resentment against this marriage to a man of inferior birth, who was also the person who had deprived her own family of royal honours. In due course she bore to Herod two sons, Aristobulus and Alexander, and two daughters, Salampsio and Cypros.

THE HIGH PRIESTHOOD

The execution of Antigonus caused a vacancy in the high-priestly office, which Herod filled by appointing to it a little-known priest of the Babylonian Jews named Hananel. But Herod's mother-in-law insisted that her own son Aristobulus was the rightful heir to the high-priesthood, and Herod yielded to her demands, deposed Hananel, and made the seventeen-year-old Aristobulus high priest. Shortly afterwards, Aristobulus was drowned while sporting with some other youths in a swimming-pool. It was widely believed that his drowning was not accidental; that Herod had persuaded the boy's companions, while they were ducking one another playfully in the pool, to hold Aristobulus's head under the water just a little too long. Herod's tears as he attended the funeral of his young brother-in-law did nothing to change this widespread belief. Hananel was restored to the sacred office which he had so recently vacated, and retained it for six years (36–30 BC).

The death of Aristobulus caused international complications. For the first six years of his reign Herod was endangered by the endless ambitions of his neighbouring ruler to the south-west, Cleopatra of Egypt, who was the last monarch of the Ptolemaic dynasty. Cleopatra hoped to regain the same control of Palestine which the first rulers of her dynasty had exercised, and anything that could weaken Herod's position was eagerly welcomed by her. Herod's position was made more insecure because of her increasing personal influence over Antony, who continued to be the dominant Roman in the Near East until 31 BC. Another difficulty was that Alexandra was Cleopatra's ally in any scheme to Herod's disadvantage. One story which blamed Herod for the death of the young Aristobulus claimed that Herod had discovered a plot by Alexandra to escape to Egypt with her son and seek Cleopatra's help to make him king of Judaea. The idea of ruling Judaea through the young Hasmonaean as her vassal would have been pleasing to Cleopatra.

CLEOPATRA'S HOSTILITY

When Aristobulus was drowned, Alexandra begged Cleopatra to do what she could to avenge his death, and Cleopatra persuaded Antony to call Herod to account. Herod was summoned to appear before Antony at Laodicea in Syria, but was acquitted of the charge of murder—partly (some said) because he paid large bribes, and partly because (as Antony told Cleopatra) 'one must not investigate too closely the official acts of a king, lest he ceases to be really a king'.[1]

But Herod's return from Laodicea to Jerusalem was followed by fresh trouble. Beforehand, unsure how Antony would treat him, he had placed his wife Mariamne in the charge of his uncle Joseph, with strict instructions to put her to death should he himself not return alive. This was a symptom of his jealous love for Mariamne. In his absence, Joseph told Mariamne of her husband's instructions; he did so to convince her of the intensity of Herod's love for her. Naturally, she was not favourably impressed by this way of showing conjugal love, and reproached Herod with it on his return. His suspicious nature immediately concluded that there must have been sexual relations between his uncle and Mariamne, or he would not have revealed this secret to her. Joseph was accordingly executed for his lack of discretion.

The circumstances of Herod's early days made him naturally suspicious, and both his political and domestic circumstances increased this tendency, until it reached the point of madness. Inevitably the reaction which his suspicions provoked in other people gave him further reasons for suspicion, and his domestic life especially became more and more unhappy.

Cleopatra was never able to achieve all her plans against Judaea, although she used her influence over Antony to acquire the revenues of some of the richest parts of Herod's kingdom, such as Jericho and its environment. She also did her best to cause a quarrel between Herod and his eastern neighbour, the Nabataean king Malichus, in the hope that they would weaken each other—to her advantage.

It was the civil war between Octavian on the one side and Antony and Cleopatra which put an end to her ambitions and her career. Defeated by Octavian's forces at the sea battle of Actium in western Greece in 31 BC, Antony and Cleopatra fled back to Egypt and both committed suicide there the following year to avoid falling into the victor's hands. By their death they avoided the humiliation of being compelled to march as prisoners in his triumphal procession in Rome.

DEATH OF MARIAMNE

Octavian was now the master of the Roman world, with no rivals. Herod had to adjust himself to these new circumstances, and did so skilfully. Shortly after the battle of Actium, he was summoned to appear before Octavian at Rhodes. He obeyed this summons in some anxiety, since it was well known that he had been Antony's friend. But he told Octavian that he was prepared to serve him as loyally as he had served Antony; and Octavian, realizing the worth of such a proved friend and ally of Rome, confirmed him in his kingdom and sent him back. In the following year, after Antony and Cleopatra's death, he went to Octavian in Egypt, and received from him the territory of Jericho, which Cleopatra had seized. The Greek cities of Hippos, Gadara, Samaria, Gaza, Anthedon, Joppa and Strato's Tower were also added to his realm.

The removal of Cleopatra and the goodwill of Octavian gave Herod much more security in his political life, but there was no improvement in his domestic life. His suspicions led to the execution of the aged Hyrcanus II just before Herod's voyage to Rhodes to meet Octavian after Actium. Hyrcanus probably had few ambitions in his old age, but Herod feared that so long as he lived, the danger existed that others might use him, since he had once been king, as the focus of a revolt against Herod. Once again, afraid that he might never be allowed to return from Rhodes, he left instructions for the safe keeping and death of Mariamne; and once again, the secret of these jealous instructions leaked out. On his return he ordered the immediate death of her guard, Sohaemus. Herod's mother Cypros and his sister Salome maliciously set out to make him suspicious of Mariamne herself; and the unfortunate queen was executed in 29 BC. In the following year her mother Alexandra was also put to death.

Some years later, when time had softened, although it could never remove, his mad longing for Mariamne, Herod married another woman of the same name, the daughter of a priest named Simon, son of Boethus. To give her noble rank, he made this second Mariamne's father the high priest, a position he held from 23 to 5 BC.

HEROD'S ACHIEVEMENTS

Herod brought peace to the territories on his north-eastern frontier in the interests of Rome, and the grateful emperor added these territories to his kingdom—Trachonitis, Batanaea and Auranitis in 23 BC and Ituraea in 20 BC.

He furthered the emperor's cultural policy by his vast building enterprises. Old cities were refounded and new cities were built; temples, hippodromes and amphitheatres were constructed—not only in his own realm but in foreign cities such as Athens as well. In his own kingdom he rebuilt Samaria and renamed it Sebaste, after the emperor (Sebastos is the Greek equivalent of the Latin Augustus, the title by which Octavian was known from 27 BC onwards).

He also rebuilt Strato's Tower on the Mediterranean coast and equipped it with a large artificial harbour, calling the new city Caesarea, also in the emperor's honour. The work occupied some twelve years, from 22 to 10/9 BC. Other settlements and strongholds were constructed here and there throughout the land, many of them bearing names in honour of members of his own family, such as Antipatris (on the road from Jerusalem to Caesarea), Cypros (at Jericho), and Phasaelis (west of the Jordan). At Jerusalem he built a royal palace for himself adjoining the western wall (c. 24 BC). North-west of the temple area he had already rebuilt the Hasmonaean fortress of Baris and renamed it (after Antony) Antonia. But the greatest of all his building enterprises was the reconstruction of the Jerusalem temple. This great project was begun early in 19 BC. A thousand Levites were trained as builders, and they carried out their work in such a way that the sacred rituals of the holy place were never interrupted while it was going on. The great outer court was enclosed, and surrounded by colonnades; the whole area was beautified with splendid gateways and other architectural structures. The temple became renowned throughout the world for its magnificence:

Far off appearing like a mount
of alabaster, topped with golden spires.

The main work of reconstruction was completed within Herod's lifetime, but the final details were not completed until AD 63, only seven years before its destruction.

Other forms of culture were patronized at Herod's court, especially the writing of history: Herod's court chronicler, Nicolas of Damascus, wrote a Universal History in 144 books. This work included a detailed record of Herod's career, which Josephus used as a principal source for this part of his history.

But even the trouble which Herod took to win the favour of his subjects by his expenditure on the temple did not please them. His Edomite ancestry was never forgotten. Though he was a Jew by religion and patronized the Jewish religion at Jerusalem, his subjects knew that he also patronized paganism in other cities by the buildings which he erected in them. Above all, his destruction of the Hasmonaean family could not be forgiven.

HEROD'S FAMILY TROUBLES

His family problems did not come end with the death of his Hasmonaean wife and her relatives. There was friction between his wives, between them and his own blood-relations (especially his sister Salome), and between their respective families. His two sons by the first Mariamne, Alexander and Aristobulus, were named as his heirs. As descendants to the Hasmonaeans, through their mother Mariamne, they were acceptable to the people in general. In view of their rank and expectations, they received a special education, much of it in Rome. When they came of marriageable age, Aristobulus married Berenice, daughter of Herod's sister Salome, and Alexander married Glaphyra, daughter of King Archelaus of Cappadocia.

These two brother considered themselves superior to their half-brothers, Herod's sons by other wives, and showed it. This was naturally resented by their step-mothers and half-brothers, who were already resentful about their privileged position. But their bitterest enemy was Antipater, Herod's firstborn, son of his first wife Doris. Antipater believed that he ought to be his father's heir, and thought that he could achieve his ambition if the two sons of Mariamne could be eliminated. So he began to poison their father's mind against them, making him believe that they were plotting against his life in order to gain his royal power. He told Herod that they planned to take revenge on him for the death of their mother; and, of course, Herod's guilty and suspicious conscience readily believed his accusations. The result of Antipater's scheming was a quarrel between them and their father. The Roman emperor was able to bring about a reconciliation, and they were formally restored to their father's favour. But Antipater continued his accusations, and at last they were put on trial before their father for conspiracy and treason, and sentenced to death. The emperor was asked to ratify the death sentence and he agreed. It was perhaps on this occasion that Augustus remarked, making a pun on two similar-sounding Greek words, and joking about the Jewish refusal to eat pork, that it was safer to be Herod's pig than his son.[2]

Antipater, however, gained no advantage from the success of his scheming. Three years later he himself fell victim to his father's suspicion in the same way, and was executed on Herod's orders only a few days before Herod's own death (4 BC).

NOTES

[1] Josephus, *Antiquities* xv. 76.
[2] A play on Gk. *hys*, 'pig', and *hyios*, 'son'.

Chapter Twenty-Five

The Sons of Herod and the Early Roman Governors (4 BC–AD 37)

HEROD'S WILL

Herod left a will in which he divided his kingdom between three of his sons—Archelaus and Antipas, the sons of his Samaritan wife Malthace, and Philip, his son by a wife named Cleopatra of Jerusalem. He bequeathed to his sister Salome the revenues of three wealthy cities of his realm.

Herod left Judaea, the most important part of his kingdom, to Archelaus, whose first task was to crush a riot in the temple courts of Jerusalem. Having done so, he set out for Rome. It was necessary that the emperor should ratify his father's will. In reality, Herod had ruled by permission of Augustus for the past twenty-seven years; so his sons needed the same permission before they could accept their inheritance.

But ambassadors from the Jews of Judaea also arrived in Rome to persuade Augustus that Archelaus should not be appointed to succeed his father. They urged that instead Judaea should regain its former temple-constitution and internal independence under a governor appointed by the emperor.

Archelaus, however, found a friend and supporter in Nicolas of Damascus, and the emperor ignored the request of the Jewish delegates. Archelaus was confirmed as ruler of Judaea (with Samaria), and his brothers Antipas and Philip, who had also come to Rome to press their claims, received their shares in the inheritance—Antipas receiving Galilee and Peraea (southern Transjordan) and Philip receiving the territory north-east of the Sea of Galilee. None of them, however, received the royal title; Archelaus was nominated ethnarch, and Antipas and Philip had to be content with the minor title of tetrarch. Salome received the revenues of Jamnia, Azotus and Phasaelis, with a castle at Ashkelon and a legacy of half a million shekels.[1]

Some scholars think that this situation is the background of the Parable of the Pounds in Luke 19:11 ff., where a nobleman, who goes into a far country to receive for himself a kingdom and to return, is hated by his subjects, who send a delegation after him, refusing to have him as their king.

During the brothers' absence in Rome, further riots and revolts broke out in Palestine. Herod's death, in fact, was the signal for many disorders throughout his kingdom. One of these centred on Sepphoris in Galilee, where Judas, son of that brigand-chief Hezekiah whom Herod had executed forty-five years before, seized the arsenal and armed his followers. These revolts were so serious that Quintilius Varus, the Roman legate in command of Syria, intervened to crush them. He severely punished the leaders: two thousand of them were crucified alongside the roads in order to warn the population that revolts in Rome's sphere of influence would not be tolerated.

ARCHELAUS

Archelaus—called Herod the Ethnarch on his coins—has the worst reputation of all the sons of Herod. He had all his father's vices but none of Herod's skills of competent statesmanship.

He continued his father's policy of appointing and deposing high priests as he pleased: during his brief rule of nine years (4 BC–AD 6) he appointed three—Eleazar son of Boethus (4–3 BC), Jesus son of See (3 BC–AD 6) and Joazar son of Boethus (AD 6).

He offended the religious feelings of his subjects when he married Glaphyra, a Cappadocian princess who had formerly been the wife of his brother Alexander (executed in 7 BC). The ancient Israelite law of the levirate marriage[2] allowed such a marriage only when the dead brother had left no children; but since Glaphyra had borne children to Alexander, this law did not apply in the present instance.

Archelaus continued his father's building policy: he restored the palace at Jericho, which had been damaged in a revolt soon after Herod's death; he built an aqueduct to water the palm-groves north of Jericho; he founded a city some six miles north of Jericho, which he called Archelais, after himself.

But his severity led to further protests. At last a deputation of Samaritan and Jewish aristocrats went to Rome to make complaints against him before Augustus, and to warn the emperor that Archelaus's continued rule in Judaea would certainly cause a full-scale revolt. Augustus summoned Archelaus to his presence, and banished him to Vienne, in the Rhône valley. He had no desire to maintain an unimportant ruler in office when his subjects were so hostile to him. From this time on Judaea (with Samaria) was given the status of a third-class province of the Roman Empire, governed by a Roman official (or prefect) appointed by the emperor.

THE EARLY ROMAN GOVERNORS

The prefects of Judaea were usually drawn from the equestrian order—the second rank of Roman society. They were subject to the general supervision of the legates of Syria, but it was only in exceptional circumstances that the legate interfered in the affairs of Judaea. In practice the prefects held independent military and political command.

Their official residence was at Caesarea, where Herod's palace was used as their praetorium or official headquarters. Only occasionally did they reside at Jerusalem—for example, during the great pilgrimage festivals of the Jewish year, when extraordinary precautions were necessary to maintain public order.[3]

Now that Judaea was to be a Roman province, its tribute was payable directly to Rome. It was necessary, therefore, that the appropriate amount of tribute should be officially assessed, and for this purpose a census was held in AD 6, under the supervision of Quirinius, the legate of Syria. The idea of paying tribute directly to a heathen ruler was offensive to many pious Jews, and two men, Judas and Sadduq, had the vigour and courage to lead a revolt against Rome. This Judas—variously called Judas of Gamala (in Transjordan) and Judas the Galilaean—is mentioned in the speech of Gamaliel reported in Acts 5:37, as having led a revolt 'in the days of the census'. He and Sadduq argued that God alone was Israel's true king, and that to him alone (through God's approved representatives in Israel) should tribute be paid.

The revolt was suppressed, but its ideals were continued by men who kept the spirit of revolt against Rome alive throughout the next two generations, until the fires of revolt, long suppressed, blazed out at last in the rebellion of AD 66. In due course they formed the Zealot party. They probably took the name Zealots in order to show that they followed the tradition of Phinehas in the early days of Israel's history,[4] and of Mattathiah and his sons in more recent times,[5] all of whom displayed 'zeal' for the honour of God's name in Israel.

When the census had been completed and the provincial tribute assessed, the first prefect, Coponius, arrived to take up office. Between AD 6 and his death eight years later, Augustus appointed three successive prefects of Judaea—Coponius (AD 6–9), Marcus Ambivius (AD 9–12) and Annius Rufus (AD 12–15). His successor Tiberius, on the other hand, during his reign of twenty-three years (AD 14–37) appointed two only—Valerius

Gratus (AD 15–26) and Pontius Pilate (AD 26–36). It was the general policy of Tiberius to leave provincial governors in office for a considerably longer time than Augustus had done.

He was asked on one occasion why he acted thus, in view of the notorious greed of provincial governors. In reply Tiberius told the story of a wounded man who lay by the roadside, covered with blood-sucking insects. A kindly passer-by began to brush away the insects, but the wounded man stopped him. 'Leave them alone', he said; 'these flies have already sated themselves with my blood and are causing me no more annoyance. But if you drive them away a new lot of hungry flies will take their place and begin to suck my blood all over again.'[6]

One of the ways in which the early Roman governors of Judaea enriched themselves was by appointing and deposing high priests. When Quirinius organized the new province of Judaea in AD 6, he deposed Archelaus's last nominee, Joazar the son of Boethus, from the high-priesthood, and replaced him by Annas the son of Seth (who plays a part in the passion narrative of the Fourth Gospel).[7] Annas held the office for nine years, but when Valerius Gratus became prefect in AD 15 he replaced him by Ishmael son of Phabi. Valerius, in fact, appointed four high priests during his prefectship; Ishmael was followed in quick succession by Eleazar (a son of Annas), Simon son of Kami, and then by Joseph Caiaphas (son-in-law to Annas). Caiaphas, who is best known today for the leading part he took in the trial and condemnation of Jesus, held the high-priesthood for eighteen years (AD 18–36); no other Jewish high priest held office for so long after the death of Herod's father-in-law, Simon son of Boethus, in 5 BC. The fact that Caiaphas was not deposed by Pilate when he became prefect in AD 26, but continued to hold office throughout Pilate's governorship, suggests that it was more profitable for Pilate to confirm him in office than to replace him by another man. When Pilate was removed from office in AD 36, Caiaphas was removed from the high-priesthood by Vitellius, imperial legate of Syria, who re-placed him by two sons of Annas—first Jonathan, and then, a year later, Theophilus. In these circumstances it is clear why only a few very wealthy priestly families, such as those of Annas and Boethus, could afford to buy and retain the sacred office. It is not surprising that the high-priesthood was no longer widely respected.

PONTIUS PILATE

Of the early governors of Judaea, the one of whom we know most is Pontius Pilate. We read of him in the New Testament as the judge who tried Jesus and sentenced him to death by crucifixion. And Josephus has given us a fairly full account of his ten years' governorship in the eighteenth book of his Jewish Antiquities. Philo, the Jewish philosopher of Alexandria, has also left us a description of Pilate as 'inflexible of nature, stubborn and harsh.'[8] But we may see it as one of the ironies of history that the only non-Jewish writer to mention him (the Roman historian Tacitus) merely names him as the judge who sentenced Christ to death.[9]

Whether intentionally or not, Pilate consistently offended Jewish public opinion. Early in his governorship he attempted to bring military standards, bearing the emperor's image at their crossbar, into Jerusalem. Out of consideration for Jewish objection to such images (in the light of the Second Commandment), imperial policy had previously given orders that the images should be removed from the standards before entering the holy city. Pilate's attempt to refuse this concession almost caused a revolt, and he was forced, very reluctantly, to yield to the Jews' insistence that the images be removed.

Similar offence was caused when he fixed golden votive shields bearing the emperor's name to the walls of Herod's palace in Jerusalem. These shields, having been dedicated to a pagan deity, were obnoxious to Jewish feelings. A Jewish deputation went to Tiberius and assured him that Pilate had placed them there, not to show honour to the emperor but simply to annoy the Jews. The emperor gave orders that the shields should be taken down.

Pilate's great service to Jerusalem was the construction of an aqueduct from the southern highlands to augment the city's water-supply. But even this action led to further trouble between the governor and the Jewish authorities. No institution in Jerusalem benefited so much from the new water-supply as the temple did, and Pilate probably thought he was fully justified in demanding that the temple treasury should make a contribution to the expense of building the aqueduct. But the priests and people were horrified at the suggestion. The temple treasury was a sacred fund, which (they argued) should not be used for such a secular purpose as paying for an aqueduct. Pilate insisted; but his insistence very nearly created another riot.

St. Luke's Gospel contains a reference to some Galilaeans 'whose blood Pilate mingled with their sacrifices'.[10] We have no other certain reference to this incident, but presumably these were pilgrims who had come to Jerusalem to attend one of the great festivals, and were involved in the temple court in a riot which was suppressed by Roman soldiers from the neighbouring fortress of Antonia. In the same context of Luke there is a brief mention of eighteen men on whom the tower of Siloam fell.[11] Perhaps a group of rioters had installed themselves in this tower in the south-east of Jerusalem which was then undermined and knocked down, killing its defenders.

Pilate was recalled to Rome in AD 36 because of a hasty action taken against a crowd of Samaritan pilgrims. The Samaritans believed that the sacred vessels from the tabernacle of Moses' time had been buried on Mount Gerizim ever since the Israelites had settled in the land. Now a Samaritan who claimed to be a prophet announced that on a certain day he would locate and unearth these vessels. So a large crowd gathered on the holy hill. Pilate suspected that they intended to start a revolt, and sent a detachment of troops against them. They were dispersed with great loss of life. The Samaritan leaders sent a complaint to Vitellius, legate of Syria, who ordered Pilate to go to Rome and explain his actions there before Tiberius. About the time of his arrival in Rome, however, Tiberius died (March, AD 37), and Pilate was replaced by a new prefect.

Tiberius was succeeded as Roman emperor by his great-nephew Gaius (better known by his nickname Caligula), whose brief reign of four years was of considerable importance because of its effect on Jewish affairs. But before we consider the events of his reign we must go back and outline the careers of the remaining heirs of Herod the Great.

PHILIP THE TETRARCH

Philip, 'tetrarch of Iturea and Traconitis',[12] governed those territories north-east of the Lake of Galilee which his father had pacified in the years 23–20 BC. He was a milder character than either his father or brothers. He rebuilt Panion, the capital of his tetrarchy,[13] and named it Caesarea in honour of the Emperor. It was called Caesarea Philippi (i.e. Philip's Caesarea) to distinguish it from other cities of the same name (especially his father's foundation of Caesarea on the Mediterranean coast of Judaea). According to Josephus, he traced the subterranean course of the Jordan between this city and Phiale. He also rebuilt Bethsaida ('Fishertown') on the shore of the Lake and called it Bethsaida Julias, in honour of Julia, the daughter of Augustus.

He married Salome, daughter of his brother Herod Philip by Herodias.[14] (Herodias herself was the daughter of Aristobulus, one of Herod's two sons by Mariamne: marriages between uncle and niece were remarkably common in the Herod family.)

Philip was the first Jewish ruler to have the face of the Roman emperor—first Augustus and later Tiberius—stamped on the coins of his realm. However, most of his subjects were Gentiles and would have no objection to a practice which Jews would have resented.

Philip had the reputation of a moderate and lenient ruler. He rarely left his tetrarchy, and made the administration of justice within its frontiers his personal responsibility. According to Josephus, when he visited the various parts of his territory, he took his judgment-seat with him, and judged on the spot any cases that were submitted to him, pronouncing sentence of acquittal or condemnation promptly, so that no-one could complain that justice was delayed.[15]

When he died in AD 34, his tetrarchy was at first added to the province of Syria; but three years later, when Gaius became emperor, it was given to another member of the Herod family.

HEROD ANTIPAS

Antipas—called 'Herod the tetrarch' in the Gospels—ruled Galilee and Peraea for over forty years. Readers of the New Testament remember him chiefly as the ruler who imprisoned and executed John the Baptist. Luke reports Jesus' description of him as 'that fox' and records Jesus' brief appearance before him in Jerusalem in AD 30 which led to the restoration of friendly relations between Antipas and Pilate.[16]

Antipas was the ablest of Herod's sons. Like his father he was a great builder: Tiberias, on the Lake of Galilee, was built by him in AD 22 and named in honour of the Emperor Tiberius. He rebuilt and fortified Sepphoris in Galilee (it had been destroyed by Varus when he crushed the revolt of Judas the son of Hezekiah in 4 BC). In his Transjordanian territory of Peraea he strengthened Beth-ramphtha to defend the area against the Nabataean Arabs, and called it first Livias and later Julias (after the empress Livia, known as Julia from AD 14 on).

His wife was the daughter of the Nabataean king Aretas IV (9 BC–AD 40). He divorced her, however, in order to marry Herodias, who was not only the daughter of his late half-brother Aristobulus but also the wife of another half-brother, Herod (sometimes referred to as Herod Philip[17]). He fell in love with Herodias on one occasion when he was lodging with her and her husband, and arranged to marry her as soon as he could make the necessary arrangements to divorce Aretas's daughter. The Evangelists tell how John the Baptist denounced the marriage of Antipas and Herodias as unlawful.[18] But John was not the only person to disapprove of his actions; King Aretas, very naturally, was angered by the insult to his daughter. Some years later he seized an opportunity to declare war on Antipas, and inflicted a heavy defeat on him (AD 36). Josephus says that many of the subjects of Antipas believed that this disaster was a divine punishment for his behaviour towards John the Baptist.

NOTES

[1] When she died in AD 10 she bequeathed her property to Livia, the wife of Augustus.

[2] See p. 172.

[3] Hence Pilate was in residence at Jerusalem at the time of the arrest, trial and execution of Jesus, because it was the Passover season.

[4] Num. 25:7–13; Ps. 106:30 f.

[5] 1 Macc. 2:24–28.

[6] Josephus, *Antiquities* xviii. 174 f.

[7] John 18:13, 24: cf. Luke 3:2; Acts 4:6.

[8] In his report of a letter written to the Emperor Gaius by Herod Agrippa I (Philo, *Embassy to Gaius*, 301).

[9] Tacitus, *Annals* xv. 44.

[10] Luke 13:1.

[11] Luke 13:4.

[12] Luke 3:1.

[13] See p. 123.

[14] See p. 203.

[15] Josephus, *Antiquities* xviii. 107.

[16] Luke 23 :7 ff.

[17] Called 'Philip' in Mark 6:17 (cf. Matt. 14:3). This son of Herod was a private citizen and is not to be confused with Philip the tetrarch.

[18] Matt. 14:4; Mark 6:18; Luke 3:19. There may also be a reference to Herodias in Jesus' ruling in Mark 10:12, that if a man's wife 'divorces her husband and marries another man, she commits adultery.'

Chapter Twenty-Six

Herod Agrippa and the Jews
(AD 37–44)

AGRIPPA'S KINGDOM

One of the children of Aristobulus (the unfortunate son of Herod the Great and Mariamne who was executed on his father's orders in 7 BC) was named Agrippa, probably because of Aristobulus's friendship with the Roman statesman of that name. At the time of his father's execution Agrippa was four years old. He was sent to Rome with his mother Berenice, and was brought up in close and friendly contact with the imperial family. But he became so heavily involved in debt that in AD 23 he had to retire to Idumaea. When his sister Herodias came to live with his uncle Antipas as his wife, she arranged for Agrippa to receive a home and a pension at Tiberias. But he quarrelled with his uncle, and at last, in AD 36, was able to return to Rome. Soon after his return he offended the Emperor Tiberius, and was imprisoned.

The death of Tiberius in the spring of AD 37 brought about a change in Agrippa's fortunes, for he enjoyed the friendliest relations with Gaius (Caligula), who succeeded Tiberius as emperor. Gaius released him from prison immediately, and recompensed him with a chain of gold equal in weight to the chain of iron with which he had been fettered. But that was a very small gift compared with the further favours which the new emperor showered upon Agrippa. He gave him the territory over which his uncle Philip had ruled as tetrarch until his death three years previously, and also the territory of Abilene to the north of that, which had formerly been the tetrarchy of Lysanias.[1] With these territories he gave him the proud title of king.

Herodias, his sister, now urged her husband Antipas to ask Gaius to raise his title from tetrarch to king. For over forty years Antipas had ruled Galilee and Peraea with efficiency. During that time he had acted as the emperor's faithful informer in that part of the world (and because of it had become very unpopular with some of his neighbours). Herodias felt that Antipas deserved to be given a royal title now, as a reward for all his services rendered to Rome. Gaius had very readily given this title to his friend Agrippa, who had done nothing to deserve it; surely he would recognize Antipas's more solid claims to equal honour.

These were the views of Herodias. Antipas hesitated to take this action, but when she insisted, he set out for Rome to make his request. It ended in disaster for him: instead of receiving the title of king, he lost his kingdom. Agrippa held a grudge against Antipas, and poisoned the emperor's mind against him. He suggested that Antipas was conspiring with the Parthians against Rome, and pointed out that his arsenal at Tiberias contained enough weapons to equip 70,000 men. So the emperor deposed Antipas and sent him into exile. The emperor offered to treat Herodias as the sister of his friend Agrippa and not as the wife of his enemy Antipas, and gave her permission to live on a private estate of her own; but she preferred to accompany her husband into exile. The regions of Galilee and Peraea, which Antipas had ruled so long, were now added to Agrippa's kingdom (AD 39).

Agrippa played an important part in imperial policy towards the Jews during the reign of Gaius. When he was on his way from Rome to his kingdom in Palestine in AD 38, he paid a visit to Alexandria in Egypt at a time when relations between the Greek and Jewish inhabitants of that city were very strained.

EVENTS IN ALEXANDRIA

Under the Ptolemies there had been little trouble between the Greek and Jewish citizens of Alexandria. The Jewish numbers grew and eventually they occupied two out of the five wards of the city.[2] They constituted a corporation within the city, enjoying a large measure of independence, and had a Jewish governor (or ethnarch).

In the closing years of the Ptolemaic dynasty, the Alexandrian Jews, partly influenced by the example of Antipater and Herod in Judaea, were friendly towards the Romans. They supported Julius Caesar in 47 BC, and later they supported Octavian (Augustus) against Cleopatra and Antony. Julius Caesar granted them many privileges, and these were confirmed by Augustus. In 30 BC Augustus arranged, through the Roman prefect of Egypt, that responsibility for Jewish affairs in Alexandria should be entrusted to an elected senate consisting (like the Jerusalem Sanhedrin) of seventy-one men. This senate was to be independent of the civic authorities of Alexandria.

However, the Alexandrian Greeks resented this exceptional favour shown to the Jews. They resented also the contemptuous attitude with which they themselves were regarded by the Romans. 'We used to hear about Alexandria', said Cicero in 63 BC; 'now we are getting to know it. That is the place where all the juggling tricks, all the frauds in the world, come from . . .'[3] It was inevitable that this resentment should eventually turn into violence. The Alexandrian Greeks saw their opportunity when Gaius became emperor in AD 37.

The Roman prefect of Egypt at the time of Gaius's accession was a man called Flaccus. He had taken part some time previously in an attack on Gaius's mother Agrippina, and so he was naturally afraid of Gaius's vengeance. The Alexandrian Greeks were well aware of this. They approached Flaccus, promising to send favourable reports about his administration to Rome if he would support them against the Jews of Alexandria (who at this time had been requesting full status as Alexandrian citizens). Flaccus agreed, and gradually developed an anti-Jewish policy, for example discriminating against Jews in the law-courts. He also deliberately held back from the emperor the loyal message which the Alexandrian Jews had written to congratulate him on his accession.

This was the situation when Herod Agrippa arrived in Alexandria. The Jews of the city greeted him warmly, for his visit seemed a godsend. They begged him to make a public procession through the city with his bodyguard. This, they hoped, would impress the Alexandrians, who already knew of the close friendship between the emperor and the Jewish king. Agrippa unwisely agreed to their request. The Greeks of Alexandria reacted by staging a counter-parade in which a local idiot named Carabas ('Cabbage') was dressed in royal robes, with mock crown and sceptre. They pretended to honour this poor fellow in the public gymnasium, hailing him with cries of *mari* (Aramaic for 'my lord').

The civic leaders were horrified at what the mob had done. They knew that Agrippa would not forgive this insult to his royal dignity, and that he would use his influence with Gaius to get vengeance. So they took hasty action in order to cause Gaius to be offended by the Jews. Roman emperors were officially considered to be gods, and Gaius was known to take his divinity very seriously. The civic leaders, therefore, with Flaccus's support, decided to place portraits of the emperor in the local synagogues. They knew that the Jewish authorities would immediately remove them, and the Greek leaders planned to report their removal as a mark of disloyalty to the emperor—in spite of the fact that Roman policy towards the Jews had always respected their objections to 'images'.

The plan proceeded. At the same time, Flaccus gave orders by decree that Jewish privileges in Alexandria should be strictly limited to existing legal arrangements. A long time previously, for example, the Alexandrian Jews had been permitted the right of residence in one of the city wards, but their residence in other wards had never been officially authorized. Now, even though their numbers were much greater, Flaccus's edict meant that they must all reside within the one ward. Those who lived in other wards were thrown out; their houses and shops were plundered; their synagogues were destroyed. Many had to take refuge outside the city. But the anti-Jewish passion of the city mob, thus enflamed, could not be restrained. Acts of violence multiplied until, on the emperor's birthday, thirty-eight members of the Alexandrian Jewish senate were publicly flogged in the theatre. Other anti-Jewish acts were carried out in the theatre, to please the mob. The civic leaders were dismayed by the excesses to which their policy had led, and they hastened to Rome to excuse themselves from any blame, claiming that Flaccus alone was responsible for what had happened. Flaccus was found guilty of treason, sentenced to confiscation and banishment, and soon afterwards executed.

Flaccus was arrested on the Day of Atonement in AD 38—a significant coincidence in Jewish eyes—and order was restored for the time being. Some steps were taken to ease the difficulties of the Alexandrian Jews, but they did not recover all the privileges which had been theirs before the riots. A delegation of five leading Jews of the city, headed by the philosopher Philo, went to Rome in the following year to request Gaius to restore in full their former privileges. Gaius, however, gave them no satisfaction. He rebuked them for failing to recognize his divinity, saying that it was not sufficient to offer sacrifices to Yahweh on his behalf (as was done daily in the Jerusalem temple); he expected his subjects to offer sacrifices to him as a god.

GAIUS AND JERUSALEM

This subject was specially important to the emperor just then, because of a crisis which was beginning to develop in Judaea. At Jamnia, in western Judaea, the Gentile population set up an altar in the emperor's honour; the Jewish inhabitants of the town pulled it down. When Gaius heard of this, he retaliated by ordering that his statue should be erected in the temple at Jerusalem. He knew that the Jews would resist this order fiercely, so he commanded Petronius, the governor of Syria, to march to Jerusalem with two legions to enforce the order.

Consternation broke out in Judaea and throughout the Jewish world; this seemed like Antiochus Epiphanes and 'the abomination of desolation' all over again. Petronius marched south, but when he arrived at Ptolemais, he was met by deputations of Jews who surrounded him and protested that the whole nation would prefer to be be killed rather than tolerate this outrage. Petronius, however, told them that he had no choice; his duty was to carry out the emperor's orders.

At this critical moment Jewish Christians in Palestine remembered some words of their Master which seemed to relate to this situation. Speaking of troubles in days to come which would lead to the destruction of both Jerusalem and the temple, Jesus had warned his disciples to flee from Judaea when they saw 'the abomination that causes desolation standing where he does not belong'.[4] It is quite likely that this warning, together with other sayings of Jesus to the same effect, was written down at this time, copied and distributed among the Christians.

However, it turned out that this crisis was not the fulfilment of these words of Jesus; the immediate danger was prevented. Thirty more years were to pass before destruction overwhelmed the city and temple. But the crisis left a deep mark on the thought of the early church, and the document circulated at that time provided a form of words which we can trace in Christian writings later in the century—in the book of Revelation for example, and also in the letters of Paul. For example, in his second letter to the Thessalonians (written in AD 50), Paul tells his readers that the second advent of Christ will be preceded by a widespread revolt against the divine government, when 'the man of lawlessness is revealed, the man doomed to destruction. He will oppose and will exalt himself over everything that is called God or is worshipped, so that he sets himself up in God's temple, proclaiming himself to be God'.[5] He reminds them that he told them this when he was with them a few months before. And there is a clear connection between his picture of lawlessness in human form enthroned in the temple of God and the earlier reference to 'the abomination which causes desolation standing where he does not belong.'

In AD 40, however, Petronius delayed before acting; he was genuinely unwilling to execute the emperor's mad command. While he was delaying, Agrippa was urgently persuading Gaius himself to withdraw his orders to Petronius. Gaius's friendship with Agrippa was strong enough for the emperor to reconsider. He yielded to him to the extent of writing to Petronius to say that, if the statue had already been erected, it must remain, but if not he was to take no further action.

But Petronius had by this time written to the emperor to say that it was impossible to carry out his order except by exterminating the Jewish people. Gaius, therefore, sent him a second letter ordering him to commit suicide as the penalty for his disobedience to orders. Before Petronius received this second letter, however, news came that Gaius had been assassinated (January, AD 41).

Gaius was assassinated by leading Romans because there was no constitutional means of removing an emperor who had become intolerable. The Roman senate thought of restoring republican government after his death, but the praetorian guards proclaimed his uncle Claudius emperor; and the senate had to accept their decision.

AGRIPPA'S REIGN

When Claudius became emperor, he issued two edicts confirming the Jews in their traditional privileges in Alexandria (and indeed throughout the Roman Empire). The Alexandrian citizens were forbidden to renew their attacks on the Jews; the Alexandrian Jews were warned not to claim further privileges than those which they already possessed. They were also warned against angering their Gentile neighbours by encouraging illegal Jewish immigration into the city either from Palestine or from other parts of Egypt. If the two parties could not learn to live at peace, they would experience the just anger of a benevolent prince, he told them. When further trouble between the two communities threatened to break out in AD 53, he suppressed it with prompt severity, thus proving that he meant what he had said.[6]

Agrippa, who was in Rome at the time of Gaius's death, was a long-standing friend of Claudius as well as of Gaius. Claudius, at the start of his reign, confirmed him in the kingdom which he had received from Gaius, and also increased its size by adding Judaea and Samaria to it. For the remaining three years of his life (AD 41–44) Agrippa ruled over a realm about the same size as that of his grandfather Herod. Like many members of the house of Herod, Agrippa bore the family name Herod in addition to his more personal name. He is the ruler called 'Herod the king' in Acts 12:1 ff, where his attack on the leaders of the Jerusalem church is described.

This narrative in Acts reveals Agrippa's eagerness to please the Jews of Jerusalem. Our other sources of information also show how eager he was to do so. He did everything possible to win the favour of his Jewish subjects, observing their customs and showing preference for their company, so that even the Pharisees thought well of him. They looked upon him rather as a Hasmonaean king (through his grandmother Mariamne) than as a member of the Edomite stock of Herod.

This is indicated in a story preserved in the Mishnah, which tells that once, as a Jewish king, he had to read the lesson Deuteronomy 17:14–20 ('the law of kingship') at the Feast of Tabernacles in a sabbatical year (probably AD 40–41). When he came to the words of verse 15, 'Be sure to appoint over you the king Yahweh your God chooses. He must be from among your own brothers', he burst into tears, as he remembered his

Edomite ancestry. But the people encouraged him by calling out repeatedly: 'Be not dismayed: you are indeed our brother!'[7]

Even so close a friend of the emperor, however, had to act in accordance with imperial policy. There were two occasions on which the Romans vetoed projects which Agrippa had started. One was the building of a third wall, north of Jerusalem, to bring the so-called 'New City' (Bezetha) inside the fortified area; the other was a conference of rulers, like himself subject to Rome, which he had called together at Tiberias.

Agrippa died suddenly in the spring of AD 44, having fallen ill five days previously, during a festival which he had inaugurated at Caesarea in honour of the emperor. The picturesque details of the occasion are related both by Josephus[8] and by Luke.[9] He left a young family, the eldest of whom, also called Agrippa, was seventeen years old. Claudius considered appointing the younger Agrippa to succeed his father; but his advisers assured him that the control of Judaea was too serious and difficult a responsibility to be entrusted to a youth. So Judaea was once again governed by Roman governors (or procurators). But some years later Claudius gave the younger Agrippa the kingdom of Chalcis, at the foot of the Lebanon range, in succession to his father's full brother Herod, who had ruled there until his death in AD 48. In AD 53 Agrippa exchanged Chalcis for the territories north-east of the Lake of Galilee over which his father had been made king by Gaius in AD 37: and when Nero became emperor in AD 54 he increased this kingdom by giving Agrippa the cities of Tiberias, Tarichaea, and Bethsaida Julias, with the surrounding districts and villages. As a compliment to Nero, Agrippa changed the name of his capital city from Caesarea Philippi to Neronias.

NOTES

[1] Cf. Luke 3:1.
[2] Philo (*Flaccus* 6, 8) estimated that in AD 38 there were a million Jews in Egypt; even if we make a substantial deduction from this estimate, their numbers were certainly very considerable.
[3] *Pro Rabirio Postumo*, 35.
[4] Mark 13:14, slightly adjusted, because the 'abomination of desolation' is personal here, and could well have been taken to refer to the emperor, represented by his image.
[5] 2 Thess. 2:3 f.
[6] See F. F. Bruce, *New Testament History* (1969), pp. 275 ff.
[7] Mishnah, *Sota* vii. 8.
[8] *Antiquities* xix. 343 ff.
[9] Acts 12:21–23.

Chapter Twenty-Seven

Troubles Multiply in Judaea
(AD 44–66)

FADUS

The Jews of Judaea strongly disliked the fact that Roman governors were imposed on them once again, after the happy years they had spent under a Jewish king. Even good and considerate governors would have found their task very difficult; but in fact the procurators from AD 44 onwards were no better than Pilate had been.

The first procurator to be appointed after the death of King Agrippa was Cuspius Fadus (AD 44–46). He claimed that, like the prefects of earlier years, he should have the right of appointing Jewish high priests, together with the custody of the high-priestly robes of office. Since then Agrippa had been in charge of these matters, and the Jews did not want pagan officials to have this twofold right again. So they appealed to the emperor, who granted their wishes by giving the privilege to Agrippa's brother Herod, who ruled the small principality of Chalcis in the Lebanon. After his death in AD 48 the privilege was given to the younger Agrippa, who retained it till the outbreak of the Jewish war in AD 66.

Early in Fadus's period of office, a man claiming to be a miracle-worker named Theudas[1] gathered a large band of followers and led them to the river Jordan. He told them that at his word of command the waters would divide, so that they might cross on dry ground. This suggests that he claimed to be either a second Joshua, who would deliver the Holy Land from the heathen,[2] or else a second Elijah, forerunner of the Messiah.[3] Fadus sent a body of cavalry against him and his followers; the multitude was dispersed and the head of Theudas brought to Jerusalem. Such 'messianic' movements (as they may loosely be called) were to become increasingly frequent in these years.

ALEXANDER

Fadus was succeeded as procurator in AD 46 by Tiberius Julius Alexander, a member of a leading Jewish family of Alexandria. His father, Alexander, was head of the Jewish community of that city; his uncle was the philosopher Philo. But he himself had abandoned the faith of his fathers, and therefore—in spite of his Jewish ancestry—could not be an acceptable figure in the eyes of religious Jews.

He, too, found it necessary to crush a revolt, which has special interest in that it was led by two sons of Judas the Galilaean, who had himself led the revolt at the time of the census in AD 6. This new revolt was defeated, and the sons of Judas (James and Simon by name) were crucified. The crucifixion of two patriotic Jews by an apostate Jew did nothing to increase Alexander's popularity in Judaea.

The end of Fadus's procuratorship and the beginning of Alexander's was a time of severe famine in Palestine. Luke tells how the church of Antioch at this time sent a relief-mission, headed by Barnabas and Paul, to their fellow-Christians in Jerusalem.[4] Josephus tells how Helena, the Jewish queen-mother of Adiabene (a district east of the Tigris) bought corn in Egypt and figs in Cyprus and brought them to Jerusalem, for distribution to its famine-stricken populace.[5]

It is interesting to note that members of the royal family of Adiabene had adopted the Jewish faith. The story shows something of the extent and character of Jewish proselytization in those days. A Jewish merchant named Ananias, in the course of commercial dealings with ladies of the royal family, discussed religious questions with them and encouraged them to worship God according to the Jewish way. About the same time Helena, the queen of Adiabene, was similarly persuaded by another Jew. Under their influence Izates, the crown-prince, also embraced the Jewish faith, and soon afterwards succeeded to the throne (c. AD 40). Ananias assured him that it was not necessary for him to be circumcised, as this might be resented by his subjects. But a Galilaean Jew named Eleazar, on a visit to Adiabene, persuaded the king that unless he was circumcised he could not hope to win divine approval, and the king accordingly submitted to the rite. Other members of his family were also circumcised, including his brother Monobazus, who succeeded him as king about AD 64. Monobazus had a magnificent tomb built in Jerusalem for his mother and brother. Some of his relatives fought on the Jewish side against the Romans in the war of AD 66–70.

The rulers of Adiabene acknowledged the Parthian king as their overlord, but they were sufficiently powerful for the Parthian king on occasion to be very grateful for their support. There were large Jewish colonies in the western part of the Parthian Empire, and for about fifteen years (c. AD 25–40) a Jewish adventurer named Asinaeus served the Parthian king as governor of his Babylonian province. This period of Jewish influence was followed by anti-Jewish riots, especially in Seleucia on the Tigris, chief city of the province, where several thousand Jews were massacred by their Gentile neighbours.

CUMANUS

Alexander was followed in AD 48 by Ventidius Cumanus. His four years as procurator of Judaea were a time of constant disturbances. The attitude of the people was such that the slightest incident might cause offence and start a serious riot. For example, during the passover celebrations in one of the years of Cumanus's procuratorship a Roman soldier from the fortress of Antonia so greatly angered the crowd of pilgrims in the Temple court by an insulting gesture that a riot followed, which could not be crushed without some loss of life.

The action of another Roman soldier during a military punitive raid in western Judaea was even more provocative. This soldier tore up a scroll of the law in a synagogue. This act of sacrilege was an attack on the Jewish religion, which had the official protection of Roman law. A Jewish deputation went to Caesarea and refused to be satisfied until Cumanus had the offending soldier executed. But the fact that the soldier was executed shows how carefully Roman law avoided giving unnecessary offence to Jewish religious beliefs and feelings.

Towards the end of Cumanus's procuratorship a frontier dispute broke out between the Samaritans and Jews. Some Galilaeans were murdered in a Samaritan village, but Cumanus took no steps to punish the offenders. Two Jews (Alexander and Eleazar by name) therefore led a group of Jews in an attack on the Samaritans. Although Cumanus had not taken steps against the Samaritan murderers, he was quick to take military action against this Jewish band. The Jewish leaders accused him of taking the Samaritan side, and made an appeal to Quadratus, the legate of Syria. Quadratus ordered leading representatives of the Jewish and Samaritan communities, together with Cumanus himself, to go to Rome and have the dispute heard there by the emperor. In the imperial court the Jews found a powerful friend and supporter, the younger Agrippa. He was a very effective advocate; Claudius acquitted the Jews, sentenced the unfortunate Samaritan delegates to death, and removed Cumanus from his procuratorship.

FELIX

Cumanus was succeeded as procurator by Antonius Felix, who appears to have held a subordinate post in Samaria under Cumanus.[6]

Felix was not a member of the equestrian order in Roman society, as the other governors of Judaea were: he belonged to the humble rank of freedman. With his brother Pallas he had once been a slave in the household of Claudius's mother Antonia. After they were given their freedom Pallas gained a position of great influence in the imperial household as head of the civil service. It was through his influence that Felix was given the extraordinary honour (for a freedman) of governing a province.

In spite of his humble birth, Felix married into the highest circles. He had three wives in succession, all of royal birth: one of them was a grand-daughter of Antony and Cleopatra. The third and last was Drusilla, daughter of the elder Agrippa, who left her former husband—Azizus, king of Emesa—to come and live with Felix as his wife (AD 54). They had a son, Agrippa, who met his death when Vesuvius erupted in AD 79.

Felix set himself energetically to crush the bands of rebels which were increasing in strength and activity in the province. His severe measures against them were temporarily successful, but they alienated large numbers of the population in whose eyes these freedom fighters were not criminals but patriots.

One method which began to be widely adopted by some rebel Jews was assassination. They mingled with the crowds at festivals and similar occasions, carrying daggers hidden in their clothing, and stabbed their unsuspecting opponents— especially Jews who were suspected of being pro-Roman. From the Latin word for dagger (*sica*) they came to be known as *sicarii* ('dagger-men'). One of their earliest victims was a former high priest, Jonathan the son of Annas, a man of moderation, who on that account was specially hated by extremists.

One of the rebel leaders who created a disturbance about AD 54 was an Egyptian who claimed to be a prophet. He led his followers, about four thousand in number, out to the Mount of Olives, east of Jerusalem, promising that at a given signal the walls of Jerusalem would fall down flat (as the walls of Jericho had done in Joshua's time), so that they might march in and seize control of the city. But Felix sent troops against him, who killed 400, captured 200, and scattered the rest.

The Egyptian disappeared. Two or three years later, when the military tribune commanding the garrison in the fortress of Antonia rescued a man from being lynched by an angry crowd in the Outer Court of the temple, he imagined for some reason that it was this Egyptian. He thought that the populace were attacking him because he had abandoned his followers. But he discovered that he was mistaken: this man was no Egyptian but a Jew of Tarsus, Paul by name.[7]

The Egyptian, however, was only one of many false leaders who in those days led people out into the wilderness of Judaea, promising to perform miracles which would repeat the wonders of the days of Moses and Joshua, and herald a new deliverance from Israel's oppressors.

Meanwhile the official leaders of the Jewish nation were rapidly losing the respect to which their office might have entitled them. The high-priesthood had become the property of a few wealthy Sadducean families, who were high-handed and arrogant and heartily disliked by the common people.

But of all the high priests, none disgraced himself more than Ananias the son of Nedebaeus (AD 47–58). He appears on one occasion in the New Testament, when as president of a judicial meeting of the Sanhedrin he acted with disgraceful lack of impartiality.[8] He is remembered in Jewish tradition mainly for his greed, which led him to seize and sell those portions of the temple sacrifices which rightfully belonged to the ordinary priests, who could have starved as a result.[9]

In the closing years of Felix's procuratorship there were fierce riots between the Jewish and Gentile citizens of Caesarea. The Jews of the city claimed special privileges because its founder was a Jewish king (Herod). When rioting broke out, Felix took the side of the Gentiles, and sent the leaders of both parties to Rome. But Nero, the stepson of Claudius, was now emperor, and Felix himself was recalled to Rome. He realized that he had caused offence to the Jews, so he tried to win their goodwill before he left by keeping Paul of Tarsus, whom they hated, in prison at Caesarea, instead of setting him at liberty. Soon after Nero's accession in AD 54 Felix's brother Pallas had been removed from his post as head of the imperial civil service; but he still retained sufficient influence to ensure that Felix suffered no other penalty than losing his post as procurator.

FESTUS

The next procurator of Judaea was Porcius Festus (c. 59–62). Soon after Festus's arrival in the province, the dispute at Caesarea was resolved in favour of the Gentiles by an imperial decision. According to the Jewish account, the Gentile Caesareans gained this favourable verdict by bribing Beryllus, Nero's secretary. Instead of receiving the special privileges which they desired, the Caesarean Jews were reduced to the level of second-class citizens. This decision, in view of the Jewish bitterness it created, must be reckoned as one of the causes of the Jewish revolt of AD 66.

Although Festus's term of office was short, it gave him time to take energetic action against a number of militant rebels. A less serious incident of his procuratorship arose from a dispute between the temple officials and the younger Agrippa. Agrippa had a town-house in Jerusalem, to which he added a tower from which he had a convenient view of the temple courts and could watch the priests performing their sacrificial duties. The priests did not like this supervision by a layman, even if he was the 'secular head of the Jewish church'.[10] So they built a high wall to block his view. Agrippa protested to Festus, who ordered the wall to be demolished. But the chief priests appealed to Caesar. They sent an embassy to Rome, where they now had a powerful friend at court, Poppaea, Nero's new wife and empress. Through her influence they obtained permission to maintain the wall which they had built to block Agrippa's view.

Festus died suddenly in office about the year AD 62, and three months passed before his successor Albinus arrived. During this interval the high priest, Annas II, seized the opportunity to take vengeance on several old enemies. He brought a number of men before the Sanhedrin and had them condemned to death. Among these the most notable person was James the Just, leader of the large Christian—or more accurately Nazarene—community in Jerusalem. This judicial murder shocked many of the Jerusalemites who were not themselves Nazarenes, for James's asceticism and piety had won him widespread respect and honour. When Jerusalem was besieged a few years later a number of Jews declared that the disaster was because James's continual intercession in prayer for the city had been so violently brought to an end.[11]

Annas's high-handed behaviour was quickly stopped by Agrippa, who deposed him from the high priesthood and replaced him by a rival, Jesus the son of Damnaeus. Street fighting followed between the supporters of the two rivals.

ALBINUS

Albinus, the next procurator, Josephus tells us, was even more ready to accept bribes than most procurators were. He arrested a large number of *sicarii*, and also those partisans of Annas II who were stirring up riots in Jerusalem in resentment at their master's loss of the high-priesthood; but he set them free when he was offered a sufficiently large bribe.

At the Feast of Tabernacles in the autumn of AD 62 a frightening impression was made in Jerusalem by the appearance of a peasant, Jesus the son of Ananias, who incessantly proclaimed the imminent doom of the city:

A voice from the east
A voice from the west,
A voice from the four winds;
A voice against Jerusalem and the sanctuary,
A voice against bridegrooms and brides,
A voice against this whole people.[12]

Like the ominous pronouncements of Solomon Eagle before the Great Fire of London, this peasant's utterances later seemed to have been prophetic, when disaster did indeed fall on the city and temple.

Albinus was recalled after three years in office. According to Josephus, before he left the province he executed convicted criminals, but set free those who were awaiting trial for less serious offences, and in this way filled the land with robbers. However, it must be kept in mind that Josephus wanted to give an unfavourable account of the last procurators of Judaea, in order to show that the Jews had some genuine grievances which partly excused their revolt against Rome in AD 66.

FLORUS

The last procurator of Judaea was Gessius Florus, who owed his appointment (or so rumour alleged) to his wife's friendship with the empress Poppaea. His appetite for bribery and extortion was such, Josephus says,[13] that he made his predecessor Albinus appear a public benefactor by comparison. He plundered whole towns and in return for bribes took no action against brigands.

Even if Josephus exaggerates Florus's wickedness, there can be no doubt that his inefficiency, together with his insensitiveness to the state of feeling in Judaea, contributed greatly to the outbreak of war in AD 66.

NOTES

[1] Not the Theudas of Acts 5:36, who probably led one of the revolts which followed Herod's death in 4 BC.
[2] Cf. Josh. 3:13 ff.
[3] Cf. 2 Kgs 2:8.
[4] Acts 11:29 f.
[5] *Antiquities* xx. 51 f., 101.
[6] Cf. Tacitus, *Annals* xii. 54.
[7] Acts 21:38, where the word 'terrorists' (NIV) or 'assassins' (NRSV) refers to the *sicarii*.
[8] Acts 23:1–5.
[9] TB *Pesachim* 57a. He plays a more commendable part in Josephus's narrative (see pp. 222 f. below).

[10] Because of his right to appoint the high priest (see p. 212).
[11] For further details of the career and death of James see F. F. Bruce, *New Testament History* (1969), pp. 349–355.
[12] Josephus, *War* vi. 300 ff.
[13] *Antiquities* xx. 253.

Chapter Twenty-Eight

The War with Rome and the End of the Second Temple (AD 66–73)

After the seventy or eighty years of independence which they had enjoyed under the Hasmonaeans, the Jews did not take kindly to the fresh imposition of foreign rule. The later Hasmonaeans had been oppressive to many of their subjects, but by now their evil deeds were forgotten, and only the fact that they were a native dynasty which had freed Israel from foreign domination was remembered.

So long as a Hasmonaean retained the high-priesthood, however, the situation was not intolerable. Even Herod was technically a Jew, although he was of Edomite stock and appointed by the Romans. While he reigned, he absorbed much of the hatred which was directed against Rome when Judaea was governed by imperial prefects and procurators.[1] Although the national leaders who requested the removal of Archelaus in AD 6 hoped that internal autonomy under a Roman governor would be preferable to his tyranny, they were in fact wrong to think so. There were, of course, those who, like Judas the Galilaean and his later Zealot disciples, found the mere fact of being directly tributary to a pagan ruler outrageous. But others might have been content if only the Roman officials had been just and sensitive. Unfortunately, the extortionate and brutal behaviour of governors like Pilate strengthened the arguments of the extremists. The situation was even more intolerable after the brief period of peaceful conditions which they enjoyed under Herod Agrippa I. After that, unjust administrators caused increasing hatred of Rome; and when riots broke out, they were crushed so ruthlessly that the people as a whole increasingly sympathized with the rioters and hated Rome even more.

It is plain, too, that many Jews were expecting God to send a deliverer. Rome began to replace the Seleucid empire in the minds of interpreters of Daniel's vision as the final Gentile power which was to be crushed to

powder by the 'rock cut out, but not by human hands.'[2] When the Hasmonaean dynasty lost its independence, the expectation began to revive of
a champion of David's line who would crush Israel's enemies and establish
dominion for his people. Even the pious, near-Essene community of Qumran cherished the hope of a final war against Rome in which, when God
gave the signal, they would play a decisive part.[3] The Zealots (who now
emerged as a distinct group) did not believe that they should wait for a
signal: the fact that they were under heathen domination was signal enough
for them. They knew their duty and believed that God must prosper their
cause and give them victory in their fight for Israel's freedom.

To a nation which was so convinced of its divinely-appointed destiny
the temptation to co-operate with destiny was great, especially when the
situation in Judaea was as intolerable as it became under the governorship
of Florus.

THE REVOLT BEGINS

The Gentiles of Caesarea, whom Nero had awarded superior civic privileges to the Caesarean Jews, who had opposed their request, took every
opportunity to insult the Jews, and annoyed them in a great variety of ways.
On one occasion they sacrificed a bird outside the synagogue door, thus
not only defiling its precincts, but also hinting delicately at the common
Gentile report that the Jews were a leprous nation (for the sacrifice of a bird
was part of the Levitical ritual for the removal of leprosy). This act was not
only insulting but also illegal, a breach of the privileges which imperial law
gave to Jewish religion; so the Jews appealed to Florus to punish the
culprits. Knowing that it was useless to appeal to Florus without bribing
him, they paid him eight talents of silver. Florus took the money, but paid
no further heed to their complaint.

Florus's greed, however, could not be endured any longer when he
raided the temple treasury and seized seventeen talents of the sacred funds.
Pilate had once taken money from the treasury, it is true, but he had taken
it for what he considered a perfectly justified purpose.[4] Florus had no such
excuse. The people of Jerusalem were unable to prevent the procurator
from robbing the sacred treasury, but two Jews humorously insulted him
by taking up a mock-collection in public for a governor who was evidently
reduced to such poverty. Florus, infuriated by this insult, sent his troops
against the populace. There was much bloodshed and looting, and several
citizens, including some who even belonged to the Roman equestrian
order, were seized at random and crucified. The people's reaction was
violent; they cut the communications between the fortress of Antonia and

the temple courts to prevent any sudden action by members of the Roman garrison in the fortress to seize and occupy the temple area.

The legate of Syria, Cestius Gallus, sent a military tribune, Neapolitanus, to Jerusalem to investigate the disturbances. During his visit the citizens remained calm, and the younger Agrippa did his best to persuade them against any thought of revolt. Rebellion would be futile, he urged; the wise and safe course was to remain obedient to Rome. But when his hearers asked him if obedience to Rome involved submission to Florus, he had to admit that it did, and they refused to listen to his further pleas.

The leader of the party in Jerusalem which wanted to fight against Rome was a priest named Eleazar, captain of the temple and son of the former high priest Ananias son of Nedebaeus. He was the man who caused the first deliberate act of rebellion against Rome. For many years a daily sacrifice had been offered in the temple on behalf of the emperor's welfare; Eleazar now put a stop to this. By doing so he was denying the emperor's authority; it was in effect a declaration of war.

There were, however, some moderate leaders in Jerusalem who contemplated with horror the turn that events had taken, and tried to check them. Chief among these were Ananias, son of Nedebaeus (father of the Eleazar just mentioned), and his brother Hezekiah. They appealed to Florus and to Agrippa for co-operation in preventing the revolt from spreading. Florus did nothing; it looked as if he had no desire to prevent war from breaking out.[5] Agrippa sent troops to reinforce the peace party. Together they were able to maintain themselves for a time in the western (upper) quarter of the city, but they were insufficient to take effective action against the rebels in the temple area. On September 5, AD 66, the rebels captured the fortress of Antonia which overlooked the temple courts, killed all the Roman soldiers there, and manned it with their own forces.

The Zealot party naturally viewed this situation as one which needed their leadership; the day of national revolt against Rome was the day for which they had waited and fought and suffered. Their leader was Menahem, last surviving son of that Judas the Galilaean who led the abortive revolt of sixty years before. Menahem and his followers had already seized the fortress of Masada, built by Herod on the south-western shore of the Dead Sea, and massacred the Roman garrison which occupied it. Now, arming themselves with the weapons which they found in the arsenal there, they marched to Jerusalem. They took charge of the attack on the western quarter of the city, and soon gained control of it. The soldiers of the peace party, along with the reinforcements sent by Agrippa, were compelled to surrender but were allowed to leave the city unharmed. The Roman forces were shut up in the three towers of Herod's palace on the western wall.

Menahem's evident ambition to be sole leader, if not indeed king, of an independent Jewish state brought him into rivalry with the priestly rebels. Moreover, he and his followers were hated by Eleazar, captain of the temple, because on September 25 they had killed his father, the former high priest Ananias, during military operations in the upper city. Even though Ananias had been a member of the peace party, Eleazar felt that he must avenge his father's death. His followers therefore attacked Menahem while he was worshipping in the temple. Menahem tried to escape but was caught and tortured to death, together with his chief lieutenants. One of his lieutenants, however—a kinsman of his own, Eleazar son of Jair—got away safely to Masada with a number of followers, and they remained in occupation of that stronghold until the spring of AD 74.

Soon after Menahem's death the rest of the Roman forces in Jerusalem were captured. They surrendered on condition that their lives should be spared, but as soon as they laid down their arms they were massacred almost to the last man.

ROMAN MILITARY ACTIONS

Florus now found himself faced with a situation completely beyond his control. The forces at his disposal were insufficient to check the revolt; it was necessary for the legate of Syria to intervene. The legate, Cestius Gallus, marched south with the Twelfth Legion and additional forces to recapture Jerusalem. He occupied the northern suburb, Bezetha, but realized that the troops he had brought with him were not numerous enough for the task of conquering the remainder of the city and temple area. He therefore withdrew, and as his army was marching north it was ambushed by Jewish rebels in the pass of Beth-horon and suffered heavy losses (November 25, AD 66).

The fact that even Cestius Gallus (as it appeared) did not dare to besiege Jerusalem and had suffered a serious defeat when retreating added great prestige to the rebel cause. The moderates who had hoped that he would restore order were discredited. Most of the Jews of Palestine were now united for a war of liberation. Joseph ben Gorion and the former high priest Annas II were put in charge of the defence of Jerusalem. Jesus the son of Sapphias and Eleazar, captain of the temple, commanded the army in Idumaea. Another Eleazar—a Zealot leader, Eleazar the son of Simon—although he was given no command, nevertheless enjoyed considerable power through gaining possession of the wealth captured from the Romans and a large part of the public treasure of Jerusalem. Among the commanding officers of the rebel forces in Galilee was Josephus, son of the priest Mattathiah (and future historian of the war). Josephus had a rival for his

Galilaean command, John of Gischala, whom he accuses of constantly plotting to undermine his position. (It is quite likely that John had no great confidence in Josephus's zeal for the rebel cause.)

Since Cestius Gallus had proved unable to deal with the revolt, Nero sent Vespasian, a veteran soldier who had held successful commands in Gaul and Britain, to Judaea with an independent command. He arrived in the province in the spring of AD 67 with three legions and auxiliary forces (about 60,000 men in all). In his first campaign he conquered Galilee, and incidentally won a surprising follower in the rebel leader Josephus. Josephus, captured by the Romans, predicted that Vespasian would become the Roman emperor; so his life was spared. (Josephus came to believe that his fellow-Jews had been misguided in expecting the messianic prophecies to be fulfilled in a Jew: the world-ruler who was to arise from Judaea was none other than the commander of the Roman forces in Judaea.)

Josephus's rival, John of Gischala, avoided capture when Galilee was conquered and escaped to Jerusalem. There he aimed at establishing his own supremacy, and encouraged the hostility of the priestly group against the Zealots, whose leader in Jerusalem was Eleazar the son of Simon. After a winter of civil strife and intrigue, he gained control of the city in the spring of AD 68. Soon afterwards the last high priest of Jerusalem entered into office—a country priest named Phinehas, son of Samuel. Unlike his predecessors he was not selected from one of the leading chief-priestly families but chosen by lot from the ordinary priests. The last survivor of the former high priests, Annas II, was killed about the same time because he was suspected of being willing to negotiate with the Romans.

By the end of spring, AD 68, Vespasian's forces had conquered Peraea, western Judaea and Idumaea, and prepared to besiege Jerusalem. But in June of that year a revolt against Nero broke out in Italy. Nero committed suicide to avoid a worse fate, and civil war raged in and around Rome as one military leader after another tried to gain control of the city and empire. Vespasian suspended military operations to see how events would turn out; and the defenders of Jerusalem were no longer under attack. They thought this was a last-minute divine intervention in their defence. Rome, they thought, was on the verge of destruction by civil warfare; the empire was about to break up. Surely the hour for which they had waited so long, the establishment of Israel as an empire ruling 'from sea to sea and from the River to the ends of the earth',[6] would soon come. The holy city would not fall: on the contrary, the time of its redemption was at hand.

By June of AD 69, however, Vespasian had resumed activity and was master of all Palestine except Jerusalem and the three strongholds of Herodion (south-east of Bethlehem), Masada, and Machaerus (in Peraea). Meanwhile further civil strife had broken out in Jerusalem. During

Vespasian's inactivity another leader, Simon bar Giora, an ally of the Zealots entrenched at Masada, had become master of Idumaea. Driven from Idumaea by the Roman forces, he entered Jerusalem and led a party hostile to the leadership of John of Gischala. Simon established control over Jerusalem and its surroundings, but John retained control of the outer court of the temple, while the Zealot leader, Eleazar the son of Simon, held the inner court with the bulk of the temple treasure. While civil strife between these three party leaders and their followers was developing in Jerusalem, Vespasian was proclaimed emperor at Alexandria in July (by Tiberius Julius Alexander, former procurator of Judaea, who was now prefect of Egypt). Caesarea and Antioch soon proclaimed him emperor, and before long Vespasian had the support of the armies in all the eastern provinces. He waited until his supporters had seized Rome for him, then left Judaea for Rome in order to restore order there, leaving his elder son Titus to finish the war in Judaea.

THE FALL OF JERUSALEM

Accordingly, in April of AD 70 Titus besieged Jerusalem. But the Jews were still sure that Jerusalem was an invincible city, and just before the siege began large numbers of Jewish pilgrims went up there as usual for the passover festival. Their presence in the city once it was closely besieged added to the difficulties of the defence. The defence was already weakened by the rivalry between the three parties mentioned above. However, the Zealot leader Eleazar was overcome by John at the passover season; and after that John and Simon were united in defence of the city and temple.

As the siege wore on, the horrors of famine, and even cannibalism, were added to the dangers of war, but the defenders had no thought of capitulating, least of all when Titus, using Josephus as his interpreter, urged the advantages of early surrender upon them. On July 24 the Romans captured the fortress of Antonia. Twelve days later the daily sacrifice in the temple was discontinued. On August 27 the temple gates were burnt. Two days later, on the anniversary of the destruction of the First Temple by the Babylonians in 587 BC,[7] the sanctuary itself was set on fire and destroyed. By September 26 the whole city was in Titus's hands. It was completely destroyed. Only three towers of Herod's palace on the western wall were left standing, with part of the western wall itself.

According to Josephus, Titus wished to save the temple, but was unable to prevent his soldiers from destroying the building which had been the centre of the resistance during the siege. This was no doubt the story which Titus wished to be believed in later years, and Josephus, who was grateful for the favours granted him by Vespasian and Titus, gave it the required publicity.

But a different story has survived in a historical fragment preserved by Sulpicius Severus (c. AD 400).[8] This account says that:

> Titus first took counsel and considered whether he should destroy so magnificent a work as the temple. Many thought that a building which excelled all mortal works in sacredness ought not to be destroyed, for if it were saved, it would serve as a token of Roman moderation, but its destruction would display an eternal mark of savagery. But others, on the contrary, including Titus himself, expressed the opinion that the temple ought most certainly to be destroyed, in order that the Jewish and Christian religions might more completely be abolished; for although these religions were hostile to each other, they had nevertheless sprung from the same founders; the Christians were an offshoot of the Jews, and if the root were taken away the whole plant would soon perish.

Whatever Titus himself thought, there were no doubt many who held this hope. But they were doomed to disappointment. The temple had outlived its usefulness. Christianity, of course, was essentially free from the limitations of the old sacrificial system; but so was all that was best in Judaism.

When the temple area was taken by the Romans, and the sanctuary itself was still burning, the soldiers brought their legionary standards into the sacred courts, set them up opposite the eastern gate, and offered sacrifice to them there, acclaiming Titus as *imperator* (victorious commander) as they did so. The Roman custom of offering sacrifice to their standards had already been commented on by a Jewish writer as a symptom of their pagan arrogance.[9] The offering of such sacrifice in the temple court was the supreme insult to the God of Israel. This action, following as it did the cessation of the daily sacrifice three weeks earlier, must have seemed to many Jews, as it evidently did to Josephus, a new and final fulfilment of Daniel's vision of a time when the continual burnt offering would be taken away and the abomination of desolation set up.[10]

THE AFTERMATH

The capture and destruction of the city were accompanied by the slaughter of many Jews; large numbers of the population were enslaved, others were destined for gladiatorial games, while seven hundred were reserved for Titus's triumphal procession.

The three remaining Jewish strongholds were captured within the following three years—Herodion with relative ease, Machaerus with greater difficulty, and lastly the almost impregnable Masada, which fell on May 10, AD 74, after the mass suicide of its defenders.

Titus did not remain in Judaea after the fall of Jerusalem. After a victorious progress from Caesarea to Antioch, followed by a visit to Alexandria, he returned to Rome in the summer of AD 71. There he was accorded a magnificent triumph, in which his father and brother also participated. In the procession were carried spoils of war, including sacred trophies from the temple, together with tableaux depicting events from the siege and capture of the city. The prisoners of war who were led in the procession were headed by Simon bar Giora and John of Gischala. Simon was executed when the procession finished while John was condemned to life imprisonment. Scenes from the triumphal procession have been preserved in Rome to the present day in panels on the Arch of Titus, which was erected as a memorial to him shortly after his death in AD 81.

With the fall of the temple and the abolition of the sacrificial ritual, the Second Commonwealth of Israel, with its priestly constitution, came to an end. No doubt many thought at the time that the nation of Israel itself had come to an end. But the event proved them wrong. The disappearance of the temple order marked the beginning of a new and glorious chapter in Israel's story, which does not come within the scope of this book.

NOTES

[1] The titles 'prefect' and 'procurator' were technical Roman terms for the governors of Judaea at different times; there seems to have been little difference in meaning.

[2] Dan. 2:34 f., 44 f.; cf. Josephus, *Antiquities* x. 210.

[3] See F. F. Bruce, *Second Thoughts on the Dead Sea Scrolls* (3rd ed.,1969), pp. 74 ff., 85 ff.

[4] See p. 201.

[5] But as L. L. Grabbe has written, 'Whatever Florus's failings—which were probably many—it seems that Josephus has given a very biased account of the events' (*Judaism from Cyrus to Hadrian* [1992], p. 117).

[6] Ps. 72:8.

[7] See p. 84.

[8] Frequently thought to be a fragment of Tacitus's *Histories*; but see H. W. Montefiore, 'Sulpicius Severus and Titus' Council of War,' *Historia* 11 (1962), pp. 156 ff.

[9] The Qumran commentator on Habakkuk 1:16.

[10] Daniel 8:11 ff.; 9:27; 11:31; 12:11. Josephus evidently recognizes the fulfilment of these prophecies in the events of AD 70 (*War* vi. 94, 311, 316).

Genealogical and Chronological Tables

N.B. Many dates in these lists are
uncertain or may vary by one year.

Genealogical and Chronological Tables

THE HOUSE OF DAVID

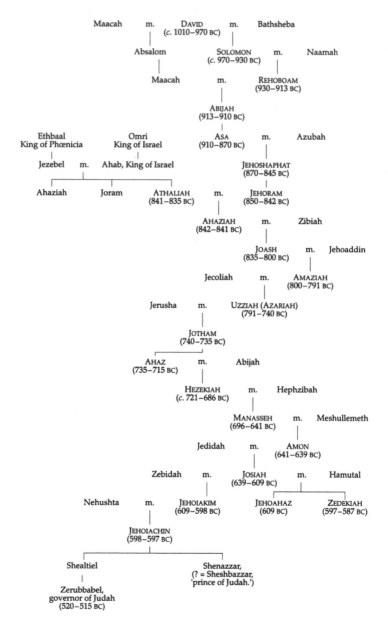

KINGS OF ISRAËL
After the disruption of the monarchy

DYNASTY OF JEROBOAM

Jeroboam I	c. 930–909 BC
Nadab	909–908 BC

DYNASTY OF BAASHA

Baasha	908–885 BC
Elah	885–884 BC

Zimri	884 BC
Tibni	884–881 BC

DYNASTY OF OMRI

Omri	881–873 BC
Ahab	873–852 BC
Ahaziah	852–851 BC
Joram	851–841 BC

DYNASTY OF JEHU

Jehu	841–814 BC
Jehoahaz	814–798 BC
Jehoash	798–782 BC
Jeroboam II	782–745 BC
Zechariah	745 BC

Shallum	745 BC

DYNASTY OF MENAHEM

Menahem	745–736 BC
Pekahiah	736–735 BC

Pekah	735–732 BC
Hoshea	732–724 BC

KINGS OF ASSYRIA
883–610 BC

Ashurnasirpal II	883–859 BC
Shalmaneser III	858–824 BC

Shamshiadad V	823–811 BC
Adadnirari III	810–783 BC
Shalmaneser IV	782–773 BC
Ashurdan III	772–755 BC
Ashurnirari V	754–745 BC
Tiglath-pileser III	744–727 BC
Shalmaneser V	727–722 BC
Sargon II	722–705 BC
Sennacherib	705–681 BC
Esarhaddon	681–669 BC
Ashurbanipal	669–627 BC
Ashuretililani	c. 627–620 BC
Sinshariskun	c. 620–612 BC
Ashur-uballit II	612–610 BC

THE CHALDAEAN DYNASTY OF BABYLON

Nabopolassar	626–605 BC
Nebuchadrezzar II	604–562 BC
Evil-merodach	562–560 BC
Neriglissar	560–556 BC
Labashi-marduk	556 BC
Nabonidus	555–539 BC

KINGS OF PERSIA

Cyrus II	559–530 BC
Cambyses	530–522 BC
Pseudo-Smerdis	522 BC
Darius I (Hystaspes)	522–486 BC
Xerxes I	486–465 BC
Artaxerxes I (Longimanus)	465–424 BC
Xerxes II	424 BC
Sekydianos (Sogdianos)	424 BC
Darius II (Nothos)	424–404 BC
Artaxerxes II (Mnemon)	404–359 BC
Artaxerxes III (Ochos)	359–338 BC
Arses	338–336 BC
Darius III (Codomannus)	336–331 BC

THE PTOLEMIES OF EGYPT

Ptolemy I Soter satrap of Egypt	323–305 BC
king	305–285 BC[1]
Ptolemy II Philadelphus	285–246 BC
Ptolemy III Euergetes I	246–222 BC
Ptolemy IV Philopator	222–205 BC
Ptolemy V Epiphanes	204–180 BC
Ptolemy VI Philometor	180–145 BC
(Ptolemy VII Neos Philopator	145 BC)
Ptolemy VIII Euergetes II (Physcon)	169–164 and 145–116 BC
Cleopatra III and Ptolemy IX Soter II (Lathyrus)	115–107 BC
Cleopatra III and Ptolemy X Alexander I	107–101 BC
Ptolemy X Alexander I and Cleopatra Berenice	101–88 BC
Ptolemy IX Soter II (Lathyrus), restored	88–80 BC
Ptolemy XI Alexander II	80 BC
Ptolemy XII (Auletes)	80–51 BC
Cleopatra VII (associated successively with her brothers Ptolemy XIII and Ptolemy XIV and with her son by Julius Caesar, Ptolemy XV Caesarion)	51–30 BC

[1] Abdicated 285 BC, died 282 BC

THE HOUSE OF SELEUCUS

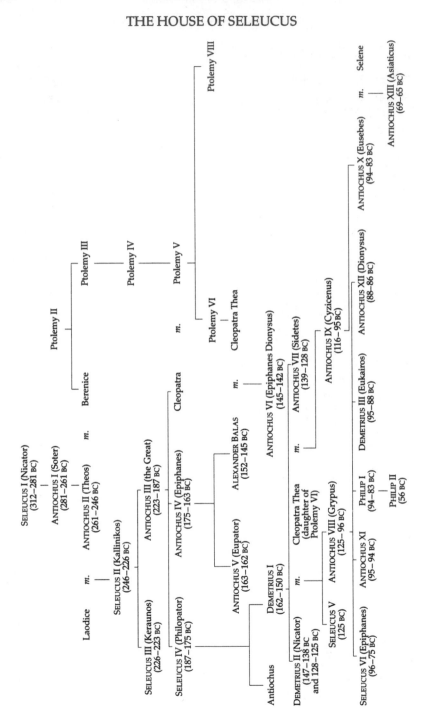

JEWISH HIGH PRIESTS IN GRAECO-ROMAN TIMES

THE HOUSE OF ZADOK

Jaddua	c. 350–320 BC
Onias I	c. 320–290 BC
Simon I	c. 290–275 BC
Eleazar	c. 275–260 BC
Manasseh	c. 260–245 BC
Onias II	c. 245–220 BC
Simon II	c. 220–198 BC
Onias III	c. 198–175 BC

APPOINTED BY SELEUCID KINGS OR RULERS

Jason (brother of Onias III)	175–172 BC
Menelaus	172–163 BC
Alcimus	162–160 BC
(Interregnum	159–152 BC)
Jonathan the Hasmonaean (also known as Jonathan Maccabaeus)	152–143 BC
Simon the Hasmonaean	143–140 BC

APPOINTED BY POPULAR DECREE: THE HASMONAEAN DYNASTY

Simon the Hasmonaean	140–135 BC
John Hyrcanus	135–104 BC
Aristobulus I	104–103 BC
Alexander Jannaeus	103–76 BC
Hyrcanus II	76–67 BC
Aristobulus II	67–63 BC
Hyrcanus II	63–40 BC
Antigonus	40–37 BC

APPOINTED BY HEROD THE GREAT (37–4 BC)

Hananel	37–36 BC
Aristobulus (last of the Hasmonaeans)	Spring–Autumn 35 BC
Hananel (restored)	c. 36–30 BC
Jesus son of Phiabi	c. 30–23 BC
Simon son of Boethus	c. 23–5 BC
Matthew son of Theophilus	c. 5 BC
Joseph son of Ellemus	c. 5–4 BC
Joazar son of Boethus	c. 4 BC

APPOINTED BY ARCHELAUS, ETHNARCH OF JUDAEA (4 BC–AD 6)

Eleazar son of Boethus	c. 4–3 BC
Jesus son of See	c. 3 BC–AD 6
Joazar son of Boethus (second time)	AD 6

APPOINTED BY QUIRINIUS, LEGATE OF SYRIA (AD 6–9)

Annas son of Seth	AD 6–15

APPOINTED BY VALERIUS GRATUS, PREFECT OF JUDAEA (AD 15–26)

Ishmael son of Phiabi	AD 15–16
Eleazar son of Annas	AD 16–17
Simon son of Kami	AD 17–18
Joseph Caiaphas, son-in-law of Annas	AD 18–36

APPOINTED BY VITELLIUS, LEGATE OF SYRIA (AD 35–39)

Jonathan son of Annas	AD 36–37
Theophilus son of Annas	AD 37–41

APPOINTED BY HEROD AGRIPPA I, KING OF JUDAEA (AD 41–44)

Simon Cantheras, son of Boethus	AD 41–42
Matthias son of Annas	AD 42–43
Elioenai son of Cantheras	AD 43–44

APPOINTED BY HEROD OF CHALCIS (AD 44–48)

Joseph son of Kami	c. AD 44–47
Ananias son of Nedebaeus	c. AD 47–58

APPOINTED BY HEROD AGRIPPA II (AD 50–100)

Ishmael son of Phiabi	c. AD 58–60
Joseph Kabi son of Simon	AD 60–62
Annas II (Ananus) son of Annas	AD 62
Jesus son of Damnaeus	c. AD 62–63
Jesus son of Gamaliel	c. AD 63–65
Matthias son of Theophilus son of Annas	c. AD 65–68

APPOINTED BY THE PEOPLE DURING THE WAR

Phinehas son of Samuel	AD 68–70

THE HASMONAEAN FAMILY

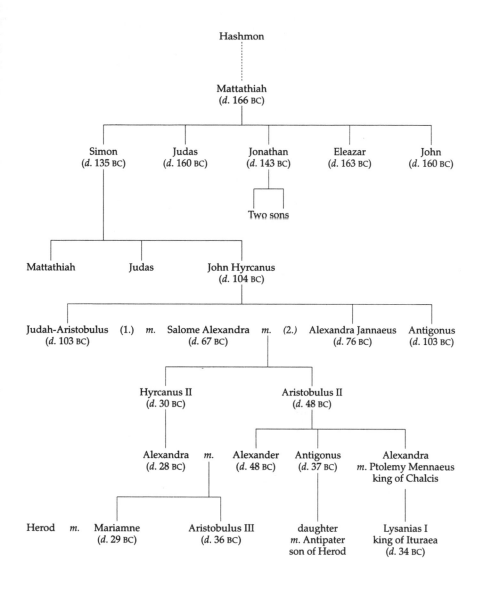

HEROD'S ANCESTRY AND KIN

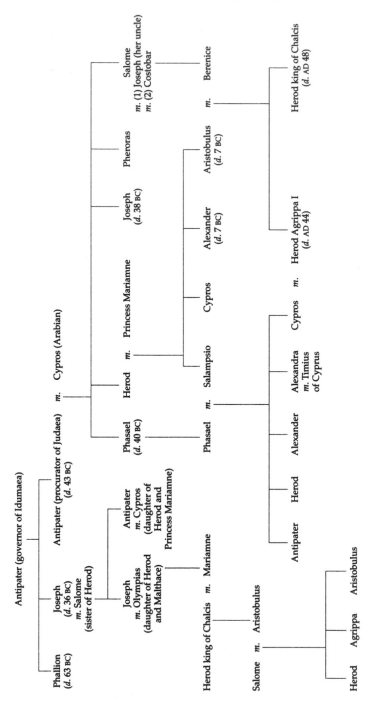

DESCENDANTS OF HEROD AND PRINCESS MARIAMNE

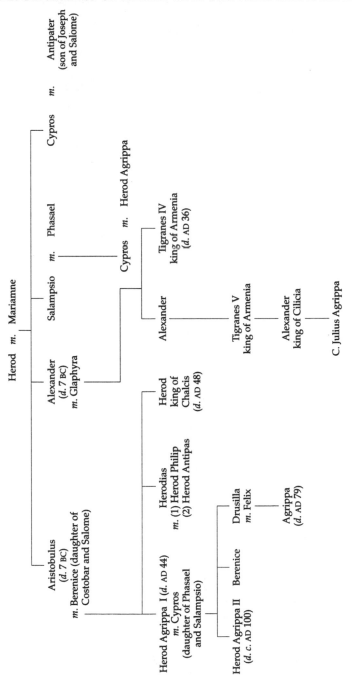

SOME DESCENDANTS OF HEROD BY OTHER WIVES

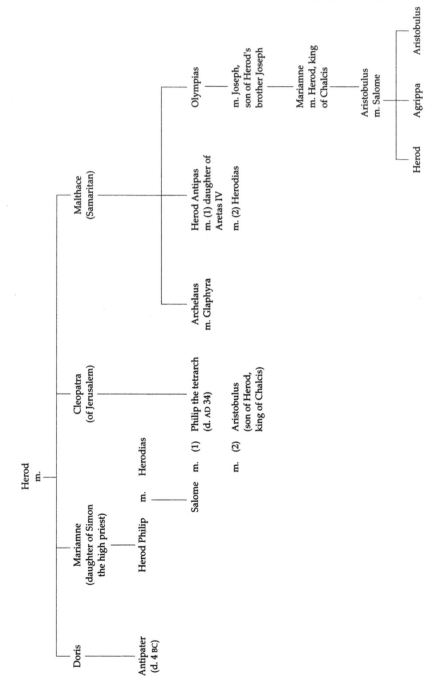

RULERS OF JUDAEA

Herod (king)	37–4 BC
Archelaus (ethnarch)	4 BC–AD 6

PREFECTS

Coponius	AD 6–9
Marcus Ambivius	AD 9–12
Annius Rufus	AD 12–15
Valerius Gratus	AD 15–26
Pontius Pilatus	AD 26–36
Marcellus	AD 36–37
Marullus	AD 37–41
Herod Agrippa I (king)	AD 41–44

PROCURATORS

Cuspius Fadus	AD 44–46
Tiberius Julius Alexander	AD 46–48
Ventidius Cumanus	AD 48–52
Antonius Felix	AD 52–59
Porcius Festus	AD 59–62
Albinus	AD 62–65
Gessius Florus	AD 65–66

ROMAN EMPERORS OF THE FIRST CENTURY AD

THE JULIO-CLAUDIAN DYNASTY

Augustus (Octavian)	31 BC–AD 14
Tiberius	AD 14–37
Gaius (Caligula)	AD 37–41
Claudius	AD 41–54
Nero	AD 54–68

Galba	AD 68–69
Otho	AD 69
Vitellius	AD 69

THE FLAVIAN DYNASTY

Vespasian	AD 69–79
Titus	AD 79–81
Domitian	AD 81–96

Nerva	AD 96–98

Bibliography

I. PRIMARY SOURCES

The primary sources for the history of Israel and the neighbouring peoples during the period covered by this survey are these:

1. The books of the Old Testament. Convenient English editions are the New Revised Standard Version (with the Apocrypha, 1989; Anglicized Edition 1995) and the New International Version (1978).

2. Contemporary inscriptions and other documents from Egypt, Palestine and Mesopotamia. For the English reader convenient selections are accessible in:

W. Beyerlin (ed.), *Near Eastern Texts relating to the Old Testament* (SCM, London, 1978).

A. K. Grayson, *Assyrian and Babylonian Chronicles* (J. J. Augustin, Locust Valley, 1975).

V. H. Matthews and D. C. Benjamin, *Old Testament Parallels* (Paulist Press, New York, 1991).

J. B. Pritchard (ed.), *Ancient Near Eastern Texts relating to the Old Testament* (Princeton UP, 1950).

J. B. Pritchard (ed.), *The Ancient Near East in Pictures relating to the Old Testament* (Princeton UP, 1954).

J. B. Pritchard, *The Ancient Near East: An Anthology of Texts and Pictures* (Princeton UP, 1959). An abridged edition of the two preceding volumes.

D. W. Thomas (ed.), *Documents from Old Testament Times* (Nelson, London, 1958).

3. Especially for the Persian and Graeco-Roman periods, the works of ancient historians: notably Herodotus, Thucydides, Xenophon, Polybius, Diodorus, Livy, Tacitus and Josephus. (Their most important works are available for the English reader in the Loeb Classical Library or the Penguin Classics.) For the last two or three hundred years of our survey the works of the Jewish historian Josephus (c. AD 37–103)—his *Jewish War, Jewish*

Antiquities, Autobiography, and *Treatise against Apion*—are of the greatest value.

Selected documents relating to the New Testament period are accessible in:

C. K. Barrett (ed.), *The New Testament Background: selected documents* (rev. ed. SPCK, London, 1987).

II. FOR FURTHER READING

G. Ahlström, *The History of Ancient Palestine* (JSOT, Sheffield, 1992).

J. J. Bimson, *Redating the Exodus and Conquest* (JSOT, Sheffield, 1978).

J. J. Bimson (ed.), *Illustrated Encyclopedia of Bible Places* (IVP, Leicester, 1995).

J. Bright, *A History of Israel* (3rd ed., SCM, London, 1981).

F. F. Bruce, *New Testament History* (Nelson, London, 1969).

R. E. Clements (ed.), *The World of Ancient Israel* (Cambridge UP, 1989).

J. D. Douglas (ed.), *New Bible Dictionary* (2nd ed., rev. N. Hillyer, IVP, London, 1982).

L. L. Grabbe, *Judaism from Cyrus to Hadrian* (SCM, London, 1994).

N. Grimal, *History of Ancient Egypt* (Blackwell, Oxford, 1992).

C. M. Jones, *Old Testament Illustrations* (Cambridge UP, 1971).

K. M. Kenyon, *The Bible and Recent Archaeology* (rev. ed. by P. R. S. Moorey, British Museum, London, 1987).

K. A. Kitchen, *The Third Intermediate Period in Egypt 1100–650 BC* (2nd ed., Aris & Phillips, Warminster, 1986).

A. R. C. Leaney, *The Jewish and Christian World 200 BC to AD 200* (Cambridge UP, 1984).

J. M. Miller and J. H. Hayes, *A History of Ancient Israel and Judah* (SCM, London, 1986).

G. Rasmussen, *The NIV Atlas of the Bible* (Marshall Pickering, Basingstoke, 1989).

N. K. Sandars, *The Sea Peoples* (Thames & Hudson, London, 1978).

D. W. Thomas (ed.), *Archaeology and Old Testament Study* (Clarendon, Oxford, 1967).

E. Schürer, *The History of the Jewish People in the Age of Jesus Christ* (3 vols., ed. G. Vermes et al., T. & T. Clark, Edinburgh, 1973–87).

W. von Soden, *The Ancient Orient* (Eerdmans, Grand Rapids, 1994).

D. J. Wiseman (ed.), *Peoples of Old Testament Times* (Clarendon, Oxford, 1973).

D. R. W. Wood (ed.), *New Bible Atlas* (IVP, Leicester, 1985).

Abbreviations

ABD	*Anchor Bible Dictionary.*
ANET	*Ancient Near Eastern Texts relating to the Old Testament* (ed. Pritchard).
BA	*The Biblical Archaeologist.*
CAH	*Cambridge Ancient History.*
CHJ	*Cambridge History of Judaism.*
DOTT	*Documents from Old Testament Times* (ed. Thomas).
IEJ	*Israel Exploration Journal.*
NIV	*New International Version.*
NRSV	*New Revised Standard Version.*
REB	*Revised English Bible.*
TB	*Babylonian Talmud.*

Index